TRAUMA,
DISSOCIATION,
AND
IMPULSE DYSCONTROL
IN
EATING DISORDERS

BRUNNER/MAZEL
EATING DISORDERS MONOGRAPH SERIES
Series Editors
PAUL E. GARFINKEL, M.D.
DAVID M. GARNER, PH.D.

BRUNNER/MAZEL EATING DISORDERS MONOGRAPH SERIES NO. 9

TRAUMA, DISSOCIATION, AND IMPULSE DYSCONTROL IN EATING DISORDERS

Johan Vanderlinden., Ph.D.
Walter Vandereycken, M.D., Ph.D.

BRUNNER/MAZEL, *Publishers*
A member of the Taylor & Francis Group

Library of Congress Cataloging-in-Publication Data

Vanderlinden, Johan.
    Trauma, dissociation, and impulse control in eating disorders /
Johan Vanderlinden, Walter Vandereycken.
        p.   cm. — (Brunner/Mazel eating disorders monograph
series ; no. 9)
    Includes bibliographical references and indexes.
    ISBN 0-87630-843-4 (hard cover)
    1. Eating disorders.   2. Adult child abuse victims—Mental
health. 3. Post-traumatic stress disorder.   4. Dissociative
disorders.   5.   Impulsive personality.   I. Vandereycken,
Walter.   II. Title.   III. Series.
    [DNLM: 1. Eating Disorders—psychology.   2. Stress
Disorders, Post-Traumatic—psychology.   3. Eating Disorders—
therapy.   4. Psychotherapy—methods.   5. Dissociative
Disorders—psychology.   6. Impulse Control Disorders—
psychology. W1 BR917D v.9 1997 / WM 175 V235t 1997
RC552.E18V36 1997
616.85'26—dc21
DNLM/DLC
for Library of Congress   97-9766
                                                                            CIP

Published by
BRUNNER/MAZEL, INC.
A Member of the Taylor & Francis Group
1900 Frost Road, Suite 101
Bristol, Pennsylvania, 19007

Manufactured in the United States of America
10   9   8   7   6   5   4   3   2   1

Contents

About the Authors

Johan Vanderlinden, Ph.D., is a clinical psychologist in the Eating Disorders Unit of the University Center St.-Jozef, Kortenberg, Belgium.

Walter Vandereycken, M.D., Ph.D., is Professor of Psychiatry at the Catholic University of Leuven. He is Clinical Director of the Department of Behavior Therapy at the Alexian Brothers Psychiatric Hospital in Tienen and consulting psychiatrist to the Eating Disorders Unit of the University Center St.-Jozef, Kortenberg, Belgium.

Acknowledgments

We are grateful to the following colleagues for their assistance, support, and criticism: Herwige Claeys, Dirk De Wachter, Alfred Lange, Ellert Nijenhuis, Jan Norré, Michel Probst, An Van de Putte, Onno van der Hart, Richard van Dyck, Veerle Van Houdenhove, Karla Van Leeuwen, Myriam Van Moffaert, Elly Van Vreckem, Hans Vertommen, Sybille Vuchelen, Glenn Waller, and Susan Wooley. We also thank the many patients who both challenged and inspired us, guided us in our work, and finally gave us new strength to help other patients.

Preface

Mary studies art history, and she has been in therapy for six months after a suicide attempt. She often writes letters to her therapist, which vary strikingly in content and style—even her handwriting varies in a peculiar way. In an early letter she told how her stepfather had raped her when she was 14. A year later, she had put on 30 pounds. She writes:

> There is someone who can be very happy and someone who no longer wants to eat and puke, but as many voices scream that I am a hypocrite, a tart, if I hurt myself I come to feel more quiet. But the beast inside me directly breaks free: give me food, I have to get food. You are a SWINE, Mary, a BEAST. Sell your BODY, put yourself NAKED in the street and have yourself FILLED UP. Let them all MAKE LOVE with you.
>
> I feel strange today. My life, the events, before and now, the things I just do. It is all a broken painting, fallen into numerous pieces. I see no connections, no unity any longer. My face is no longer recognizable. Yet I know that it exists. Between the debris of my life I still see the lines of my face. I think it was attractive and I want to restore

the painting. Will I ever see that face together again? My painting has been broken for so long.

Each day I try to imprint on myself that I have to be happy. A week ago I still binged and puked. I study hard. The girl next door often comes to me to have a good cry, because she doesn't trust anybody else. But yet I feel alone and I am afraid that nobody is there anymore. Perhaps I earned all this, is it all my fault. I cannot trust anyone and nobody puts his trust in me. Nobody, no body! I only have my own body. . . .

Mary belongs to a group of eating-disordered patients we have been seeing more and more in recent years. In the last decade increasing attention has been paid to the possible relationship between serious traumatic experiences (especially physical and sexual abuse) and the development of an eating disorder. It often is difficult to label these patients as having anorexia or bulimia nervosa because they often show comorbidity, especially in the form of impulse control problems and dissociative symptoms. These cases can be difficult to treat and warrant special diagnostic and therapeutic attention.

Presently there are no monographs addressing theory, assessment, and treatment of traumatic and dissociative experiences in eating disorders. This book aims to fill that gap. We discuss the complexity of the issue from the viewpoint of theory, research, and treatment. Illustrated with many examples (case vignettes), we offer practical guidelines for assessment and treatment. Finally, we discuss critical issues concerning contraindications and pitfalls of treatment as we reflect on the outcome of our treatment approach. The rationale behind our work could provide a subtitle of this book—it would be *Back to Reality*. It means that first of all, we want to help our patients to cope with the reality of their present lives. For many this implies that they have to turn their backs to the past and head toward the future. But it also means that in order to achieve these goals therapists have to face the emotional reality of traumatic life histories. For many victims of abuse, treatment will be a learning process about how to go backward into the future. Therapy should then close old doors and open new windows. "Only in the context of supportive and politically conscious advocacy can a survivor begin to accept that recovery is always partial in a patriarchal culture. With support one can begin to work through the aftermath of trauma, focusing on constructively resisting and preventing abuse. As survivors take small steps toward their own partial wholeness, they often find connections that lead them to work for social change" (Manlowe, 1995, pp. 133–134).

Taking into account the controversies around trauma therapies ("recovered" and "false" memory), we have tried to present a balanced and realistic presentation from a therapist's viewpoint, based on our own clinical experience.

- *Chapter 1* gives an overview of studies on trauma and dissociation in eating disorders in both clinical and nonclinical samples. Special attention is paid to the research carried out at our center.

- *Chapter 2* presents a multidimensional model that shows how different factors play a mediating role between the trauma experience in childhood and the development of adult psychopathology, such as dissociative symptoms and eating disorders.

- *Chapter 3* discusses those comorbid behaviors that in our experience are often linked to the combination of an eating disorder and a trauma history. These are problems with controlling impulses to perform acts that are harmful to oneself ("impulse dyscontrol"). Original research data on stealing and self-injurious behavior in eating disorders are presented.

- *Chapter 4* presents the assessment methods and instruments we prefer to use in our work with eating disorder patients. Special emphasis is laid on assessing trauma histories and dissociative symptoms.

- *Chapter 5* first briefly describes the treatment principles we consider essential for patients suffering from an eating disorder. Next, and in more detail, we discuss specific clinical guidelines for regaining self-control and dealing with patients whose eating disorder appears to be connected with a history of trauma, dissociation, and/or impulse dyscontrol.

- *Chapter 6* focuses on the possibilities of using hypnotherapeutic techniques for various therapeutic aims: regaining self-control and exploring and managing trauma experiences and dissociative symptoms.

- *Chapter 7* discusses some special family and marital issues that are relevant in dealing with trauma and dissociation in eating-disordered patients, but that often are neglected.

- *Chapter 8* closes the discussion with the risks, complications, and pitfalls a therapist can encounter in this often complex and demanding psychotherapeutic work. Special attention is given to possible contraindications of trauma exploration.

- For the interested readers we present a separate and exhaustive list of *references* on trauma, dissociation, and hypnosis in eating disorders. As an additional aid we have reproduced some new questionnaires in the *Appendices*. Also, *Appendix A* reports the data of our own follow-up study, designed to answer the question of whether trauma experiences are risk factors that affect the treatment outcomes of eating disorder patients.

Shortly before the end of two years of intensive therapy, Mary wrote the following note to her therapist:

Why did I starve myself so much? Why did I stuff myself so much? Fortunately I could get out of the straitjacket of pounds. I threw off the chains, but the journey remained to be difficult. We were together on our way, all the time, together. Every step requires a counter step. If the left foot leads, the right should follow. If right is tired, left should check its step. So to every question there belongs an answer. For a long time I was wondering where the journey would lead. To nowhere, I often thought. Or yet to myself?

I do know it now: the arrival isn't the meaningful element of a journey, but being on the way. Having arrived, one only has the past. I want to go on, on my way to the future.

1

Trauma History and Dissociative Experiences

Some case studies in the 1980s stimulated interest in the possible relationship between a history of traumatic experiences—especially physical and sexual abuse—and the development of an eating disorder (Goldfarb, 1987; Kearney-Cooke, 1988; McFarlane, McFarlane, & Gilchrist, 1988; Schechter, Schwarts, & Greenfeld, 1987; Sloan & Leichner, 1986; Torem, 1986a, b. The first reports suggested a higher frequency of traumatic experiences in bulimia nervosa patients than in patients with anorexia nervosa of the restricting type.*

Soon a rapidly growing number of studies on this subject appeared in the scientific literature together with a more general trend in psychiatry to look for a possible relationship between sexual abuse and the development of mental disorders.

---

*"*Restricting*" anorexia nervosa patients lose weight through strict food restriction, often combined with physical hyperactivity, whereas those with "*mixed*" anorexia nervosa also resort to self-induced vomiting and/or the use of laxatives, often combined with binge eating. The latter therefore resemble patients with bulimia nervosa. However, if body weight is low, the diagnosis of anorexia nervosa is given priority.

STUDIES IN CLINICAL SAMPLES

After the first case reports, several retrospective studies on larger samples—both clinical and nonclinical—have been carried out. Oppenheimer, Howells, Palmer, and Chaloner (1985) published the first large-scale study of 78 female eating-disordered outpatients, and they reported sexual abuse during childhood and/or adolescence in 70% of these patients. They found no relationship between a history of sexual abuse and the type of eating disorder diagnosed. Finn, Hartman, Leon, and Lawson (1986) studied the relationship between sexual abuse and the prevalence of an eating disorder in a sample of 87 eating-disordered women. Prevalence of sexual abuse in the latter was 57%, but comparisons of women with and without histories of sexual abuse suggested no association between the occurrence of an eating disorder and a history of sexual abuse. Kearney-Cooke (1988) found a history of sexual trauma in 58% of 75 bulimic patients. Root and Fallon (1988) reported that 65% of women in a group of 172 eating-disorder patients had been physically abused, 23% raped, 28% sexually abused in childhood, and 23% maltreated in relationships. Hall, Tice, Beresford, Wooley, and Hall (1989) found the number of sexually abused women (50%) in a group of 158 eating-disordered patients to be significantly higher than in a control group of 86 other patients (28%). Bulik, Sullivan, and Rorty (1989) investigated childhood sexual abuse and family background in 34 bulimics: 34% of this sample had been sexually abused. Interestingly, when comparing abused with nonabused subjects, no differences were found in eating pathology and related characteristics.

Steiger and Zanko (1990) compared the prevalence of sexual abuse in a group of 73 eating-disordered subjects with two other control groups: 21 psychiatric patients and 24 "normal" women. About 30% of the eating disorder group reported sexual abuse histories, versus 33% in the psychiatric control group and 9% in the normal controls. Within the eating disorder group, restricting anorexia nervosa patients had significantly lower abuse rates (6%) than all other eating disorder subgroups. Palmer, Oppenheimer, Dignon, Chaloner, and Howells (1990) extended their first series of eating disorders (Oppenheimer et al., 1985) and studied the sexual abuse histories of 158 patients; of these, 31% reported childhood sexual abuse and another 27% reported other unpleasant or coercive sexual events. Again they did not find a significant association between rates of abuse and the particular type of eating disorder. In a systematic study of 112 consecutive referrals of normal-weight bulimic women, Lacey (1990) found that only eight patients (7%) mentioned a history of sexual abuse involving physical contact. Four of these (3.6%) described incest, but only in two cases (1.8%) did this occur during childhood. Lacey concluded that his therapeutic work confirmed the "impression that incest and child sexual abuse mostly occurred in multi-impulsive bulimics" (these are bulimic patients who show additional forms of impulse dyscontrol, as discussed in more detail in Chapter 3). DeGroot, Kennedy, Rodin, and McVey (1992) reported a sexual abuse rate of approximately 25% in a sample of 184 female outpatients with a DSM-III-R eating disorder diagnosis.

In Waller's (1991, 1993a) series of 100 eating-disordered women, 50% were sexually abused and the prevalence of abuse appeared to be associated with diagnostic category: Women with bulimic disorders reported significantly higher rates of unwanted sexual experiences than did restricting anorectics. Waller (1992a) further showed that the frequency of bingeing and vomiting is significantly greater in women who report sexual abuse with particular characteristics: when the abuse was intrafamilial, involved force, or occurred before the woman was 14 years old. In another study of 100 anorectic women, Waller (1993b) found that 37% of the women reported that they had been subjected to unwanted sexual experiences. Again, the results showed a strong association between reported unwanted sexual experiences and purging behavior (vomiting and abuse of laxatives). Anorectics who did purge had lower reported rates of abuse.

Waller further studied the influence of other factors that might mediate the link between childhood sexual abuse and the development of an eating disorder. Waller's (1994) study suggested that borderline personality disorder was associated with the report of sexual abuse and might be a psychologial factor that explains a small part of the causal link between sexual abuse and bulimic behavior, especially the frequency of bingeing. In other studies (Everill & Waller,

1995; Waller & Ruddock, 1993), the importance of the experience of initial disclosure as a mediator in eating disordered women was considered. The extent of psychopathology (particularly the frequency of vomiting and the presence of symptoms of borderline personality disorder) was associated with the nature of the perceived response to an attempted disclosure. A perceived lack of response or a negative, hostile response was associated with greater levels of both borderline and bulimic symptoms (particularly vomiting).

Folsom, Krahn, Nairn, Gold, Demitrack, and Silk (1993) published a well-controlled study in which they compared rates of physical and sexual abuse in 102 women with eating disorder and 49 with general psychiatric disorders. No differences in abuse rates were found between the two groups: sexual abuse on the one hand and physical abuse on the other were reported in 69% and 51%, respectively, of the eating disorder sample and in 80% and 56% of the psychiatric sample. No relationship between a history of sexual abuse and severity of the eating disorder was found. However, within the eating disorder group, sexually abused subjects reported more severe psychiatric disturbances of an obsessive and phobic nature than nonabused subjects. According to Folsom and colleagues, their findings suggest that although sexually abusive experiences may be related to increased psychological distress, they do not serve to increase eating disorder symptomatology.

Miller and McCluskey-Fawcett (1993) compared 72 bulimic women with 72 age-matched controls who had no signs of eating disorders on measures of sexual abuse, dissociation, and early family mealtime experiences. Rates of self-reported sexual abuse after the age of 12 with an adult relative as the perpetrator were significantly greater in the bulimics than the control women: 15.3% versus 1.4%. Nonsignificant but high rates of sexual abuse prior to the age 12 were also found in this group: 11.1% versus 1.4%. Dissociative experiences were significantly more common in the bulimic group overall, and higher still for bulimic women who reported sexual abuse in their childhood. Bulimic women had more negative and unusual mealtime experiences than nonbulimic women. The authors concluded that sexual abuse may be related to the subsequent onset of bulimia nervosa for some women.

Welch and Fairburn (1994) carried out one of the best controlled studies. They investigated four individually matched groups: 50 community cases of bulimia nervosa, 50 community controls without an eating disorder, 50 community controls with other psychiatric disorders (mostly depression), and 50 inpatients with bulimia nervosa. Assessment of abuse histories before the onset of the eating disorder was established by interview in the subjects' own homes. Results showed that significantly more community cases of bulimia nervosa had been abused before the onset of their eating disorder (26%) than the community controls (10%). However, there was no difference between the rates of sexual abuse in the community cases of bulimia nervosa and the psychiatric controls (24%). A surprising result was the smaller number of inpatient cases of bulimia nervosa who had been sexually abused (16%). Welch and Fairburn concluded that childhood sexual abuse does increase the risk of psychiatric disorders including bulimia nervosa but that the increased risk is not specific to the eating disorder.

Though a history of sexual abuse may be not a specific risk factor for the development of an eating disorder, the follow-up study by Gleaves and Eberenz (1994) demonstrated that the presence of sexual abuse might be related to a poor prognosis in eating disorders. The authors studied 464 bulimic women in treatment at a residential facility for women with eating disorders, and they examined the connection between a history of sexual abuse and symptoms suggestive of poor prognosis including a history of multiple therapists or hospitalizations, self-injury or suicide attempts, and alcohol or drug problems. Of the women with all of the indicators of poor prognosis, approximately 71% reported a history of sexual abuse, versus 15% reported by subjects in the sample who did not have any predictors of poor outcome.

While most of these studies have focused on the incidence of sexual abuse, some researchers point also to the need to examine the full range of possible abusive experiences in women with eating disorders (Schmidt, Tiller & Treasure, 1993). Rorty, Yager, and Rossotto (1994a & b) compared 80 women with long histories of bulimia nervosa with 40 women who had never had an eating disorder or related difficulties. The bulimics reported higher levels of childhood physical abuse, psychological abuse, and multiple abuse. The authors concluded that their findings underscore the importance of examining the full range of possible abusive experiences in eating disorder patients, rather than focusing simply on sexual abuse alone.

Another interesting report, which is slightly tangential to the rest of this literature, is the study done by Kaner, Bulik, and Sullivan (1993). They assessed the presence of abuse (repeated physical battery) in the adult relationships of 20 bulimic women and 17 control women. Significantly more bulimic women than controls reported having been in relationships in which repeated physical battery occurred. Battered bulimic women were significantly more depressed than the controls. The authors stressed the need for a heightened sensitivity on the part of therapists to the presence and implications of recurrent abusive experiences in adult relationships.

STUDIES IN NONCLINICAL SAMPLES

Besides these studies in clinical populations—except for the Welch and Fairburn study (1994) comparing inpatients with community subjects—other studies have been conducted exclusively in nonclinical populations. Calam and Slade (1989) administered questionnaires to 130 female undergraduate students: 20% reported unwanted sexual experiences before the age of 14, with 13% reporting intrafamilial abuse. The experience of sexual events involving force was associated with abnormal eating attitudes and behaviors. Only early sexual intercourse (before age 14) against the participant's wishes showed a significant correlation with bulimic tendencies. Bailey and Gibbons (1989) studied the relationship between bulimia nervosa and abuse histories in a sample of 294 college students: 13% reported childhood sexual abuse, 11% rape, 8% battery, and 6% other physical abuse. Only physical abuse correlated significantly with the presence of bulimic symptoms.

Smolak, Levine, and Sullins (1990) administered questionnaires to 298 undergraduate women: 23% reported child sexual abuse and this subgroup showed more eating disorder symptoms and related problems than the nonabused group. The eating pathology was related neither to the severity or type of abuse, nor to the identity of the perpetrator. Beckman and Burns (1990) investigated the relation between self-report of prior sexual abuse and current eating behaviors consistent with bulimia in 340 college women. Bulimic women in this sample did not report a higher incidence of past (intra/extrafamilial) childhood sexual experiences than did the control group. However, bulimic women did report significantly more experiences of extrafamilial sexual abuse after age 12 (during adolescence) than normal eaters. Strikingly, Abramson and Lucido (1991) obtained nearly identical percentages of bulimics and non-bulimics reporting childhood sexual abusive experiences (69%), and they found a significant correlation between eating behaviors and the total number of childhood adversive sexual experiences.

Two other studies focused on the relationship between family background, sexual abuse, and eating disorders. Kinzl, Traweger, Guenther, and Biebl (1994) found a sexual abuse incidence rate of 21% in a sample of 202 female university students. There were no differences in symptoms or related features of an eating disorder among women with no, one, or repeated incidents of sexual abuse. However, women who reported an adverse family background displayed significantly more eating disorder pathology than did women who assessed their family backgrounds as secure. The authors concluded that childhood sexual abuse is neither necessary nor sufficient for the later development of an eating disorder, while an adverse family background may be an important etiological factor. Hastings and Kern (1994) investigated the presence of sexual abuse and bulimia in a sample of female college students (N=786) and its relationship with past family experiences (before the age of 12). Their findings appear to show that the association of sexual abuse and a chaotic family environment increase in an additive manner the probability of bulimia.

In contrast to previous reports, Schaaf and McCanne (1994) found no evidence that childhood sexual or physical abuse was associated with the development of body image disturbance in a sample of 670 female college students screened for childhood abuse. Furthermore, the results did not support the hypothesis that childhood sexual abuse and physical abuse are related to eating disorder symptomatology. It is suggested that victims of childhood sexual abuse manifest higher rates of a number of different types of psychopathology, including eating disorders.

DISSOCIATIVE SYMPTOMS IN EATING DISORDERS

At the end of the 19th century, the eminent French philosopher and psychiatrist, Pierre Janet, was probably the first author to systematically study the relationship between traumatic experiences and dissociation in the etiology of a wide range of psychiatric problems, including eating disorders. He described dissociation as a crucial psychological mechanism with which the organism reacts to overwhelming trauma. Memories and *idées fixes* (fixed ideas), referring to the traumatic experience, can be split off from conscious awareness and result in a wide variety of dissociative ("hysterical") symptoms (Janet, 1907; Van der Kolk & van der Hart, 1989). Hence, Janet described dissociation as a kind of mental avoidance ("escape") technique; in his view the resulting amnesia for the traumatic event was the most specific clinical characteristic in pathological dissociation.

After Janet the interest in the concept of dissociation in eating disorders disappeared for more than half a century, but reemerged in recent decades (for a detailed review, see Vanderlinden & Vandereycken, 1988). The presence of minor dissociative "hysterical" mechanisms in bulimic patients was reported by Russell in 1979. In the mid 1980s, Torem was among the first clinicians pointing again to the possible presence of dissociative mechanisms and symptoms in eating disorders. In a study in 30 eating disorder patients, Torem (1986a), found that 12 of them had dissociated ego-states that were in disharmony with one another. Consequently, Torem (1986 a & b, 1990) stressed the importance of systematic screening for dissociative symptoms in eating disorder patients. Based on a case report, Chandarana and Malla (1989) also suggested a relationship between dissociation and bulimia.

In recent years, researchers have begun systematically to study the presence of dissociative symptoms in eating disorders. Sanders (1986), who developed a new scale for the measurement of dissociation (the Perceptual Alteration Scale or PAS), demonstrated that binge-eating college students reported a higher degree of dissociative phenomena than normal controls. Demitrack, Putnam, Brewerton, Brandt, and Gold (1990) studied dissociative experiences in 30 female eating disorder patients, compared to 30 age-matched "normal" women, and found that the patients demonstrated significantly higher levels of dissociative psychopathology than the control subjects. This finding has been replicated by Covino, Jimerson, Wolfe, Franko, and Frankel (1994), who found higher scores on a self-reporting dissociation questionnaire in bulimics, compared to controls. A study by Goldner, Cockhill, Bakan, and Birmingham (1991) corroborates these findings. Significantly higher scores on a dissociation questionnaire were reported in eating-disordered patients compared to age-matched female controls. McCallum, Lock, Kulla, Rorty, and Wetzel (1992) demonstrated in a sample of 38 eating-disordered patients that dissociative symptoms frequently occur in subgroups of eating disorders, particularly those with multiple psychiatric comorbidity. The authors found a 28% rate for dissociative disorders, including a 10% rate for multiple personality disorder (MPD). The presence of dissociative disorder was significantly related to a history of self-harm.

Herzog, Stoley, Carmody, Robbins, and van der Kolk (1993) studied the presence of both sexual abuse and dissociative symptoms in 20 eating disorder patients: 65% of the subjects reported childhood sexual abuse, and those with more comorbidity reported abuse more often. Subjects with a history of abuse had significantly higher scores on a dissociation scale. In another study with a rather small number of patients, Greenes, Fava, Cioffi, and Herzog (1993) assessed dissociative features in bulimics with and without depression and in depressed subjects with and without bulimia. In contrast with earlier findings, an association was found between depression and dissociation, confounding the previously noted relationship between bulimia nervosa and dissociation. Another study in 142 college women by Rosen and Petty (1994) suggested that dissociation might be associated with eating problems and that treatment of eating-disordered individuals should include a component directed toward teaching patients to recognize their ability to dissociate.

A study carried out in Japan by Berger and colleagues (1994) in a sample of 41 eating disorder outpatients found a combined physical and sexual abuse rate of 45% for the total sample. Of these patients 22% fulfilled the criteria for MPD (multiple personality disorder according to DSM-III-R) and 15% showed scores on a dissociation scale that indicate a high likelihood of MPD or posttraumatic stress disorder.

A relationship between dissociative experiences and eating disorders has also been reported by Everill, Waller, and Macdonald (1995). They investigated the links between dissociation and eating pathology in a clinical group of bulimic women and a nonclinical group of female undergraduates. In the nonclinical group, specific dissociative styles were found to be linked with bulimic tendencies. In the eating-disordered group, there was an association between the scores on a dissociation scale and the frequency of binge eating. The authors further concluded that the presence of both dissociation and bulimic symptomatology may be particularly suggestive of a history of early abusive or stressful experiences, or of a significant loss.

Dalle Grave, Rigamonti and Todisco's (1995) study confirmed the findings of earlier studies. They found dissociative symptoms to be significantly more prevalent in a sample of 103 eating disorder patients than in female controls. Twenty percent of the eating-disordered women reported high levels of dissociative symptomatology. An association between dissociation and eating disorder was found particularly in patients with a bulimic component (normal-weight bulimics and "mixed" anorectic bulimics). Surprisingly enough, obese binge eaters reported less severe trauma experiences and showed low levels of dissociative symptoms.

OUR OWN RESEARCH FINDINGS

In a first study (Vanderlinden & Vandereycken, 1993), the relationship between traumatic experiences and dissociative phenomena was explored in a group of 98 eating disorder patients, all diagnosed according to DSM-III-R criteria. Traumatic experiences were assessed by means of a self-report questionnaire on unwanted sexual events in childhood (Lange, Kooiman, Huberts, & van Oostendorp, 1995) and clinical interview; dissociative experiences were assessed with the newly developed self-reporting *Dissociation Questionnaire* or DIS-Q discussed in Chapter 4. Besides (intra/extrafamilial) sexual abuse varying from fondling to rape, the following situations were also considered as seriously traumatic: physical abuse (repeated beating or torture), complete emotional neglect or abandonment in childhood, and loss of a close family member. Only the trauma situations that occurred before the onset of the eating disorder were assessed.

The total trauma prevalence rate was 28%: 20% reported childhood sexual abuse, of which 8% was incestuous. Anorexia nervosa patients of the "mixed" type (with bingeing and/or purging), bulimics and atypical eating disorder patients had significantly higher trauma rates (respectively 25%, 37%, and 58%), compared to restricting anorectics (12%). Sexual abuse was significantly lower in the latter (only 3%), compared to the three other eating disorder subgroups (20%). Hence these data showed a relationship between the presence of a traumatic experience and the type of eating pathology. The trauma group reported significantly higher scores on the DIS-Q, compared to the nontrauma group.

The highest scores on the DIS-Q were reported by the sexually abused subjects, especially on the subscale for amnesia. The latter turned out to be the most specific characteristic to differentiate the sexually abused patients from the nonabused subjects. On the DIS-Q about 12 % of our eating disorder sample mentioned dissociative experiences to a degree as high as in a group of patients with dissociative disorders. Of this subgroup 5 patients reported sexual abuse by others, 4 subjects reported incest with father (starting before the age of ten) and 1 subject mentioned neglect and physical abuse; in only two patients with dissociative features was no history of trauma detected.

These data suggested that trauma-related dissociative experiences may play an important role in a subgroup of patients with eating disorders. When comparing several forms of trauma, the results suggested a possible relationship between the seriousness of the trauma and the occurrence of dissociative experiences. Only the patients with a history of incest and sexual abuse reported higher total DIS-

Q score (p<.05) and a higher score on amnesia (p<.002), compared to the nonabused group.

A second study addressed the relationship between childhood trauma (sexual abuse and other traumatic experiences such as emotional abuse and neglect and/or physical abuse) and psychiatric comorbidity (general neuroticism, borderline psychopathology) in a sample of 80 eating disorder patients, all diagnosed according to DSM-III-R criteria. This study had three aims: (1) to replicate the findings from our first study on the relationship between childhood trauma and dissociative experiences, assessed with the DIS-Q; (2) to determine whether there existed a relationship between childhood trauma and eating pathology, assessed with several questionnaires developed to assess typical eating pathology, including the *Eating Disorder Evaluation Scale* or EDES (Vandereycken, 1993a described in Chapter 4); and (3) to study the association between childhood trauma, dissociation, and psychiatric comorbidity, assessed with the *Hopkins Symptom Check List* (SCL-90) (Derogatis, 1983) and the *Borderline Syndrome Index* (BSI) (Conte, Plutchik, Karasu, & Jerret, 1980). Since we discovered that many patients disclosed trauma experiences only after several months of intensive psychotherapy, information on childhood trauma was based not only on data from a self-report questionnaire on unwanted sexual events in childhood (Lange et al., 1995) and on information gathered from a clinical interview, but also on trauma experiences that came to light during the treatment.

Results showed an overall trauma prevalence rate of 53%, much higher than in our first study: 20% reported sexual abuse (of which 7% was incestuous abuse), 35% emotional neglect, and 27% physical abuse. When comparing different subgroups of eating disorders (restricting and mixed type anorectics and normal-weight bulimics), sexual abuse was found to be significantly more present in anorexia nervosa of the mixed type (50%) and patients with bulimia nervosa (18%), than in restricting anorectics (10%); physical abuse was more present in patients with bulimia nervosa (37%) than in restricting (23%) or mixed type anorectics (21%).

These findings again showed a relationship between sexual abuse and the subtype of eating disorder, specifically bulimic behaviors. When comparing the sexually abused subjects (*N*=16) with the nonabused sample (*N*=64), again only bulimic behavior (EDES subscale) was found to be more prevalent in the former group (p<.06). The sexually abused patients also scored significantly higher (= more abnormal) on the following questionnaires: total SCL-90 score (p<.01), yielding a general psychoneuroticism score; the SCL-90 subscales anxiety (p<.02) and depression (p<.01); the total DIS-Q score (p<.01) and subscales identity confusion (p<.01) and amnesia (p<.005); the total score on the BSI (p<.05) and the first subscale negative self-esteem and depression (p<.05).

To elaborate on this finding, correlations (Pearson's R) were carried out between sexual abuse and the scores on the different questionnaires. Only one significant correlation was found between sexual abuse and all eating disorder subscales, namely with the EDES bulimia subscale (r=.21, p<.05). Other positive correlations with sexual abuse were found with the total score on the SCL-90 (r=.29; p<.008), the SCL-subscales on anxiety (r=.25; p<.026) and depression (r=.29; p<.009), and the total DIS-Q score (r=.28; p<.012) and subscales on identity confusion (r=.28; p<.01) and amnesia (r=.32; p<.004).

The data of the DIS-Q confirmed the results of our first study with the amnesia subscale being the most significant differentiating variable between sexually abused and nonabused patients. Compared with the scores of a patient group with dissociative disorder, 16.5% of the subjects showed DIS-Q scores above the cut-off point of 2.5. Trauma prevalence rate in this group was 75%: 50% sexual abuse and 33% physical abuse. The majority of these patients had a diagnosis of either mixed anorexia nervosa or bulimia nervosa, while only 12% of the restricting anorectics scored above the cut-off score. Besides higher scores on the DIS-Q, sexually abused subjects reported significantly more psychoneurotic symptoms, especially anxiety and depression, and borderline pathology. This finding corroborates the results from many other studies, and again demonstrates the serious link between childhood abuse and psychiatric sequelae during adolescence and/or adulthood (see Briere & Zaidi, 1989; Ensink, 1992; Herman, Perry & van der Kolk, 1989).

With regard to borderline pathology, 53% of the eating disorder sample scored above the BSI cut-off point, suggesting a high presence of borderline symptoms in this group. A high correlation was found between the total DIS-Q score, the total BSI score (r=.68, p<.0001), and the total SCL-90 score (r=.65; p<.0001), suggesting an important overlap between these symptoms. Only a moderate correlation was found between the prevalence of trauma and BSI scores (r=.25; p<.05).

DISCUSSION

Overviewing all these data on the prevalence of traumatic experiences and features of dissociation in eating-disordered patients, we have to question what we can learn from all these findings. Most studies have focused on sexual abuse alone, although evidence suggests that probably many different factors, such as parental lack of care, inappropriate parental control, physical abuse, loss of significant others, and emotional abuse may play an important role in the development in the eating disorder. Even when studies are limited to sexual abuse, it is very difficult to draw unequivocal conclusions from them because reported prevalence rates range from 7% (Lacey, 1990) to 70% (Oppenheimer et al., 1985). How can these divergent findings be explained? The following methodological factors appear to play a role.

1. *Heterogeneity of the eating disorders.* Samples can vary considerably with respect to clinical features: type and severity of eating disorder, age of onset and duration, and comorbidity (additional diagnoses). Research data clearly suggest that sexual abuse may be related to higher levels of comorbidity, in particular mood disorders, anxiety disorders, personality disorders (especially of the borderline type), and dissociative disorders.

2. *Definition of trauma and/or sexual abuse.* Some studies report only those sexually abusive experiences that took place before the onset of the eating disorder and when the perpetrator was at least five years older than the victim. Some investigate only childhood sexual abuse, while other studies

also include more recent traumatic experiences involving peers during adolescence or adulthood. We clearly need a consensus about definitions of sexual abuse.

3. *Severity of the abuse.* One important, although very complex, factor that has not been assessed in most studies is the severity and duration of the abuse. Research data (e.g., Boon & Draijer, 1993) show a relation between the degree of adult psychopathology and the severity of sexual abuse—for instance, abuse starting before the age of five years, abuse combined with violence or physical abuse, and abuse involving multiple perpetrators who are close relatives. Evaluation of severity remains a difficult issue, however, because it concerns first and foremost the subjective experience of the victim. Furthermore, studies must take into account the perceived response to attempts at disclosure. A lack of reaction or a hostile response may be at least as traumatic as the event itself (Waller & Ruddock, 1993).

4. *Assessment of sexual abuse.* The investigator's own personal characteristics (male or female, involved in the therapy or not), the timing of the assessment (before, during, or after therapy), and the methods used to gather information may have an impact on the results (see Chapter 4). Currently, no data are available that support the use of a specific assessment method—for instance, a self-report questionnaire rather than a standardized interview. Moreover, there always remains the problem of memory distortion and induction, especially in this group of highly vulnerable, suggestible, and emotionally labile patients.

Taking into account the methodological problems, we can summarize the major findings as follows:

• Sexual abuse is reported by a substantial number of women with an eating disorder. Approximately 20 to 50% report a history of childhood sexual abuse, but such rates also have been found in other psychiatric patients. Compared to the general female population, the rate of abuse appears to be higher in eating disorder patients.

- The rate of sexual abuse seems to be higher in patients with bulimic symptoms compared to restricting anorectics.

- Sexual abuse is more often associated with comorbidity, especially borderline personality disorder and dissociative symptoms.

A *specific and direct* connection between sexual abuse (or other traumatic experiences) and the subsequent development of an eating disorder has not been demonstrated yet. But both the available research data and our own clinical experiences in therapeutic work with these patients seem to lead to at least one general conclusion: serious sexual and/or physical abuse in childhood and early adolescence puts the individual at special risk for developing psychiatric disorders, including eating disorders.

In the next chapter we propose a multidimensional model with different levels and factors that might be important in understanding the relationship between sexual abuse and eating disorders, including, for example: (a) the functioning of the subject prior to the trauma (e.g., age and vulnerability of the child at the time when the abuse occurred); (b) family background and educational atmosphere; (c) the nature, severity, and extent of traumatization (e.g., sexual abuse versus physical abuse alone, or a combination of both); (d) the initial response to the trauma, such as the child's coping resources and parental reactions to the trauma; and (e) other factors, including later life events and self-image.

2

The Link Between Trauma and Dissociation in Eating Disorders

Most of the research on psychotrauma and dissociation has been focused exclusively on three issues: (1) the exploration and/or uncovering of traumatic experiences (especially in childhood); (2) the assessment of dissociative symptoms; and (3) the relationship between these trauma experiences (input) and psychopathology such as dissociative disorders and eating disorders (output). In these studies, a link has been found between severity and duration of the trauma on the one hand and severity of the dissociative symptoms on the other (e.g., Boon & Draijer, 1993). However, a frequently made and important misinterpretation is confounding the association or correlation between (childhood) trauma and dissociation with a *causal relationship.* The fact that in many studies high levels of dissociative symptoms have been found in severely traumatized patients does not automatically mean that childhood trauma causes dissociative symptoms. The existing research does not allow us to consider a direct and causal link between the two phenomena.

Despite extensive research on the adverse effects of reported sexual abuse, the process linking abuse and dissociative phenomena remains unclear. It has been suggested that other factors may interfere or mediate between the trauma input and the psychopathology outcome (Waller, 1993a). This chapter will discuss the most important factors that may play a mediating role between the trauma experience in childhood (or early adolescence) and the development of adult psychopathology, such as dissociative symptoms and eating disorders. These mediating factors also must be evaluated in the diagnostic process and may provide the clinician/therapist with important information and guidelines for the planning of the treatment.

DEVELOPMENTAL PHASE

Several studies have shown a link between the age at onset of the abuse and later psychological sequelae, including dissociative symptoms and eating disorders, not only in general population studies (Putnam, 1989; Ross, 1989), but also in eating disorders (Waller, 1993b). Abusive experiences at a younger age seem to be associated with more severe problems. How can we explain this finding? We assume that the lower the age at the time when the abuse started, the more primitive the defensive mechanisms activated by the traumatic experience. Once installed, these reactions—including radical changes in eating behavior—are maintained through learning processes (especially classical conditioning) and thus are quite resistant to change. This assumption is based on the ideas of Van der Kolk (1987) and Van der Kolk, Greenberg, Boyd, and Krystal (1985), who have stressed the many apparent behavioral and biological similarities between human responses to traumatic events and animal responses to an inescapable electric shock. The (experimental) animal model of inescapable shock has been proposed as a fruitful biological model for posttraumatic stress disorder and dissociative disorder in human beings.

Human responses to psychotraumas involve physiological and behavioral hyperreactivity (hyperarousal, intrusive reliving of traumatic events in flashbacks and nightmares), alongside numbing (emotional constriction, social isolation, anhedonia, a sense of estrangement). Following this model, when they are confronted with trauma at a very young age, human beings may react as if they were frozen—they may seem immobilized, as if they were paralyzed. Such a reaction is typical in animals facing a life-threatening situation and can be experimentally elicited by such methods as confronting rats in a cage with inescapable electric shocks. According to Nijenhuis and Vanderlinden (1995) the analogy between animal and human defenses in the face of serious threat may be extended to include, apart from the dominant defensive reaction of freezing, other animal defensive behaviors such as a radical change in eating patterns.

The defensive system of a prey-animal consists of several subsystems; that is, of discrete states in which characteristic behavioral patterns and physiological responses are shown (Fanselow & Lester, 1988). Depending upon the stage of imminent danger, radically different behaviors and physiological reactions are evoked, each of which is adapted to provide optimal survival chances. For example, prey-animals instantly display a radical change in eating patterns when they are placed at risk during foraging. They become highly aroused in those situations, and show prolonged abstinence from food that is occasionally interrupted by a short and rapid intake of large quantities of food. Food abstinence allows the aroused animal to pay full attention to the imminent danger, while bingeing compensates for loss of body weight. Nijenhuis and Vanderlinden (1995) assume that the various defensive states, such as freezing, and specific eating patterns, such as bingeing and vomiting, may reflect human analogies to animal subsystems of defense.

Research has further demonstrated that brain structures involved in cognitive information processing (such as the hippocampal system) need several years to maturate, but that the affect processing system (with the amygdala as a central unit) is functioning already from birth on (Jacobs & Nadel, 1985; LeDoux, 1989). It is assumed that the amygdala is responsible for the freezing reactions. Hence, due to immaturity of the hippocampal system, that primitive reaction will be the dominant response when the trauma takes place to a very young child (someone below five years old). In other words, very young children have, besides the freezing reaction and/or changes in their eating patterns, little or no other coping mechanisms available to deal with overwhelming trauma experiences. In contrast, children who are abused for the first time in late childhood can rely more on cognitive-oriented strategies; for example, they can blame others for the abuse or they can rationalize, and they can use more sophisticated defenses as a means of coping with the trauma.

Based on these findings, we assume that in some patients there might be remarkable similarities between bingeing and vomiting on the one hand and the so-called freezing-like states in animals on the other. Some patients will binge as a way to escape from conscious awareness when they are confronted with an inescapable emotional state or intrusive negative thoughts. Patients tell us, for instance: "While bingeing and vomiting, I have no feelings anymore"; "I am in a kind of hypnotic trance-like state"; "The bingeing/vomiting is a way to emotionally anesthesize myself; while I binge my mind is totally blank"; "When bingeing it is just like somebody else is taking over control and all negative feelings are disappearing."

Research has further demonstrated that these defensive reactions are quickly and strongly conditioned, following the classical pattern (Nijenhuis & Vanderlinden, 1995), and hence may become therapy-resistant. This means that specific situations and stimuli will immediately evoke these freezing-like reactions and their accompanying eating behaviors. These stimuli may be internal or external. Some examples of internal stimuli are feelings such as loneliness, depression, or aggressiveness and thoughts or images (flashbacks) that refer to the trauma experience. External stimuli may be all kinds of specific situations that refer to the original trauma experience, for instance a specific way of being looked at by a man, a smell, a specific environment (for example, a bedroom or a bathroom), specific dates, and so on. These findings may help us to better understand why patients who have been abused at a very young age may have such a great difficulty stopping their eating disorder symptoms.

NATURE OF THE ABUSE

Several studies have indicated that the specific characteristics of abuse may affect the severity of psychological problems encountered during adolescence and adulthood. The perpetrator's relationship to the child, the number of perpetrators, the frequency of the abuse, and the use of physical force have been found to be related to the extent and severity of dissociative symptoms and other adult psychological problems (Boon & Draijer, 1993; Briere & Zaidi, 1989; Carlin & Ward, 1992; Herman, 1992). Similar evidence is emerging from research in patients with eating disorders. Calam and Slade (1989) showed that eating-disordered women were more likely than women in comparison groups to have had a number of specific unwanted sexual experiences such as forced intercourse, intercourse with an authority figure, and abuse by a close male relative. As mentioned in the previous chapter, Waller (1992a) found that symptoms such as bingeing and vomiting were more marked when the abuse was intrafamilial, involved force, and occurred before the victim was 14 years old.

It is therefore important to explore the specific details of the abuse, including the type of contact (for example, exposure, touching, oral sex, or intercourse), the degree of threat or violence involved, the victim's relationship to the offender(s), and the frequency and duration of the abuse.

DISCLOSURE OF THE ABUSE

Recent studies have demonstrated that an important mediating factor between the abuse and later psychological sequelae may be the initial response to the disclosure of the trauma (Everson, Hunter, Runyon, Edelsohn, & Coulter, 1989; Friedrich, 1990). Roesler (1994) found that for those who disclosed their trauma experience in childhood, primarily to close family members, the reaction to the disclosure had a mediating effect between the abuse and the later development of symptoms. Those who had experienced a bad reaction from the first person to whom they disclosed their traumatic event turned out to have worse scores on symptoms of posttraumatic stress disorder and dissociation.

Everill and Waller (1995) also investigated how perceived responses to (attempted) disclosure of abuse were related to psychological functioning. A perceived adverse response to disclosure was associated with greater levels of psychopathology, particularly oral control, dissociation, and self-denigration. The reaction from family members to a disclosure of abuse has been shown to contribute to adult psychopathology in a sample of eating-disorder patients. Waller and Ruddock (1993) found that a perceived lack of response or a negative, hostile response was associated with specific patterns of symptomatology, particularly the frequency of vomiting and the symptoms of borderline personality disorder.

These data clearly underline the importance of systematically asking questions about earlier attempts of disclosure: when, to whom, and what was the response. A negative reaction may be related to intensified self-blame, feelings of guilt, and higher levels of psychopathology in the eating-disordered patient. Therefore, clinicians and researchers should be aware of their personal reactions when they encourage disclosure of abusive experiences (Everill & Waller, 1995). Ignoring the abuse stories, reacting in a neutral way, or showing a critical response might be harmful for these patients.

FAMILY VARIABLES

Family studies (e.g. Kog, Vertommen, & Vandereycken, 1989) have demonstrated that anorectics with a bulimic component report more conflict and disorganization and less cohesion in the family than do their restricting anorectic counterparts. Hence it makes sense to assume that this chaotic family structure may mediate between childhood trauma (input) and adult psychological sequelae (outcome). Case studies clearly indicate that parental support is a significant factor in the outcome of treatment of children who experienced abuse. However, systematic research with regard to the relationship between exposure to traumatic experiences and family variables has only recently drawn attention from researchers. Remarkably enough, all studies in the field of psychotrauma have focused exclusively on the possible impact of past family experiences. None examine the impact of actual family relationships on current psychological functioning (Faust, Runyon, & Kenny, 1995).

Some data are available in support of the hypothesis that perceived family environment might be an important mediating variable in abused subjects in determining the general level of adult psychological distress (Nash, Hulsey, Sexton, Harralson, & Lambert, 1993). A study by Dalgard, Bjork, and Tambs (1995) in Norway has demonstrated that social support—especially within the family—protects individuals exposed to negative life events against psychiatric disorders such as depression. This appeared to be the case, especially in subjects with an external locus of control (that is, subjects who attribute their well-being to external events). Wiesmann Wind and Silvern (1994) found that poor parental warmth, childhood stress, and abuse were each separately associated with current functioning in a nonclinical sample of 259 working women. Lack of parental warmth strongly mediated the relationship of intrafamilial child abuse to levels of depression and self-esteem. In contrast, abuse was associated with posttraumatic stress disorder independently of the variation in perceived parenting. Thus both factors, unfavorable parenting and abuse, independently contributed to the development of symptoms. The authors conclude that dissociative symptoms may be influenced by the abuse itself, while other symptoms, such as depression and low self-esteem, may be more affected by lack of parental warmth.

Similar studies have also been carried out in eating disorder samples. Schmidt, Tiller, and Treasure (1993) wanted to study whether childhood experiences and the quality of childhood care have an impact on the course of eating disorders. They used a semistructured interview for retrospective assessment in four groups of eating-disordered patients. The childhood family environment was rated on parental indifference, parental control, intrafamilial discord, and intrafamilial violence. The normal-weight bulimics reported higher levels of parental indifference and excessive parental control, physical abuse, and violence against other family members than did restricting anorectics. Overall, the findings suggest that negative life events, together with negative family experiences, may affect the course of illness; patients with a bulimic component reported more childhood adversity than restricting anorexia nervosa patients.

Hastings and Kern (1994) found some significant connections

between bulimia, sexual abuse and a chaotic family environment. Kinzl and colleagues (1994) examined the possible relationship of negative early family experiences and childhood sexual abuse to the later development of eating disorders in a sample of 202 female students. Their data suggested that sexual abuse in childhood is neither a necessary nor a sufficient factor for the later development of an eating disorder, but an adverse family background may be an important etiological factor. Hence the abuse-related factors may be less influential than the continuing family processes, such as the quality and amount of family support given to the child. However, Waller (1992b) could find no evidence in an eating disorder sample that perceived family dysfunction acted as a mediator between abuse and bulimic symptoms. Therefore, more research is needed to study the possible mediating influence of both past and actual family experiences on the relationship between trauma and eating pathology.

When the various studies on parenting in eating disorders are reviewed (Vandereycken, 1994), they show that bulimic patients report a striking pattern. These patients recall their rearing in childhood as being characterized by a lack of care from both parents and most clearly from the mother. The mothers are not perceived as being overprotective; rather, in the eyes of the patients they seem to have practiced neglectful parenting. Because the fathers were more often seen as overprotective, their rearing practices tended to be viewed by the patients as closer to the pattern of affectionless control. This perception by the bulimics of the parenting style they experienced should be viewed in the broader perspective of family (dys)functioning. The perception of parenting practices can also be linked to particular communication patterns. It was found, for example, that the level of critical comments (expressed emotion) from parents toward bulimic offspring were significantly higher than those toward anorectic offspring (Vandereycken, 1994). Hence, a dysfunctional form of parenting or a distorted perception of parenting (or both) can be seen as epiphenomena of a more general negative atmosphere within families of bulimic patients. In distressed parent–child relationships, chronic negative emotion can be both a cause and a consequence of interactions that undermine parents' concerns and children's development. (Vandereycken, 1995).

However, even if we had found a particular family interaction pattern, its specificity and causal significance in each particular patient remain to be demonstrated. Nothwithstanding these warnings, we believe that the screening of past and actual family experiences and dynamics—for instance, through a semistructured interview and/or questionnaires such as the Parental Bonding Instrument and the Leuven Family Questionnaire (see Chapter 4)—should belong to the usual diagnostic process. Special care must be given to the chaotic, less cohesive and/or disorganized families that are often encountered in work with bulimic patients.

Finally, patients' recently developed intimate relationships should not be forgotten. Not achieving or maintaining intimacy in the relationship with a partner may negatively influence a person's physical, emotional, or psychological well-being. In order to explain such negative effects of a failure to achieve intimacy it is assumed that the emergence of specific complaints or symptom behavior serves the purpose of avoiding something that the partners perceive as threatening their individuality or their relationship. Hence, in accounting for the relationship between a low degree of marital intimacy and the emergence of physical or psychiatric symptoms, the avoidance function of symptom behavior must be assigned a crucial role. More specifically, the emergence of symptoms may be regarded as an avoidance reaction to situations that are perceived as threatening the patient's identity (for example, the partner's attempts to achieve more intimacy), or alternatively, the existence of the relationship itself (overt conflicts that arise as a result of the low level of intimacy). Marital as well as sexual problems may both reveal and conceal old traumatic experiences. (Van den Broucke, Vandereycken, & Norré, 1997).

LIFE EVENTS

All too often events in the (remote) past are being linked as explanatory factors to current conditions as if nothing had happened in between. Everyone has to cope with all kinds of life events, from daily hassles to extreme stress. Moreover, the abuse victim may be more vulnerable and/or less prepared to handle stressful situations. Research suggests that many victims of abuse in childhood are at high risk for revictimization experiences—that is, a repetition of physical and sexual abuse by people other than the original perpetrators (Briere & Runtz, 1988; Wyatt & Newcomb, 1990). The serious impact of a traumatic event often increases the probability that a series of other stressors will follow the occurrence of the first stressor. For example, the social withdrawal and increase in fearfulness seen initially eventually may be identified as school refusal and subsequent decrease in academic achievement (Friedrich, 1990). Physical and sexual abuse of a child also has an impact on the parental relationship, possibly leading to marital dissolution and the increased likelihood of economic stressors. Single-parent families (mostly mothers and their children) seem to be especially vulnerable.

In addition to asking about revictimization experiences, such as sexual abuse and physical abuse in actual relationships (partner, friend, boss, therapist), a therapist should also ask about other kinds of life events that may have functioned as triggers in the development of the eating disorder and dissociative symptoms. In many patients, we notice that the eating disorder starts when the young adolescent girl is confronted with her own sexuality and more intimate contacts, even when these experiences are positive and not abusive at all. These situations may function to elicit memories of abuse and related feelings and thoughts. The eating pathology may then function as a way to escape from these feelings and thoughts.

Our experience points to the importance not only of focusing on old traumatic experiences, but also of gathering information about recent stressful events and revictimization experiences. As the example in Chapter 4 shows, these experiences may even be more crucial to deal with in the psychotherapeutic treatment. Finally, we like to state that attention should be paid to positive life events and social support as well. The experience of being respected or—even better—of being loved in a trustful and safe relationship might help the patient to regain self-confidence and find a way out of the pathology.

SELF-IMAGE

Victims of sexual and physical abuse often have low self-esteem and blame themselves for what happened (Herman, 1992; Jehu, 1988). Therefore, it seems plausible that the degree to which abused children and/or adolescents have a chance to talk about the traumatic events and to receive emotional support will affect their self-esteem. Most frequent, and most crucial, are feelings of guilt, shame, and self-blame, including self-denigratory feelings and beliefs of worthlessness, powerlessness, stigmatization, and inferiority (Jehu, 1988), together with a profound sense of being different (Finkelhor & Brown, 1985). Here, we assume that a negative self-image, based on self-blame in combination with poor self-esteem, may also mediate between the input (trauma) and outcome (dissociative symptoms and eating disorders). The more the girl blames herself for the abuse (eventually reinforced by negative comments from others: "It's your fault") the greater the likelihood that the abusive experience will be dissociated from conscious awareness. Moreover, children who view themselves in a negative way will become isolated from their peer group (which normally serves as an important socializing arena), or they will become involved in a marginal group of troubled youngsters, where their negative self-image will be confirmed (Friedrich, 1990).

Research data show divergent findings about the importance of the victim's self-image. Waller (1992b) did not find self-esteem to function as a mediating factor, but he argues that future research should focus on specific cognitions related to the abuse, rather than on general measures on self-esteem. Therefore, we hypothesize that self-esteem in eating disorders might be strongly related to the way these patients perceive their bodies. In our own study of 62 eating disorder patients, we found that negative perceptions and cognitions of the subject's own body, assessed with the *Body Attitude Test* (BAT), were the best predictors of dissociative symptoms at follow-up after treatment (Vanderlinden, Vandereycken, & Probst, 1995). Eating disorder patients who reported very negative feelings toward their bodies at the start of treatment turned out to show the highest scores on the DIS-Q six months and one year after admission to our inpatient unit. Moreover, very high and significant correlations (p<.0001) were found between the scores on the DIS-Q and the BAT at the three evaluation moments (r=.48 at admission; r=.73 after 6 months; r=.68 after 1 year). These data suggest that in eating disorder patients dissociative symptoms are strongly related to the way these patients perceive, experience and/or evaluate their own bodies. Hence, in eating disorders, the negative body experience may function as a mediator between the trauma experience and the development of dissociative symptoms.

A MULTIFACTORIAL MODEL

The described mediating factors between childhood abuse (input) and later psychological problems (outcome) are of course interrelated in many ways and will vary greatly from person to person. Whether the traumatic experiences will be integrated in or dissociated from the victim's conscious psychological life will depend on a combination of these factors (see Exhibit 2.1). In this model the psychosocial adjustment of a trauma victim is conceptualized on a continuum that ranges from the constructive integration of the traumatic experience into the subject's cognitive and emotional functioning at one end to a maladaptive dissociation leading to all kinds of related psychopathological symptoms on the other.

In this model, the place of the eating disorder that has developed in a patient with a history of traumatic experiences can be viewed in different ways. The bulimic behavior (bingeing, vomiting, purging) can be considered as a way of coping with feelings, memories, sensations, and cognitions closely related to the trauma. The bulimia may be viewed as a form of impulse dyscontrol in a dissociated state. The eating disorder can also be understood as a way to cope with a negative self-image, and more particularly a negative body experience, resulting from physical and/or sexual abuse. In many cases this negative body-image will also be expressed in other self-destructive acts (see Chapter 3).

EXHIBIT 2.1
A Multifactorial Model of Trauma and Dissociation

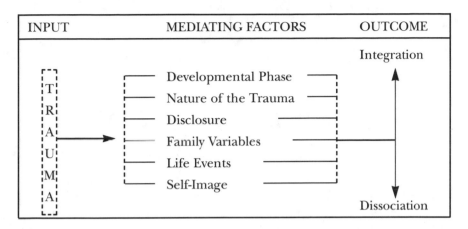

3

Impulse Dyscontrol

An association between reported childhood abuse and later psychopathology has been found in a significant number of studies in both nonclinical and clinical samples (see Chapter 1). In eating disorders the seriousness of the trauma history seems to be related to a greater bulimic symptomatology (Waller, 1993a; Wonderlich, Swift, Slotnick, & Goodman, 1990) as well as to a greater comorbidity, especially with respect to mood disorders, borderline personality features, and problems with impulsivity. To cite just a few recent investigations: Braun, Sunday, and Halmi (1994) found that in a sample of 105 eating disorder inpatients, depression, anxiety, substance dependence, and personality disorders were the most common comorbid diagnoses. Andrews, Valentine, and Valentine (1995) reported that in a community sample, sexual abuse and physical abuse were often associated with chronic and recurrent depression and bulimic behaviors. Studying 87 bulimic women in a clinial trial, Sullivan, Bulik, Carter, and Joyce (1995) found more depressive symptoms, suicide attempts, alcohol and drug dependence, and avoidant personality disorder in the subgroup (44%) of women who reported childhood sexual abuse (see Table 3.1).

In this chapter we will not discuss the often described and investigated association between eating disorders and mood disorders (for a critical view, see Cooper, 1995). Because the focus in this book is on patients with a history of traumatic experiences, we will address those comorbid behaviors that in our experience are more closely

TABLE 3.1
Clinical Characteristics Often Found in Bulimic Patients

Negative body experience
Impulsivity (aggressiveness)
Tendency to addiction
Mood instability
Dissociative experiences
Increased suggestibility
History of psychotrauma

and/or typically linked to the combination of an eating disorder and a trauma history. In this subgroup of patients the central issue seems to be a maladaptive struggle with controlling the impulse, drive, or temptation to perform acts that are harmful to themselves or others. The DSM-IV category of "impulse-control disorder" is only one variation of this spectrum that we like to call problems of *impulse dyscontrol* (see also Edelstein, 1989; Hollander & Stein, 1995; Lowe & Eldredge, 1993).

IMPULSIVITY AND BORDERLINE PERSONALITY

The association between substance abuse and bulimic behavior has been documented in several studies (for a critical review, see Wilson, 1995). The combination of eating disorders and abuse of alcohol in women has been gaining attention recently. Very often researchers forget to ask women with alcohol problems about eating problems, while in bulimic patients the use of alcohol often is overlooked. Binge-eating in particular may fairly often go together with abuse of alcohol, although we don't yet know exactly which of the two is cause and which is consequence. The simultaneous occurrence of these problems is often used as an argument to consider the eating disorder itself as an *addiction*.

The "addiction model" (see Vanderlinden, Norré, & Vandereycken, 1992) has become a popular approach in both the self-help movement and specialized treatment centers. Anorexia as well as bulimia nervosa patients appear to struggle in vain with an overwhelming urge. Anorectic patients seem to be addicted to slimming and many bulimic patients speak about a "food addiction." We have already pointed out that many also show various disturbances in impulse control and an inclination to abuse alcohol and/or drugs. Just like addicts they experience an uncontrollable urge to eat and would do anything to get the necessary food. As the alcoholic seems blind to the consequences of drinking, food addicts continue to eat and vomit or purge despite the health risks. If they cannot binge in time, they become so tense, irritable, or even aggressive that it almost looks like withdrawal symptoms. The bingeing then has a calming effect on some, and others experience it as a kick, although usually it is followed by a hangover.

The occurrence of binges also can be regarded as a form of conditioned addictive behavior. In particular circumstances (loneliness, tension, or sadness), or as soon as the patient comes into contact with certain stimuli (especially smelling, seeing, and tasting), she "automatically" reaches for food, without thinking. Once the patient puts herself on a diet, her susceptibility to these stimuli could increase. That binges almost always occur after a period of dieting or fasting might have to do with this. But regardless of the explanation, the major consequence is that patients should learn to develop a better self-control over their eating behavior.

The latter also applies to many comorbid behaviors. Therefore, instead of emphasizing the addictive component in the behavior, we want to stress that a great deal of comorbidity in (traumatized) eating disorder patients can rather be regarded as an expression of a *disturbed self-control.* Thus, the patient is no longer able to suppress a strong urge (impulse) to perform undesired acts. Other signs of a similar failure in impulse control are stealing (usually of food, or of money to get the required food), self-inflicted injury (for instance, a patient's cutting herself without the intention to commit suicide), and sudden outbursts of anger. Along a similar line of reasoning, Lacey and Evans (1986) have proposed the term "multi-impulsive" bulimia, referring to those patients who not only binge, vomit, and purge, but who also have problems with alcohol and drug abuse, kleptomania, self-mutilation, and promiscuous sexual activity.

In a long-lasting bulimia, some patients over the course of time exhibit several of the above described behavioral disorders. In other cases the phenomena alternate and patients are given different diagnoses according to the disturbing behavior that is prominent at that moment. The combination of eating disorders and other mental disturbances may point to the existence of a *borderline personality disorder*, which is characterized mainly by great instability in mood, behavior, and relationships. Much has been written about this association (see Dolan, Evans, & Norton, 1993; Garfinkel & Gallop, 1992; Vitousek & Manke, 1994). Again, here we limit our discussion to the issue of impulsivity, which not only must be considered as a key feature in eating disorders with a bulimic component, but seems to be closely related to the lack of stability in borderline cases and to the maladaptive behavioral repertoire of victims of childhood trauma (Boon & Draijer, 1993). The many possible interrelations between eating disorder, abuse, and personality disorder are summarized in Exhibit 3.1.

EXHIBIT 3.1

Interactions Between Sexual/Physical Abuse,
Eating Disorder, and Personality Disorder

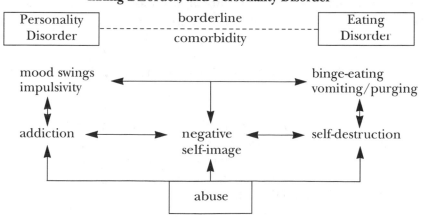

The frequently reported connection between childhood sexual abuse and adult borderline personality disorder, often in combination with dissociative features and self-destructive behaviors (see, e.g., Zweig-Frank, Paris, & Guzder, 1994), has led to the view that it concerns a variant of posttraumatic stress disorder (Kroll, 1993). Others (Waller, 1993a, 1994) have suggested that borderline personality disorder may function as a mediating factor between abusive experiences in childhood and psychological problems during adolescence and adulthood. It is assumed that the presence of these characteristics significantly enlarges the risk for revictimization. Hence, probably due to their impulsiveness, identity disturbances, mood shifts, and unstable relationships, these patients run a greater risk of being confronted with new traumatic experiences in and out the family environment. Whatever its theoretical interpretation, the association itself will have important practical implications for therapeutic management. Hence, what has been written about the treatment of borderline cases will be of great value for the group of patients we are dealing with, especially with regard to enhancing their self-control within a well-structured daily life (see Chapter 5).

In the following paragraphs we will describe in detail two behavioral problems of impulse dyscontrol we often encounter in traumatized eating disorder patients, stealing and self-mutilation. The reason for doing so is threefold: (1) there is a relative lack of research on this subject (compared to other forms of comorbidity in these patients); (2) therapists tend to overlook these problems in their assessment; and (3) there are many shortcomings or mistakes in the therapeutic management of these patients.

STEALING IN EATING DISORDERS

In anorexia nervosa patients, stealing behavior was first connected with their habit of hoarding foods or objects, and as such it was considered a form of kleptomania for which patients should be treated, not punished (Norton, Crisp & Bhat, 1985). The association of stealing and anorectic behavior even in non-Western countries has stimulated various interpretations, ranging from biological to psychodynamic views (Lee, 1994). Using the analogy with "compulsion" or "poor impulse control," early researchers on bulimia had already made a connection between compulsive eating and stealing (Ziolko, 1988). Soon after the official nosographic recognition of bulimia in DSM-III (renamed as bulimia nervosa in DSM-III-R), several reports mentioned stealing behavior as an aspect of "impulsivity" in these patients (McElroy, Hudson, Pope, & Keck, 1991a; Wellbourne, 1988). And, coming from the opposite direction, in recent years studies on kleptomania paid attention to its frequent connection with eating disorders (McElroy, Pope, Hudson, Keck, & White, 1991b). Finally, stealing was related to the new phenomenon of "compulsive buying": a lifetime diagnosis of an eating disorder was found in 17% (Schlosser, Black, Repertinger, & Frect, 1994) to 20.8% (Christenson, Faber, deZwaan, & Raymond, 1994) of those studied.

Inspired by these various reports, we wanted to pay more specific attention to this issue, but we soon realized that the research literature showed serious shortcomings. Therefore, we planned a study with two major aims. First, we wanted to investigate in a systematic way the occurrence of stealing behavior in a large group of eating-disorder patients. We assumed that it would be more frequent in patients who suffer from binge eating. We also supposed that at first assessment, patients—particulary anorectics—might show a tendency to deny this behavior (Vandereycken & Vanderlinden, 1983), and that they would be more willing to admit it after a period of treatment. Our second aim was to find various patterns of stealing behavior. We assumed that in some patients it was a well-planned action to get food (or the money to buy it), while in others it would have the characteristics of an impulse dyscontrol and/or show dissociative features, as in kleptomania (Goldman, 1991).

Study

One hundred and fifty-five women, all of whom met DSM-III-R criteria for eating disorders (the only selection criterion), were recruited at three different treatment settings: 65 had been admitted to a specialized eating disorders unit of a university hospital; 56 were inpatients at a behavior therapy unit of a general psychiatric hospital known for treating eating disorders; and 34 were outpatients from a private practice of a clinical psychologist who specialized in the treatment of eating disorders. The cases of anorexia nervosa were subdivided (in accordance with the DSM-IV subtyping) into a restricting group of pure fasters (N=51), and a mixed type with binge-eating and/or vomiting/purging (N=62). Of the 39 bulimia nervosa patients, 10 showed an overweight of at least 15%. Finally, three patients were diagnosed as "atypical" (eating disorder not otherwise specified). Except for obvious features (such as weight and eating behavior), there were no significant differences between restricting anorectics, mixed anorectics, and bulimia nervosa patients with respect to age (23.5 ± 7.3 vs 22.5 ± 5.7 vs 23.0 ± 3.8 years) or duration of illness (5.9 ± 5.4 vs 4.7 ± 3.5 vs 5.3 ± 3.2). Although applied in different settings, the basic ideas of the multidimensional therapy were the same for all patients (see Vanderlinden, Norré, & Vandereycken, 1992).

All data have been gathered and analyzed by a researcher who was not involved in the treatment. Confidentiality of the results was guaranteed to all patients—it was explicitly stated that their therapists would not be informed. At the first assessment, before starting treatment, all patients were asked to fill out a series of self-reporting questionnaires. A first set of validated questionnaires was aimed at assessing features directly related to the eating disorder itself (see also Chapter 4). The *Eating Disorder Evaluation Scale* (EDES) (Vandereycken, 1993a) is an easy and comprehensive self-reporting instrument for the clinical judgment of the severity of eating disorders, containing four subscales: anorectic preoccupation, bulimic behavior, sexuality, and psychosocial adjustment. Contrary to the other instruments used in this study, a lower score on the EDES points in the direction of more pathology. The *Body Attitude Test* (BAT) (Probst, Vandereycken, Van Coppenolle, & Vanderlinden 1995) is a self-report questionnaire developed for female patients suffering from eating disorders. It measures three aspects of body experience: negative appreciation of body size, the patient's lack of familiarity with her own body, and general body dissatisfaction.

A second set of self-reporting instruments was chosen to assess psychopathology in general, and specific comorbidity in particular.

The *Symptom Checklist* (SCL-90) (Derogatis Lipman, Rickels, Uhlen-hutz, & Covi, 1974) is a well-known measure for the assessment of a wide array of psychiatric symptoms (for example, anxiety, depression, somatization, sensitivity, and hostility). Another classical instrument is the *Beck Depression Inventory* (BDI) (Beck, Ward, Hendelson, Mock, & Erbaugh, 1961), measuring the degree of depression. The *Dissociation Questionnaire* (DIS-Q) (Vanderlinden, VanDyck, Vandereycken, & Vertommen, & Verkes 1993) is aimed at assessing dissociative experiences: identity confusion and fragmentation (referring to experiences of depersonalization and derealization), loss of control (over behavior, thoughts and emotions), amnesia (memory lacunas), and absorption. Details on these questionnaires may be found in Chapter 4.

Finally, for the purpose of this study we developed an exploratory instrument, the *Stealing Behavior Questionnaire* (SBQ) (see Appendix C). The subject is first asked whether he or she has ever stolen anything. In the introduction we state, "By stealing we mean taking without permission any object, regardless of its value, that doesn't belong to you. If this happened at your family's home it should also be considered as stealing, except for foods and drinks." If the subject answers that he or she has never stolen, the next question is "Have you ever felt the urge to steal, without doing it?" If the answer is again no, the subject is then asked to answer the last question: "Do you think that stealing (or the urge to do it) has something to do with having an eating disorder?" Subjects who admit to stealing are asked to skip question 2 and fill out the rest of the questionnaire. A group of 80 patients was asked to complete the SBQ a second time after about two months (a period during which all were in either inpatient treatment or outpatient weekly psychotherapy).

Results

First Versus Second Assessment

As a first step, we compared the results on our experimental questionnaire SBQ at first assessment and after two months treatment (N=80). To our great surprise there were almost no differences in the admission of stealing: three patients changed their answer from yes to no, and two others made the opposite change. There were also few changed responses to more concrete questions about stealing (questions about frequency, places, ages, and objects taken). Twelve patients (15%) admitted to a higher frequency of stealing during the past year on the second questionnaire; this could be interpreted as a sign of greater honesty and/or that they did more stealing in the period since the first assessment (the SBQ was now covering these two treatment months). On the question of whether they had talked with someone about their stealing, 10 (12.5%) patients changed their answers from no to yes, and 16 (20%) now included a therapist in the list of people with whom they had discussed the situation (in both cases we think these were clear effects of the current treatment). Most probably the two months of therapy influenced the answering patterns with respect to questions related to feelings and thoughts about stealing. In general, about 25% of the patients answered differently the second time, showing more psychological insight now. Although we cannot exclude a bias of false negatives, we have to reject our denial hypothesis with the fortunate implication that we feel justified in using the findings at first assessment for further analysis.

Characteristics of "Stealers"

A total of 73 patients (47.1%) admitted to having stolen (we will refer to them as "stealers"): 35.3% of the restricting anorectics, 54.8% of the mixed anorectics, and 48.7% of the bulimia nervosa patients. Only the difference between restricting and mixed anorexia nervosa patients reached statistical significance (p<.05). There was no significant difference with respect to the clinical setting (inpatient versus outpatient). Of the patients who reported never having stolen, 8.5% admitted that they had once had the urge to do it. Compared to the other patients, the stealers did not differ in age, but their mean duration of illness was greater (5.8±4.1 vs 4.3±4.2; p<.05) and a smaller proportion of them was married (9.9 vs 16.7%; p<.01). On the self-reporting questionnaires related to aspects of the eating disorder (EDES, BAT) no significant differences were found, but there was one important exception that confirmed our hypothesis: on the bulimia subscale of the EDES (the lower the score, the more abnormal) the stealers were scoring significantly (p<.0001) lower than the others (9.8+5.0 vs 13.4+5.2). With regard to various psychopathological complaints (assessed with SCL-90) or depression (BDI) no significant differences were found. But the stealers showed more pronounced features of dissociative experiences and behaviors, with the most distinct difference on the DIS-Q subscale "loss of control" (see Table 3.2).

Aspects of Stealing

Details about the stealing behavior are summarized in Table 3.3 (percentages refer to stealers only). In about 45% of the cases, stealing started before the eating disorder, and in more than half of the patients it occurred more than once during the past year. In about two thirds of the cases all kinds of food had been stolen, and in one third of the cases money, too, was taken. The vast majority did make use of the stolen goods, whereas only 17% did keep the goods without using them (suggesting some form of kleptomania or hoarding?). Stealing occurred most often at home or in a shop or supermarket. Two thirds of the patients said that the stealing had not been planned at all. Just before stealing, most patients felt tense or anxious; at the moment itself tension or anxiety prevailed; afterwards 88% felt guilty. About 40% of the stealers have been caught at least once, and about half of the time they were caught in a shop or supermarket (one third of them were fined). Only a minority—36%—never spoke about the stealing with someone, and in only one fifth of the cases was it revealed to a therapist. Asked whether they

TABLE 3.2
Stealing and Scores on the Dissociation Questionnaire (DIS-Q)

DIS-Q scales	Stealers (N=73)	Non-stealers (N=82)	p
Total	2.29 (0.63)	1.87 (0.43)	.0020
Confusion	2.37 (0.78)	1.89 (0.59)	.0007
Loss of control	2.52 (0.77)	2.00 (0.54)	.0002
Amnesia	1.65 (0.58)	1.37 (0.33)	.0034
Absorption	2.69 (0.74)	2.46 (0.71)	.0111

TABLE 3.3
Aspects of Stealing

	Total N (%)	A N (%)	B N (%)	p[c]
First time, how long ago?	[N=73]	[N=45]	[N=27]	
< 5 years	29 (39.7)	20 (44.4)	9 (33.3)	
5–10 years	20 (27.4)	12 (26.7)	7 (25.9)	
>10 years	24 (32.9)	13 (28.9)	11 (40.8)	
Last time, how long ago?	[N=66]	[N=40]	[N=25]	***
< 4 months	28 (42.4)	22 (55.0)	6 (24.0)	
4–10 months	7 (10.6)	7 (17.5)	0 (-)	
>10 months	31 (47.0)	11 (27.5)	19 (76.0)	
Total number of times	[N=73]	[N=45]	[N=27]	***
once	14 (19.2)	0 (-)	13 (48.2)	
2–5 times	24 (32.9)	17 (37.8)	7 (25.9)	
> 5 times	35 (47.9)	28 (62.2)	7 (25.9)	
Frequency in past year	[N=73]	[N=45]	[N=27]	***
none	33 (45.2)	12 (26.7)	20 (74.1)	
1–10 times	25 (34.2)	18 (40.0)	7 (25.9)	
> once a month	7 (9.6)	7 (15.5)	0 (-)	
> once a week	8 (11.0)	8 (17.8)	0 (-)	
Goods stolen[a]	[N=68]	[N=45]	[N=22]	
food items	44 (64.7)	36 (80.0)	7 (31.8)	***
money	23 (33.8)	14 (31.1)	9 (40.9)	
toilet items, clothes	17 (25.0)	9 (20.0)	8 (36.4)	
others	24 (35.3)	15 (33.3)	9 (40.9)	
Use of stolen goods[a]	[N=71]	[N=45]	[N=25]	
used it	62 (87.3)	42 (93.3)	19 (76.0)	*
kept without use	12 (16.9)	9 (20.0)	3 (12.0)	
given away or restored	11 (15.5)	6 (13.3)	5 (20.0)	
thrown away	5 (7.0)	4 (8.9)	1 (4.0)	
Where or from whom?[a]	[N=72]	[N=45]	[N=26]	
parents, siblings	28 (40.0)	18 (40.0)	11 (42.3)	
other family or friends	22 (31.4)	18 (40.0)	4 (15.4)	*
shop or supermarket	31 (44.3)	17 (37.8)	14 (53.8)	
school or work site	13 (18.6)	10 (22.2)	3 (11.5)	
others	9 (12.9)	8 (17.8)	1 (3.8)	
Did you plan it?	[N=70]	[N=45]	[N=24]	
not at all	45 (64.3)	26 (57.8)	18 (75.0)	

Table 3.3 (*continued*)

	Total N (%)	A N (%)	B N (%)	p^c
more or less	21 (30.0)	16 (35.5)	5 (20.8)	
well planned	4 (5.7)	3(6.7)	1 (4.2)	
Feelings just before^a	[N=58]	[N=40]	[N=17]	
tense	38 (65.5)	25 (62.5)	13 (76.5)	
anxious	30 (51.7)	22 (55.0)	8 (47.1)	
guilty	12 (20.7)	5 (12.5)	7 (41.2)	*
depressed	12 (20.7)	9 (22.5)	3 (17.6)	
others^b	24 (41.4)	18 (45.0)	6 (35.3)	
Feelings during stealing^a	[N=68]	[N=45]	[N=22]	
tense	49 (72.1)	36 (80.0)	12 (54.5)	*
anxious	45 (66.2)	27 (60.0)	17 (77.3)	
guilty	19 (27.9)	11 (24.4)	8 (36.4)	
depressed	5 (7.4)	3 (6.7)	2 (9.1)	
others^b	25 (36.8)	21 (46.7)	4 (18.2)	*
Feelings afterwards^a	[N=68]	[N=44]	[N=23]	
tense	26 (38.2)	17 (38.6)	8 (34.8)	
anxious	37 (54.4)	25 (56.8)	12 (52.2)	
guilty	60 (88.2)	38 (86.4)	21 (91.5)	
depressed	21 (30.9)	15 (34.1)	6 (26.1)	
others^b	26 (38.2)	19 (43.2)	7 (30.4)	
Have you ever been caught?	[N=73]	[N=45]	[N=27]	
never	44 (60.3)	24 (53.3)	19 (70.4)	
yes, at least once	29 (39.7)	21 (46.7)	8 (29.6)	
yes, more than once	12 (16.4)	9 (20.0)	3 (11.1)	
To whom did you reveal it?	[N=72]	[N=45]	[N=26]	
no one	26 (36.1)	14 (31.1)	12 (46.1)	
family member	25 (34.7)	19 (42.2)	6 (23.1)	
spouse or boyfriend	11 (15.3)	6 (13.3)	5 (19.2)	
friend	25 (34.7)	14 (31.1)	10 (38.5)	
therapist	16 (22.2)	14 (31.1)	2 (7.7)	
Stealing in the future^c	[N=73]	[N=45]	[N=27]	**
never again	28 (38.4)	10 (22.2)	17 (63.0)	
very unlikely	17 (23.3)	11 (24.4)	6 (22.2)	
might happen again	14 (19.2)	12 (26.7)	2 (7.4)	
don't know	14 (19.2)	12 (26.7)	2 (7.4)	
Reason for stealing^a	[N=70]	[N=45]	[N=24]	
to get food	27 (38.6)	24 (53.3)	3 (12.5)	***
lack of money	19 (27.1)	13 (28.9)	6 (25.0)	

(*continued*)

Table 3.3 (*continued*)

	Total		A		B		
	N	(%)	N	(%)	N	(%)	p^e
anger or revenge	14	(20.0)	9	(20.0)	5	(20.8)	
for fun or sensation	11	(15.7)	4	(8.9)	6	(25.0)	
uncontrollable urge	9	(12.9)	9	(20.0)	0	(-)	*
Related to eating disorder?^{d}	[N=71]		[N=45]		[N=25]		***
not at all	20	(28.2)	5	(11.1)	14	(56.0)	
possibly	15	(21.1)	10	(22.2)	5	(20.0)	
certainly	33	(46.5)	28	(62.2)	5	(20.0)	
no idea	3	(4.2)	2	(4.5)	1	(4.0)	

A = "stealing related to eating disorder"; B = "other form of stealing" (see paragraph on types of stealing)
^{a} On these questions the patient could mark more than one possibility
^{b} Other feelings: excited, confused, or ashamed.
^{c} Do you think that, in the future, stealing could happen to you again?
^{d} Do you think that stealing (or the urge to do it) has something to do with having an eating disorder?
^{e} A vs B, Chi-square: * p<.05; ** p<.01; *** p<.001

might steal again, about 62% of the patients were quite confident that they would not. Although the majority had stolen food items and/or money, for about one third obtaining the stolen object was not the main motive. Rather, the act of stealing itself had a special meaning. Perhaps this is related to the fact that almost one third of the patients excluded any relationship between stealing and having an eating disorder.

Types of "Stealers"

Two independent assessors analyzed the questionnaires in order to find different types of stealing. First they agreed upon four types of theft: (1) simple thefts, (2) stealing related to an eating disorder, (3) stealing as a form of antisocial behavior, and (4) stealing related to other psychological problems. Next, independently from each other, they grouped all the stealers into one of these four types. The correspondence in subgrouping for the total sample was 82.2%. Because our criterion of 90% was only reached for group 2, we decided to simplify the subtyping into two groups. Combining three questions—stolen object, motive of stealing, and the patient's idea about its relationship with anorexia/bulimia nervosa—the same assessors obtained a correspondence of 93.2% in subdividing the sample in "stealing related versus unrelated to eating disorder." After having reached a consensus about where to put the hard-to-classify cases (one case was dropped for lack of important information), the characteristics of the stealers (N=72) in the two types were compared: 45 cases (62.5%) belonged to group A (stealing related to eating disorder) and 27 (37.5%) to group B (other kinds of stealing). Except for the aspects directly related to the subgrouping (goods stolen, reason for stealing, was it related to eating disorder?), group A showed some differences in comparison with group B that can be understood because of their "eating-related stealing" (see Table 3.3). In most cases, the thefts still happened with a marked frequency during the past year. Patients in group A did steal more from friends, felt less guilty before but more excited or confused while stealing. The fact that only half of group A was convinced that stealing would not occur again can be seen as expressing their uncertainty as to the likelihood that their eating disorder (and hence the urge to steal) would disappear.

With respect to age, marital status, duration of illness, body mass index, and treatment setting, no significant differences were shown between group A and B. The same applied to the scores on all questionnaires (EDES, BAT, SCL-90, DIS-Q, BDI). This means, for example, that "eating-related stealing" was not associated with more bulimic tendencies, and that contrary to our expectation, the type of "stealing unrelated to eating disorder" did not show specific psychopathological features such as more dissociation or impulse dyscontrol.

Comments

A self-report study in eating disorder patients always must face the bias of expectancy ("social desirability") and the problem of denial, especially in anorexia nervosa patients (Vandereycken & Vanderlinden, 1983). One might expect that such a distortion of answering patterns *a fortiori* would take place when patients are questioned about such socially unacceptable behaviors as stealing. A classical test–retest procedure can be useful to check the reliability of a questionnaire, but only under the condition that the subject basically is willing to admit to the problematic behavior in question. We supposed that some eating-disorder patients would first need to build up a trustful therapeutic relationship and/or to gain some psychological insight before being ready to reveal information that would put them in a vulnerable position. Unexpectedly, however, at second assessment with our Stealing Behavior Questionnaire (SBQ) after two months intensive treatment, virtually the same number of patients as the first assessment admitted to stealing. On the other hand, changes in the content of some answers can be seen as influenced by the ongoing treatment: a greater openness, and different feelings and thoughts about stealing and its significance.

The rather limited influence of therapy on the answers to the SBQ might be related to the *selection* of our sample. The great majority of respondents already had been in treatment elsewhere, and now had agreed to start a specialized and demanding treatment. Hence, our patients might have shown greater psychological insight, and a more-than-average willingness to reveal delicate information about themselves. One should keep this selection factor in mind in the interpretation of our data and their comparison with other studies. Furthermore, differences in findings may be due to the definition of stealing and the assessment method (we preferred an anonymous questionnaire instead of the more embarrassing confrontation with an interviewer).

Another stumbling block in comparing data are the diagnostic criteria used. Even if we look only at studies in which nothing other than DSM-III-R criteria have been used, there remains the problem of subdividing anorexia nervosa, as acknowledged now in DSM-IV. As we had advocated more than a decade ago (Vandereycken & Pierloot, 1983), we always make a firm distinction between *classic* anorexia nervosa (the pure fasting/restricting type) and the *mixed* form (where patients also show binge-eating and/or vomiting and/or laxative abuse—the "binge-eating/purging type" according to DSM-IV). The problem with most pre-DSM-IV studies is that if they speak about mixed anorexia nervosa they refer to binge-eating anorectics and thus include the nonbulimic purging anorectics within the "restricting" type.

Garner, Garner, and Rosen (1993) have clearly demonstrated that purging behavior (that is, self-induced vomiting and/or laxative abuse) is an important distinguishing characteristic for subtyping anorectic patients, regardless of whether they report binge-eating; recently Beumont, Kopec-Schrader, and Toyuz (1995) confirmed this observation. Although details are lacking, Garner and colleagues (1993) give the following figures on "history of stealing" in anorexia nervosa subgroups (data on a large sample of patients attending a specialized treatment program): 2% nonpurging restricters, 7% purging restricters, and 17% bulimic anorectics.

If we take *DSM-III-R criteria* as the basis for a comparison, only a few studies have systematically examined stealing behavior in eating disorders. Current and lifetime psychiatric diagnoses in 229 female patients seeking treatment for an eating disorder have been studied by Herzog and colleagues (1992). Using a structured interview, kleptomania as defined in DSM-III-R was diagnosed in only 7 patients (3% of total sample)—1 of the 41 anorexia nervosa and 1 of the 98 bulimia nervosa patients—whereas the other 5 cases belonged to the group of 90 mixed anorexia/bulimia patients.

Krahn, Nairn, Gosnell, and Drewnowski (1991) classified patients as "stealers" if they answered yes to the interview question: "Since the onset of your eating problem, have you been involved in stealing?" A history of stealing was admitted by 28.2% of the total sample: 6.3% of the 16 anorexia nervosa patients, 30.8% of the 13 patients with anorexia and bulimia nervosa, and 32.6% of the 95 bulimia nervosa patients. Of the 57 patients with "eating disorder not otherwise specified" (mainly including patients who did not meet the criterion of binge-eating frequency for bulimia nervosa), 26.3% also reported a history of stealing. Stealers showed more psychopathology (SCL-90), and more dysfunctional eating and purging behaviors, although they did not differ from nonstealers on the Eating Disorder Inventory. "The idea that a subgroup of bulimics have multiple impulse control problems was partially supported by the finding that MAST [Michigan Alcoholism Screening Test] scores were higher in the stealing patients, although this difference was not statistically significant" (Krahn et al., 1991).

Other systematic investigations of stealing behavior in bulimia nervosa (according to DSM-III-R criteria) are scarce. Christenson and Mitchell (1991), studying "repetitive behavior" in 65 bulimic patients, found 12% "compulsive stealing" (no details given) reported on a written survey. Information taken from a study of self-damaging and addictive behavior in 112 bulimic women who all were from the same catchment area, Lacey (1993) reported the following figures: "Forty-six women (41%) gave a history of stealing; 23 (21%) had stolen on two or more occasions. The 46 women included 20 who were shoplifters, 16 who had stolen money from family or friends, four who had stolen from their employers, and one who had been involved in a major crime involving gross bodily harm. With the exception of the latter case, none had stolen significant amounts of money. Shoplifting occurred in both food and clothes shops, the former being more common. Only two had been prosecuted." Repeated stealing did not occur as an isolated behavior, but always in the presence of alcohol or drug abuse. As mentioned above, Lacey called this type of bulimia nervosa patient "multi-impulsive bulimics." Fichter, Quadflieg, and Rief (1994) examined a group of multi-impulsivists—patients with bulimia nervosa and an additional impulsive behavior (suicide attempt, alcohol/drug abuse, autoaggressive behavior, promiscuity, stealing). They found that the lifetime incidence for shoplifting (other than food) was 34.7%. These impulsive bulimics, all patients at a specialized treatment center, showed more general psychopathology and overall had a less favorable course of illness.

If we compare our own results with those just discussed, the summary in Table 3.4 shows that the most comprehensive comparisons can be made for bulimia nervosa patients. The low figure in the study by Christenson and Mitchell (1991) might be attributed to their stricter definition of "compulsive stealing" and/or the fact that they had recruited their sample through advertisement. The restriction in definition of stealing by Krahn and colleagues (1991) and Fichter and colleagues (1994)—the latter had also selected a sample of "impulsive" bulimics—might explain their figures being somewhat lower than those found by Lacey (1993) and in the present study. All studies, however, show the same basic finding: Stealing is

TABLE 3.4
Stealing in Eating Disorders: A Comparison of Studies

	Pure AN	Mixed AN	BN
Krahn et al. (1991)[a]	6.3%	30.8%	32.6%
Garner et al. (1993)	2.0%	12.0%[b]	-
Christenson & Mitchell (1991)[c]	-	-	12.0%
Lacey (1993)	-	-	41.0%
Fichter et al. (1994)[d]	-	-	34.7%
Present study	35.3%	54.8%	48.7%

[a] Stealing since the onset of eating disorder
[b] Averaging two figures: 7% in purging restricters and 17% in bulimic anorectics
[c] "Compulsive stealing"
[d] Shoplifting other than food

more likely when the eating disorder includes "bulimia-like" behavior (binge eating, vomiting, and/or laxative abuse).

Both Krahn and colleagues (1991) and Fichter and colleagues (1994) conclude that stealing is related to other psychopathology. We could confirm this only with regard to dissociative experiences. Generally speaking, stealing behavior seems to express some form of loss of control or impulsivity. Most often, however, it appears to be related to the eating disorder itself, although in several cases it may be ordinary shoplifting. Mitchell, Fletcher, Gibeau, Pyle, and Eckert (1992) published an interesting comparison between the stealing patterns of 27 bulimics and 25 nonbulimic shoplifters: "the majority of the bulimic shoplifters reported most commonly stealing something involved with their eating disorder: food, money, laxatives, diuretics, or diet pills. The nonbulimic shoplifters were more likely to endorse reasons for stealing that one might consider antisocial, e.g., to 'get back' at the store or for excitement. The bulimic shoplifters as a group indicated that a more important reason for them to shoplift was embarrassment over buying certain items." The pattern of "non-eating-related stealing" in our own study seems to resemble the nonbulimic shoplifting in Mitchell and colleagues' (1992) study.

Krahn and colleagues (1991) suggested that "assessing the presence or absence of associated symptoms such as stealing or other impulse control problems might be a better strategy for determining severity of the bulimic syndrome." In fact, this is in accordance with the recently growing attention paid to comorbidity in eating disorders as being probably one of the most important indicators of response to treatment and long-term outcome. According to Lacey (1993), recognition of impulsive behavior "would allow the development of treatments to deal with the interchangeable nature of the symptoms" because "only by concentrating on *all the symptoms* can the underlying psychopathology be tackled." These arguments should justify more systematic studies of stealing behavior in eating disorders.

SELF-INJURIOUS BEHAVIOR

The starving anorectic and the purging bulimic may be viewed as people who deliberately harm their bodies. Therefore, eating disorders might be part of the spectrum of self-mutilative behaviors (for an overview see Walsh & Rosen, 1988). Although various forms of self-injury, especially self-cutting, have been reported in eating-disorder patients (Favazza, DeRosear, & Conterio, 1989), to our knowledge no specific and systematic study of this issue has been carried out. Because we saw more and more patients who displayed a coexistence of eating disorders and self-injurious behaviors, we started a research project to examine the issue. Preliminary results of this study are reported in the next section.

Study

We carried out an exploratory investigation in a sample of 94 patients from two psychiatric hospitals in Belgium. The patients were all women between 14 and 50 years of age (85% between 15 and 35), all recently admitted for a nonpsychotic and nonorganic psychiatric disorder, and all willing to fill out a series of questionnaires (informed consent). The diagnosis (Axis 1 and 2, according to DSM-IV) was made by the psychiatrist in charge of each patient; because we expected frequent comorbidity, the psychiatrist was also asked to specify which diagnosis was of primary concern at the moment of assessment.

To assess self-harm we developed a *Self-Injury Questionnaire* (SIQ; see Appendix D), which consists of two parts. First, using a 4-point scale ranging from "never" to "very often," subjects are asked to rate certain behaviors that are likely to occur in a state of tension, as well as "urges" or "inclinations" toward self-injurious behavior they have experienced in the last six months. Secondly, subjects are asked if they deliberately injured themselves in the past year (hair pulling, scratching, bruising, cutting, burning); if so, they are to specify how often this happened, if they felt some pain, and what kind of emotional experiences they had at the moment of self-injury (being nervous, bored, angry, sad, scared, or some other feeling).

Additionally, patients had to complete a series of questionnaires assessing several aspects of their psychological (dys)functioning: the Symptom Checklist (SCL-90), the Impulsiveness Scale (IS), the Munich Alcohol Test (MALT), the Dissociation Questionnaire (DIS-Q), the Body Attitude Test (BAT), the Eating Disorder Evaluation Scale (EDES). Details on these self-reporting instruments can be found in Chapter 4.

Results

The most striking finding was that almost half of the women reported the occurrence of at least one form of self-injury during the past year (see Table 3.5). Comparing these "mutilators" (N=43) with the "nonmutilators" (N=51), we did not find any statistical difference in age, marital status, or educational level. With regard to the psychiatric diagnoses, only two major differences have to be stressed: almost 85% of the borderline patients belonged to the group of mutilators, and 80% of the mood disorders were found in the group of nonmutilators. In half of the cases, the age at onset of the self-injury was before 18 years. The first time such behavior occurred was situated in the following periods (calculated from the moment of assessment): in the last 6 months (48.5%), between 6 and 12 months earlier (9.1%), from 1 to 5 years earlier (21.2%), and more than 5 years earlier (21.2%).

TABLE 3.5
Study of Self-Injury in Psychiatric Patients

Primary diagnosis (total of 94 women)
  Eating disorder (N=31)
  Substance abuse (N=18)
  Mood disorder (N=13)
  Borderline personality disorder (N=13)

Frequency of self-injurious behavior

	YES	NO
Hair pulling	24.0%	76.0%
Scratching	24.7%	75.3%
Bruising	13.4%	86.6%
Cutting	23.7%	76.3%
Burning	9.4%	90.6%
At least one	45.7%	54.3%
Two or more	21.3%	-

The vast majority of the mutilators experienced no or just mild pain. Except for nervousness in self-scratching and anger in self-bruising, patients reported the self-injury to be related to more than one specific emotional state. The following parts of the body were self-injured: arms and hands (48.5%), head and neck (18.2%), legs and feet (3.0%), or a combination (30.3%). Most patients (46.9%) considered the self-injury as an uncontrollable act; 16.6% reported that it happened unexpectedly; 6.3% didn't remember afterwards how it occurred, while the same percentage knew it was going to happen; 3.1% admitted that the self-injury was planned. In 31.9% a combination of these descriptions applied.

With regard to the psychopathological variables, as assessed with the other questionnaires, the general picture is quite clear: on most of the measures the mutilators appeared to be significantly more dysfunctional than the nonmutilators (see Tables 3.6 and 3.7). Although the clinical features related to eating disorders (EDES) were only to a limited extent more pronounced in mutilators (for example, being more bulimic), these subjects reported a significantly more negative body experience (BAT). Patients admitting no self-

TABLE 3.6

**Body Dissatisfaction and Features of Eating Disorders in Patients
With/Without Self-Injurious Behavior**

	With (N=43)	Without (N=51)	p
EDES[a]			
Anorectic	11.2 (6.8)	13.8 (6.9)	ns
Bulimic	12.0 (4.4)	14.7 (3.9)	< .005
Sexuality	10.1 (5.3)	10.6 (4.9)	ns
Psychosocial	10.8 (4.8)	13.5 (4.6)	< .01
Total	44.0 (12.0)	52.1 (12.2)	< .01
BAT[b]			
Body size	16.6 (8.5)	11.0 (8.9)	< .005
Familiarity	15.1 (6.1)	11.4 (4.4)	< .005
Dissatisfaction	12.3 (5.3)	9.0 (5.5)	< .01
Total	50.9 (16.5)	38.1 (15.7)	< .005

[a] The higher the scores, the more normal
[b] The lower the scores, the more normal

TABLE 3.7

Psychopathology in Patients With/Without Self-Injurious Behavior

	With (N=43)	Without (N=51)	p
SCL-90			
Anxiety	32.0 (11.5)	23.0 (9.2)	< .001
Depression	55.8 (15.6)	41.2 (14.7)	< .001
Total	268.1 (79.5)	205.1 (54.1)	< .001
DIS-Q			
Identity	2.7 (1.0)	1.8 (0.7)	< .001
Loss of control	3.0 (1.0)	2.1 (0.7)	< .001
Amnesia	2.3 (1.1)	1.6 (0.5)	< .001
Absorption	2.8 (1.0)	2.2 (0.7)	< .005
Total	2.7 (0.9)	1.9 (0.5)	< .001
MALT	5.5 (6.7)	2.7 (4.6)	< .05
IMPULSIVENESS			
State	14.3 (8.8)	7.2 (6.4)	< .001
Trait	13.5 (6.1)	9.6 (3.1)	< .005

Note: The higher the scores, the more abnormal.

injury at all clearly showed fewer neurotic complaints (SCL-90); they were less anxious and generally less depressed (although a primary diagnosis of mood disorder was more common in this group according to the psychiatrist in charge). The mutilators had a greater likelihood of drinking behaviors that might develop into alcohol abuse (MALT). Predictably, self-injury was significantly related to a more general pattern of impulsiveness (IS). Finally, a most striking difference was found with regard to dissociative experiences (DIS-Q): the average scores of the nonmutilators were all within the normal range, whereas many mutilators clearly showed characteristics of dissociative pathology (identity confusion, loss of control, and amnesia).

Comments

Although our study has a selection bias (female psychiatric inpatients), the results confirm what is known from the research literature: self-injury probably is a much-overlooked problem in psychiatric patients in general and in eating-disordered women (especially bulimics) in particular. Part of the neglect may be due to the concealment of such behaviors by the patients themselves. But our questionnaire clearly shows that when they are confronted with specific and direct questions, patients are prepared to reveal their self-harming behaviors. Even such a seemingly innocent behavior as hair pulling (in serious forms known as trichotillomania), might be related to a more general pattern of impulsiveness, especially when it occurs in bulimics. It may lead the assessor to other self-harming behaviors and/or signs of psychological disturbances, each one representing a piece of one complex chain (refer back to Table 3.1).

The finding that self-injury is often connected with a negative attitude towards the patient's own body and with a greater likelihood to have abnormal dissociative experiences raises the question of etiology. More generally, and related to the possibility of a trauma history, this theoretical issue is summarized in the final conclusion of this chapter. Several explanations for the self-injurious behavior of eating-disordered women can be put forward. On a diagnostic phenomenological level, this behavior is considered to be manifestations of a "deliberate self-harm syndrome" (Favazza, DeRosear & Conterio, 1989) or symptomatic of a "multi-impulsive" behavior (Lacey, 1993). It may be explained within a biological model (Yaryura-Tobias, Neziroglu, & Kaplan, 1995), or a psychodynamic feministic framework (Cross, 1993). Many other interpretations may be found in the literature (Suyemoto & MacDonald, 1995): the result of a learning process, the reflection of a dysfunctional family system, a replacement or avoidance of suicide, an attempt to cope with sexual conflicts and maturation, a way of expressing emotions or controlling affective needs, a means to end depersonalization, or an attempt to create psychological boundaries between self and others.

From a more pragmatic and clinical viewpoint with practical implications for therapeutic management (see Chapter 5), we pay attention to the many possible functions the self-mutilation can have. They are summarized in Table 3.8 on a functional scale according to the direct consequence of the behavior upon the psychological status of the patient: from a highly rewarding effect (positive reinforcement) to a highly destructive impact (enhancing a negative self-image).

In many patients the repetitive self-injury seems to have developed into a kind of addictive behavior because of its immediate rewarding effects. Some enjoy the pleasure of pain or the feeling of warm blood on their skin. But most often the direct reinforcing element of the self-mutilation is the *relaxation* or diminishment of tension in a form of direct abreaction; it is a discharge (almost a purging) of negative sensations or affects. In a more indirect way, the self-injury may be used as a means to divert attention from a distressing situation or emotional state. For example, when they are confronted with painful memories, patients may distract themselves through self-mutilation (they seem to prefer controllable pain). Another escape mechanism may be some form of dissociative experience or trance-like state induced by the self-injury at a moment of high tension.

A second function of deliberate self-harm may be to get *attention* from (significant) others. Although this certainly is a frequent motive (and some patients are well known in hospitals for their almost exhibitionistic behavior), all too often the caregivers—from family members to health care professionals—consider this desire

TABLE 3.8
Maladaptive Functions of Self-Mutilation*

Relaxation   ++ EFFECT
  • Enjoying (pain, warm blood)
  • Diminishing tension by:
      direct abreaction
      diverting attention
      inducing dissociation
Attention
  • Obtaining self-affirmation
  • Getting protection
Stimulation
  • Feeling one's body/identity
  • Escape from dissociation
Punishment
  • Because of guilt feelings
  • For being weak/undisciplined
Self-destructiveness
  • To be unattractive
  • Parasuicidal act   – – EFFECT

*Excluding organic disorders, psychoses, and mental retardation

for attention to be the only or main function. Hence, in case of repetitive self-mutilations, caregivers are inclined to react in a negative, rejecting way. Of course some patients want to be special and resemble people with factitious disorders. In many cases, however, patients use this behavior in a helpless attempt to obtain self-affirmation. In others it is a cry for help or a clear expression that they need protection.

A third major goal of the self-injurious behavior may be to use an intense physical *stimulation* (deliberate induction of specific stimuli such as feeling pain or watching the seeping blood) to escape from a dissociative state, especially depersonalization (this is the opposite of self-mutilation leading to dissociation, as mentioned above). In other cases, closely related to this motive, the physical stimulation is intended to induce the feeling of being alive, having an intact body, or being one and the same person.

As a fourth possibility, now clearly leading to more negative effects, the self-injury is meant as a form of the *punishment* patients feel that they deserve. It may be connected to guilt feelings that often can be found in patients who have a history of abuse where they consider themselves responsible for what happened. Other patients punish themselves for being weak or undisciplined: some behavior, for example binge eating, is then looked upon as a sign of a lack of willpower.

Fifth, the self-injury may reflect a tendency toward *self-destructiveness* connected with a negative self-image. Here patients can mutilate themselves to become physically (sexually) unattractive. For others it comes close to a suicidal act; in patients with a history of suicide attempts it can be sometimes very difficult (and frightening for those taking care of them) to make a distinction between self-injury as a suicidal gesture on the one hand and as a means to avoid suicide on the other.

Finally, we would like to remark that in one and the same patient different forms of self-injury may have the same function but that the opposite may also be the case: the same repetitive self-mutilation could have different meanings. It is unnecessary to stress that the management of such cases should vary accordingly (see Chapter 5).

CONCLUSION

Together with Lowe and Eldredge (1993), we conclude that data on the comorbidity of eating disorders indicate a special link between bulimic behavior and impulsivity: studies with substance abusers, self-mutilators, and kleptomaniacs have strongly suggested a higher-than-expected prevalence of binge eating, whereas studies with eating-disorder patients have shown a higher frequency of impulsive behavior among binge eaters and vomiters/purgers. In a considerable number of these patients, the impulse dyscontrol seems to be related to dissociative experiences and/or a history of trauma (sexual/physical abuse).

Although we are concerned about too easy an etiological generalization, as happened with the concept of "Trauma Reenactment Syndrome" as coined by Dusty Miller (1994), the phenomenological links described by this author are quite recognizable in the group of patients we are discussing here: "(1) the sense of being at war with one's own body; (2) excessive secrecy as a central organizing principle of life; (3) inability to self-protect, often evident in a specific kind of fragmentation of the self; and (4) relationships in which the struggle for control overshadows all else" (Miller, 1994, p. 26–27). Each of these problematic characteristics should become the focus of the treatment, as will be illustrated in the following chapters.

4

Multidimensional Assessment

This chapter will present the assessment methods and instruments we prefer to use in our clinical work with eating-disordered patients. (See Table 4.1 for a list of available assessment instruments.) Special emphasis will be laid on the assessment of trauma histories and dissociative experiences.

EATING DISORDER

The *Eating Disorder Inventory* (EDI) (Garner, Olmsted, & Polivy, 1983) is a widely known questionnaire that has eight scales measuring attitudes and psychological features relevant to anorexia and bulimia nervosa: drive for thinness, ineffectiveness, interoceptive awareness, bulimia, perfectionism, maturity fears, body dissatisfaction, and interpersonal distrust. Although there exists a newer extended version (Garner, 1991), the original one is still the most used and best investigated questionnaire (with translations in many languages). The EDI is certainly much better for clinical work than the *Eating Attitudes Test* (EAT) (Garner & Garfinkel, 1979), which is often used to detect anorectic attitudes and behaviors (dieting, bulimia and food preoccupation, and oral control) in epidemiological studies.

TABLE 4.1

Questionnaires for a Multidimensional Assessment

Eating Disorder
      Eating Disorder Inventory (EDI)
      Eating Disorder Evaluation Scale (EDES)
      Body Attitude Test (BAT)
      Anorectic Behavior Observation Scale (ABOS)

Psychiatric Comorbidity*
      Symptom Checklist (SCL-90)
      Beck Depression Inventory (BDI)
      Borderline Syndrome Index (BSI)

Dissociation
      Dissociative Experience Scale (DES)
      Dissociation Questionnaire (DIS-Q)

Psychotrauma
      Traumatic Experiences Questionnaire (TEQ)
      Childhood Unwanted Sexual Events (CHUSE)

Family Background
      Leuven Family Questionnaire (LFQ)
      Parental Bonding Instrument (PBI)
      Marital Intimacy Questionnaire (MIQ)
      Maudsley Marital Questionnaire (MMQ)

*Additional instruments for the assessment of impulse dyscontrol (alcohol abuse, stealing, self-injury) are described in Chapter 3.

The *Eating Disorder Evaluation Scale* (EDES) (Vandereycken, 1993a) has been designed for clinical use to judge the severity of an eating disorder. It was deliberately kept short and practical to facilitate its use for repetitive judgments. On the other hand it aims at assessing both the specific symptoms and the broader psychosocial aspects of eating disorders. Preferably this judgement is based on an interview with the patient. To help the clinician in structuring and systematically scoring the interview, we developed a questionnaire version, which may also be used as self-reporting instrument by the patient. The latter possibility is practical but probably less reliable than the interview version.

As a global measurement of severity the total EDES'score can be used: the higher the score the more healthy the subject (maximum score is 90). A comparative study between 370 eating disorder patients and 174 normal women (see Vandereycken, 1993a) yielded a cutoff score of 55 (that is, 55 is the critical score that marks the boundary between patients and normals), showing a sensitivity of 93 (referring to the percentage of subjects scoring in the pathological range, and correctly detected as patients) and a specificity of 96 (the percentage of subjects scoring within the normal range who are correctly categorized as normal). If used as an evaluation instrument for repeated assessments it is advised to look at changes on the four subscales found in a factor analytic study of the results in 370 eating disorder patients: (1) anorectic preoccupation, (2) bulimic behavior, (3) sexuality, and (4) psychosocial adjustment.

The *Body Attitude Test* (BAT) (Probst, Vandereycken, Van Coppenolle, & Vanderlinden, 1995) is a new self-report questionnaire developed for female patients suffering from eating disorders. Its psychometric characteristics have been tested in a large number of patients and control subjects (people with eating disorders, members of Weight Watchers, and normal subjects). Repeated analyses yielded a stable four-factor structure: negative appreciation of body size, lack of familiarity with respondent's own body, general body dissatisfaction, and a rest factor. Repeated tests in different subgroups have shown the BAT to be reliable and valid, as well as easy and practical, with only 20 items to be scored on a 6-point scale: from "always" (score = 5) to "never" (score = 0). The maximum total score is 100: the higher the score, the more deviating the body experience. The cut-off point of 36 leads to a sensitivity of 69% and a specificity of 75%. Originally drafted in Dutch, the BAT is presently available in English and many other languages.

Because some patients, especially anorectics, show a tendency to deny or minimize problems, an observation from a closely involved outsider (particularly a parent or spouse) may yield valuable information. The *Anorectic Behavior Observation Scale* (ABOS) (Vandereycken, 1992) is a self-reporting questionnaire developed to obtain information from parents about specific behaviors and attitudes in their children that might be symptomatic for anorexia or bulimia nervosa. A total of 30 items are to be answered by "yes" (2 points), "?" (1 point), and "no" (0 point); the higher the total score (maximum 60) the more pathological the result. Using a cut-off point of 19, the ABOS has a sensitivity of 90% and a specificity of 89.6%.

PSYCHIATRIC COMORBIDITY

A striking characteristic of patients with a history of trauma may be the large variety of psychiatric symptoms actually present. Besides dissociative phenomena and the eating disorder, the patient may show symptoms of depression, anxiety, sexual dysfunction, substance abuse, obsessive compulsive behaviors and thoughts, and many more. Within this complex picture of comorbidity (see Chapter 3) special attention must be paid to impulse dyscontrol and features of borderline personality disorder (BPD). Before exploring a trauma background, the clinician should always assess the complexity of the psychiatric problems and, with it, evaluate the risk for acting-out behavior (including auto- and heteroaggressiveness) at future psychotherapeutic interventions, such as a confrontation with a trauma experience. In general, the more comorbid behaviors are present, the more careful the therapist must be in dealing with the trauma history (see Chapters 6 and 8 on contraindications and risks of trauma exploration).

To assess general neurotic psychopathology, the widely known *Symptom Checklist* (SCL-90) (Derogatis, 1983) can be very useful, especially for repetitive evaluations. Along with a global measure for psychoneuroticism, it measures complaints of anxiety, depression, somatization, insufficiency, sensitivity, hostility, and sleeplessness. The *Beck Depression Inventory* (BDI) (Beck et al., 1961) is a more specific measure of the degree of depression. To assess BPD we use the self-reporting *Borderline Syndrome Index* (BSI) (Conte et al., 1980) which consists of four subscales: negative self-esteem, hampered interpersonal relationships, lack of social skills, and severe identity problems.

DISSOCIATIVE EXPERIENCES

The *Dissociative Experiences Scale* (DES) (Bernstein & Putnam, 1986) is a brief self-reporting 28-item scale. Subjects are asked to indicate on a 100-mm line the percentage of time they experience the feelings or behaviors concerned. The score ranges from 0-100 and represents the mean of all items. The DES score is therefore an index of the number of different types of dissociative experiences and the frequency of each experience. The questionnaire has been developed to quantify dissociative experiences in both normal and clinical populations. The questions have been developed from data gathered in interviews with patients meeting DSM-III-R criteria for dissociative disorders and from consultations with clinical experts. The items refer to experiences of disturbance in identity, memory and awareness, and cognition and feelings of depersonalization and derealization. A factor analytic study has been carried out (Bernstein, Carlson, & Putnam, 1993) and the results show that the DES measures three different components: amnestic dissociation, depersonalization and derealization, and absorption and imaginative involvement.

In several studies the DES has been shown to have an excellent split-half reliability and test-retest reliability, and good internal consistency (for an overview see Bernstein, Carlson & Putnam, 1993). In addition, the scale is able to differentiate between subjects with and without a clinical diagnosis of dissociative disorder.

Boon and Draijer (1993) investigated the utility of the DES as a screening instrument for the identification of patients at high risk for dissociative disorders. Their results indicate that a total score of 25 is the optimal cutoff point, yielding good-to-excellent sensitivity (the ability of the test to correctly identify true positive cases of patients with a dissociative disorder) and specificity (the ability of the test to correctly identify true negative cases or subjects without a dissociative disorder). For clinical use, to identify patients who are likely to have a dissociative disorder, a score of 40 predicts a dissociative disorder in all cases. But in Boon and Draijer's (1993) study, 37% of all patients with a dissociative disorder scored below 40. The reader must keep in mind that the DES (like any other self-reporting questionnaire) is not to be used as a diagnostic instrument, but as a screening tool to identify those subjects who may experience high levels of dissociation.

The development of our own *Dissociation Questionnaire* (DIS-Q) (Vanderlinden, Van Dyck, Vandereycken, Vertommen, & Verkes, 1993; Vanderlinden, Van Dyck, Vertommen, & Vandereycken, 1992; see Appendix A) was encouraged by the pioneering work of Bernstein and Putnam (1986). After we began to use the DES questionnaire, we learned that some patients found the answering method (indicating on a line the percentage of time they had this particular experience) difficult. Therefore, five different answer categories were chosen: the subjects have to circle one of the five numbers, indicating to what extent that particular item or statement is applicable to them (1 = not at all; 2 = a little bit; 3 = moderately; 4 = quite a bit; 5 = extremely).

Several factor analytic studies have been carried out on different subject samples. They always show the same four factor structure (Vanderlinden, 1993) accounting for 77% of the common variance: (1) identity confusion or fragmentation (referring to experiences of derealization and depersonalization); (2) loss of control (referring to experiences of losing control over behavior, thoughts, and emotions; this subscale also contains a few items about control over eating behavior); (3) amnesia (referring to experiences of memory lacunas); and (4) absorption (referring to experiences of enhanced concentration, which are supposed to play an important role in hypnosis).

The DIS-Q has a good internal consistency and test-retest reliability. When administered to different groups of psychiatric patients (diagnosed according to DSM-IV criteria), the results showed that the dissociative identity disorder subgroup obtained a significantly higher score than all other psychiatric categories. A study using DES and DIS-Q in a sample of 100 psychiatric patients strongly supported the construct validity of both questionnaires (a correlation of .85 between the total DES and DIS-Q scores).

The reliability and validity of the DIS-Q have been studied in a North American setting (Sainton, Ellason, Mayran, & Ross, 1993). The DIS-Q and DES were administered to subjects with a DSM-IV diagnosis of dissociative identity disorder (DID) (n=87), to inpatients with a primary substance dependency (n=26), and to undergraduate students (n=83). The internal consistency of the DIS-Q was very good and a high correlation (.87) with DES scores was found. The total DIS-Q scores of American undergraduate students and dissociative identity disorder patients closely resembled the average scores of their European counterparts, both students and DID patients: respectively 1.79 (SD 0.58) versus 1.70 (SD 0.50) for the students and 3.63 (SD 0.58) versus 3.5 (SD 0.4) for the patients. Sainton and colleagues (1993) concluded that no other area of psychiatry has produced self-report measures with greater reliability and validity than the DES and the DIS-Q.

The DIS-Q can be used as a screening device for dissociative symptoms not only in psychiatric patients but in general population samples as well (Vanderlinden, Van Dyck, Vandereycken & Vertommen, 1993). A cutoff score of 2.5 has an excellent sensitivity of 91% and specificity of 97%. Our studies have shown that the subscales identity confusion/fragmentation and amnesia are the best at differentiating between patients with a dissociative disorder and all other psychiatric categories (Vanderlinden, 1993). More details on the use and interpretation of the DIS-Q may be found in Appendix A.

Psychiatric diagnoses cannot be based on questionnaires alone. In recent years, structured interviews have been developed and tested for this purpose. A well-established example is the *Structured Clinical Interview for DSM-IV Dissociative Disorders* (SCID-D) (Steinberg, Cichetti, Buchanan, Hall, & Rounsaville, 1993; Steinberg, Rounsaville, & Cichetti, 1990). This is a semistructured interview for the assessment of five dissociative symptoms: amnesia, depersonalization, derealization, identity confusion, and identity alteration. The interview schedule contains direct and indirect questions about the presence or absence of symptoms. Severity of each of the dissociative symptoms is rated in terms of the frequency and duration of episodes and the presence or absence of precipitating stressors provoking dissociative phenomena. The symptoms are scored on a 4-point scale (1=absent; 2=mild; 3=moderate; 4=severe), and the total SCID-D score can range from 5 to 20. The assessment of the full interview may take between half an hour and two hours, and therefore is somewhat time-consuming. However, it has good reliability and validity, clearly differentiating between patients with a dissociative disorder and those with other psychopathology, including borderline and histrionic personality disorders (Boon & Draijer, 1993). Administration of the SCID-D may be recommended in all patients who score above the cutoff point on either the DES or the DIS-Q.

The *Dissociative Disorder Interview Schedule* (DDIS) (Ross, 1989) has been developed to make DSM-III-R diagnoses of somatization disorder, major depressive episode, borderline personality disorder, and all the dissociative disorders. The DDIS has an interrater reliability of .68, a sensitivity of 90%, and a specificity of 100% for the diagnosis of dissociative identity disorder (Ross et al., 1990). This structured interview takes only 30 to 45 minutes to administer to most subjects. More information with regard to the administration and scoring of this instrument is available in Ross (1989).

PSYCHOTRAUMA

Screening of trauma experiences has become a highly controversial issue in the psychiatric and psychotherapeutic field. Especially with regard to the reliability of the trauma memories clinicians, researchers and the lay public alike seem to be split up into two irreconcilable camps, the "believers" and the "nonbelievers." The often highly emotional discussions usually put the truth on trial, and eventually some end in a real courtroom. But a clinician's or therapist's first task is to accept the patient's subjective experience and "narrative truth" within a relationship of growing mutual trust. Testing the "factual truth" is not a primary function of therapists, or they would act like detectives or judges. In some instances, however, therapists can be forced to consider the implications of information revealed to them: when there is enough reason to believe that the patient's story contains reliable evidence that either the patient or another person was or still is the victim of a serious violation of personal rights and integrity. Then the first step is to ensure protection of the (potential) victim against repetition of abuse. The patient's "safety" should always be a primary concern, whatever the therapy. One must protect patients against dangerous or destructive acts either from themselves or from someone else. This must be a basic condition for the therapy itself.

If actions outside the therapeutic context are necessary, the therapist should remain in the therapeutic role and leave the other actions to an otherwise uninvolved colleague who:

- evaluates the information on its factual reliability;

- involves other parties when and where needed without violating the rights of the patient or of significant others;

- discusses these actions and all their implications with the patient ("informed consent").

Starting from these principles, our discussion will stay within the context of health care, and we will address the screening of traumatic experiences only from a clinical viewpoint. First, there is no solid research available to decide whether a questionnaire or a standardized interview should be recommended (Waller, 1991). Next, many patients will disclose their trauma histories only after several months of intensive treatment. It is crucial then to question whether the act of disclosure itself or the disclosed information or both might have a special meaning within the therapeutic process. Because any retrospective information is colored by the context within which it is revealed, a therapist should always pay attention to the moment and circumstances of disclosure. Often, therapists are blamed for being "naive" in this sense (if not actually accused of "producing" the trauma), but researchers, too, appear to forget the context when they collect facts!

We now use the *Traumatic Experiences Questionnaire* (TEQ) (Nijenhuis, van der Hart, & Vanderlinden, 1995), a newly developed instrument that includes the following categories: several kinds of emotional neglect and abuse; physical abuse; sexual abuse (by family members and others); family problems (such as alcohol abuse, poverty, psychiatric problems of a family member); decease or loss of a family member; bodily harm; severe pain; war experiences. For 28 items the subject is asked to indicate: (1) whether he or she has had this kind of experience; (2) the age when it started and stopped; and (3) the degree of burden the experience has posed or the subjective "severity" of the trauma experience (rated on a Likert-type 5-point scale). The items contain short descriptions of the events of concern. For instance, sexual harrassment is defined as "troublesome sexual approach that did not result in actual sexual contact," while sexual abuse is described as "being forced to perform sexual acts." Further questions include information about the perpetrators, eventual disclosure of the event, and response to it.

Additionally, we use the *Childhood Unwanted Sexual Events* questionnaire (CHUSE) (Lange et al., 1995), which contains detailed questions about negative sexual experiences in the past, asking about the nature of the abuse, age at onset and final occurrence, frequency, relation to abuser(s), type of impact, degree and type of pressure used.

The clinician should be aware that such questionnaires or detailed interviews may function as a trigger of old memories and feelings associated with the trauma. Hence, the patient again may be overwhelmed with these negative experiences, become very anxious as to further treatment, and even develop a dissociative-like state or other reactions as a way to cope with the relived trauma. In all cases, the therapist must try to debrief the patient of the painful material (Kearney-Cooke & Striegel-Moore, 1994).

FAMILY BACKGROUND

As discussed, family characteristics may mediate between childhood trauma (input) and adult psychopathological sequelae (outcome). Using the *Leuven Family Questionnaire* (LFQ) (Kog, Vertommen, & Vandereycken, 1987; see also Vandereycken, Kog, & Vanderlinden, 1989) we pay special attention to poorly organized, chaotic, less cohesive, and highly conflictual family interactions (more often encountered in eating disorder patients with a bulimic component). The *Parental Bonding Instrument* (PBI) (Parker, 1983) assesses the subject's recollections of relationships with both parents during the first 16 years of his or her childhood. The subject has to judge each parent's behavior and attitude as described in 25 items (4-point Likert-type scales) that contribute to the dimensions "care" (empathic responsiveness) and "protection" (support and tolerance of autonomy). Combining these two dimensions a therapist can situate a parental rearing style in one of the following quadrants: "optimal parenting" (high care and low protection), "neglectful parenting" (low care and low protection), "affectionate constraint" (high care and high protection), and "affectionless control" (low care and high protection).

As a first warning we want to stress that the assessment of family variables is not intended to find a scapegoat or declare parents to be guilty. A therapist should be very careful in reaching conclusions. When addressing parental features or quality of parenting, for example, it is difficult for the therapist to distinguish between evaluations of the actual relationship with parents and the actual perception of experienced interaction with parents during childhood. The perceived past or present relationship with parents may be influenced by the subject's actual degree of attachment to or emotional separation from the parents. Since separation–individuation can be seen as a core issue in many anorectics and bulimics, the therapist should take this into account when analyzing the patient's family perceptions. The patient's age, and perhaps more importantly the actual stage in the family life cycle—for example, the leaving home phase—also play an influential role. (For a discussion of these influences on family perceptions, see Vandereycken, Kog, & Vanderlinden, 1989).

A final methodological remark especially concerns the attitude of anorexia nervosa patients towards psychological assessment. These patients, particularly in the acute stage or before being engaged in treatment, often deny any problem and thus make the use of self-reporting instruments questionable (Vandereycken & Vanderlinden, 1983). Moreover, their tendency to please others and their concern with appearances may distort their answering pattern in the direction of social desirability. This is closely connected to the well-recognized tendency of patients with anorexia nervosa to idealize their parents.

When patients are married or patients live with a partner, that relationship should be evaluated as well. For this kind of assessment we have developed and validated a new self-report inventory, the *Marital Intimacy Questionnaire* (MIQ) (Van den Broucke, Vertommen, & Vandereycken, 1995). This questionnaire consists of 56 items (to be scored on a five-point Likert-type scale) and examines five factors: (1) intimacy problems, (2) consensus, (3) openness, (4) affection, and (5) commitment. The questionnaire has sufficient internal consistency and validity. We recommend that therapists combine the MIQ with a broader judgment of the marital (dis)satisfaction, including the sexual relationship. For example, they can use the *Maudsley Marital Questionnaire* (MMQ) (Crowe, 1978).

CASE EXAMPLE: LAURA

Laura, a 27-year-old bulimic woman, was referred to our inpatient unit by her psychotherapist. Laura had been living on her own for the three years since her separation from her husband (their official divorce was soon to come). She had no children. After six months of intensive outpatient psychotherapy, no positive evolution had taken place; Laura was still bingeing and vomiting every day. Her symptoms made it impossible for her to continue working and her eating disorder also caused serious financial problems. She had lived in isolation for the past three months. Hospitalization seemed indicated to break the vicious cycle.

Eating Disorder Symptoms

On the Eating Disorder Inventory (EDI) Laura scored very high in total (94) and on the following subscales: drive for thinness (21), bulimia (15), perfectionism (15), and body dissatisfaction (23). On the Eating Disorder Evaluation Scale (EDES) she also scored in the pathological range (a total of 34), especially on the subscale anorectic preoccupation (8), bulimia (6) and psychosocial adjustment (4).

Comorbidity

On the Symptom Checklist (SCL-90; Dutch version) the total score was very high (313) and comparable with scores of a psychiatric population. The following subscales displayed the highest scores: anxiety (45), depression (60), and somatization (50). During the last months before admission, Laura regularly abused alcohol to help her to fall asleep at night. She also showed a subtle form of self-destructiveness, waking up every morning at 5 AM and working till midnight. With only 4 to 5 hours of sleep, she soon reached complete exhaustion.

Trauma

On the Childhood Unwanted Sexual Events questionnaire (CHUSE) Laura admitted sexual violation by her husband when he was drunk. At first she reacted violently, but after a while she stopped and became apathetic. On the Traumatic Experiences Questionnaire (TEQ) Laura reported a long list of trauma experiences, many of which she did not report at the intake interview.

Early trauma experiences included:

- suffering emotional neglect and abuse in the family of origin between the ages of 5 and 17 years;

- being forced to take care of her mother and brother between the ages of 8 and 17 ("parentification");

- undergoing physical abuse in her family of origin between the ages of 6 and 17 years;

- suffering severe stress (a brother's psychiatric problems) between the ages of 8 and 17.

Traumatic experiences in later life included:

- loss of a child (an abortion after 7 months of pregnancy due to physical violence by her husband) at the age of 22;

- sexual abuse (rape) in her marriage;

- life-threatening circumstances (her husband said he would kill her if she refused sexual intercourse) at the age of 22;

- physical abuse by her husband: she was frequently beaten by him.

Dissociation

On the Dissociation Questionnaire (DIS-Q) Laura obtained a total score of 2.7, a score of 2.8 on the subscale "identity confusion," 3.1 on "loss of control," and 1.3 on "amnesia." These scores are similar to those found in patients with posttraumatic stress disorder, borderline personality disorder, and dissociative disorder not otherwise specified (DDNOS). A similar result was found with the SCID-D interview: Laura obtained a score of 10.

Developmental Phase

Laura reported both emotional neglect and physical abuse, but only after the age of 5. The absence of trauma experiences in very early childhood is considered to be a good prognostic factor. Revictimization experiences were frequently reported, especially in her marriage (for example, the loss of a child and physical abuse). Higher severity scores on the TEQ indicate that these experiences were more traumatizing and still are distressing her life to a greater extent than her past family experiences. But the fact that these traumatic events took place in late adolescence and early adulthood makes them less pathogenic.

Nature of the Abuse

As is often the case, Laura experienced different kinds of trauma. First, there was a combination of emotional abuse and physical abuse in her family of origin. Her father, in particular, is described as dominating and very aggressive, both physically and verbally (making humiliating remarks). Most stressful for Laura were family burdens such as her brother's psychiatric problems and the parentification (taking care of her mother and brother).

During her treatment, Laura realized that she had married as a way of fleeing the problems in her family of origin. Her husband, however, soon turned out to be an alcoholic, who frequently beat her and forced her to have sexual intercourse. The only time she became pregnant, she had a miscarriage after 7 months probably due to the physical violence of her husband. This experience was particularly traumatizing for Laura and still played a major role in her life at the time she was admitted to our hospital.

Disclosure

Laura never spoke about her experiences to friends or relatives. When she started outpatient treatment six months before her admission to our hospital, she disclosed them for the first time. Before, her way of coping with these experiences was trying to avoid thinking about the past and working very hard. However, at night she regularly was awakened by a nightmare, often related to one or more of these trauma experiences. In the evenings, especially when she was with her husband, she became very anxious without knowing why. Bingeing in secret became her special way to anesthesize herself emotionally and to stop thinking.

Family Variables

Laura grew up under the tyranny, as she called it, of an aggressive father. As a child, she felt more and more hate toward her father. The relationship with her mother was much better, although little affection was shown and there was almost no physical contact. Conflict avoidance was very high and mutual support was lacking. However, an important evolution in her family of origin took place after her father retired some years ago. He became more and more interested in Laura's life. At first she remained very distant and cautious toward him. But the more she saw her father, the more her feelings of anger and hate progressively diminished. An important factor in this positive evolution seemed to be that her father showed some regret for what he had done in the past.

When therapists looked at her actual relationship with her husband, the pattern of avoiding conflicts and poor communication present in her relationship with her father emerged again. Her husband had great difficulty in communicating his feelings and was afraid to face open conflicts. He himself had grown up in a very troubled family with a violent and alcoholic father.

Life Events

Laura's marriage can be considered as a revictimization experience. Most of the time she felt emotionally neglected by her husband, and often there was a lot of physical violence combined with sexual abuse. Moreover, the loss of her unborn child was very traumatizing.

But in recent years, some positive—possibly healing—experiences occurred. First, she started to establish a better relationship with her father, who showed some regret for his violent behavior in the past. This enabled Laura to forgive her father for his conduct. Another important life event was her actual relationship with a new boyfriend. Now she had chosen a man who really cared for her and showed a lot of affection. It was the very first time in her life that she felt really loved and respected. At moments, it was difficult for her to accept this new experience. She looked at herself as not worthy enough to be loved.

Self-Image

The results of Laura's Body Attitude Test (BAT) confirmed the body dissatisfaction reported on the EDI. Her total BAT score of 64 corresponds with the average score found in a large group of bulimia nervosa patients. The highest scores (above the average of an eating disorder sample) were found on subscale "negative appreciation of body size" (21) and "lack of familiarity with one's own body" (20). In combination with this negative body image, Laura also showed a negative self-esteem: she had the feeling of being totally incapable of controlling her life and that she had failed in everything both professionally and personally (in intimate relationships).

Summary

Laura showed all characteristics of DSM-IV bulimia nervosa, purging type (307.51), with a normal body weight and daily episodes of bingeing, vomiting and abusing laxatives. The eating disorder symptoms had existed for about six years. Other typical eating disorder characteristics were her drive for thinness, her perfectionism, and a strong body dissatisfaction in connection with a low self-esteem. As comorbid problems she reported alcohol abuse, depressive mood, anxiety, and tendency of somatization. There is no clear evidence of a personality disorder, but she showed dissociative features similar to those found in patients with posttraumatic stress disorder, borderline personality disorder, and dissociative disorder not otherwise specified.

Laura disclosed a large list of traumatic experiences both in her family of origin and later during marriage: a repetition (revictimization) of physical, emotional, and sexual abuse. Disclosure and support were totally absent till the moment she went into psychotherapy. Several important life events are considered as positive factors, including the reconciliation with her father and her relationship with her boyfriend.

5

Regaining Self-Control

In this chapter we first present the treatment principles we consider essential in any patient suffering from an eating disorder. Because most of its applications have been described elsewhere in detail (see other volumes of the Brunner/Mazel Eating Disorders Monograph Series, especially our own book: *A Practical Guide to the Treatment of Bulimia Nervosa*, Vanderlinden, Norré, & Vandereycken, 1992), we will limit ourselves to a brief presentation of our treatment philosophy. Next, we will discuss the use of psychotropic medication within our psychotherapeutic framework. Finally, we will describe in more detail the clinical guidelines for dealing with patients whose eating disorder appears to be interwoven with a history of trauma, dissociation, and/or impulse dyscontrol.

GENERAL PRINCIPLES IN THE
TREATMENT OF EATING DISORDERS

In our treatment of eating disorders we apply a directive and multidimensional approach, integrating strategies from different therapeutic models. Based on our clinical experience with both in- and outpatient treatment of eating disorders, we propose seven basic guidelines. We consider these principles essential in creating the necessary condition for therapeutic change.

1. *Therapy should be based on a biopsychological assessment.* A multi-dimensional assessment includes an examination of the patient's physical condition and a functional analysis of the disturbed eating pattern, and also an assessment of the patient's psychosocial functioning (relationships with family and friends, studies or occupation, and sexuality). A one-sided viewpoint or model inevitably neglects the complexity of an eating disorder.

2. *Therapy should interrupt the perpetuating influences.* The treatment plan does not start with hypotheses about possibly causal factors, but focuses first on the factors that appear to perpetuate the eating disorder. The interventions are meant to interrupt these vicious circles.

3. *Therapy should give maximum responsibility to the patient.* In our treatment approach we try to give the patient maximum responsibility for the therapy and limit the external control as much as possible. We elaborate this principle in a treatment contract in which the patient is asked to make her own treatment goals.

4. *Therapy should improve self-esteem and body-experience.* If therapy is aimed only at changing the eating behavior or the body weight, the improvement most probably will be only superficial, partial, and temporary. As an essential long-term goal we want to improve the patient's self-esteem as expressed in a positive body-experience.

5. *Therapy should include the family context.* Often distorted family interactions are part of the perpetuating influences of the eating disorder. Therefore, as early as possible in the beginning of treatment we try to establish a collaborative alliance with the patient's parents (or partner). Although the separation issue is usually quite central, therapy should avoid "parentectomy."

6. *Therapy should be well-structured but transparent.* Therapy is structured in different phases and all agreements are written down in the treatment plan. This is done in a very concrete and clear (transparent) way to avoid discussion with the pa-

tient and her parents at the moment when certain rules must be applied. The therapist should beware of on the spot improvization because it can lead easily to manipulation.

7. *Therapy should be time-limited with regular evaluations.* Treatment of eating disorders is a complex and difficult matter that may require a long-lasting therapeutic engagement, but its cost–benefit ratio should be regularly evaluated. Therapeutic goals should be shaped accordingly, including an evaluation of whether it is worthwhile to continue this form of treatment.

OUTPATIENT TREATMENT

Our treatment rationale is that a striking behavior, such as binge eating, is only the tip of an iceberg. Such an eating pattern is signaling other problems. This means that a treatment focused purely on the eating pathology offers few or limited chances of success. We make the patient see clearly that the bulimia conveys an important message about her life. We therefore invite the patient to scrutinize her feelings about bulimia to learn to decipher hidden significances. The outpatient treatment consists of three phases (see Vanderlinden, Norré, & Vandereycken, 1992).

First, in *individual sessions,* preferably twice a week, we try to build up a healthy eating pattern and to restore the patient's control over the bingeing–purging behavior. Following a nonabstinence approach (that is, we aim at only gradual decrease of the bulimia), we use cognitive-behavioral therapeutic strategies to reach these goals. Using a diary, the patient has to find the function of her disturbed eating. Working with a diary also creates the opportunity for the therapist to gather a lot of information about the patient's daily life.

As early as possible we plan an interview with the partner and/or her parents (even when the patient lives on her own). If her parents are not informed about the disturbed eating pattern, this situation constitutes a primary motivational task for the patient, who must bring the problem into the open. This contact with the family or partner is to prepare for the involvment of these significant others in treatment, if necessary and if possible.

The individual phase is time-limited. Once therapy evolves favorably, we prefer to switch patients to group therapy (if possible with the same therapist). Family or marital therapy can take place at the same time if indicated (see Vandereycken, Kog, & Vanderlinden, 1989). If the first phase has not resulted in clear amelioration, outpatient therapy is stopped according to the therapeutic contract; at this point an admission to a specialized eating disorders unit can be proposed.

The main purpose of the *group therapy* (a two-hour session once a week) is to achieve effective changes in the patient's life toward autonomy and sufficient self-esteem so that the bulimia becomes superfluous. Again our approach is directive, pragmatic, and eclectic. Making use of behavioral, cognitive, and interactional components, the group therapy is aimed at well-defined goals within a particular period of time. This directive approach necessitates the active participation of both patient and therapist. We prefer to restrict the group size to six patients (eight at most) in order to keep control over escaping maneuvers and to enlarge the possibility of active participation.

After three months, each patient has to evaluate her progress and judge the cost and benefit of further group therapy. For this purpose we use a system of "goal-attainment evaluation." At the start and after each evaluation, the patient has to specify concrete treatment goals on each of the three levels of her problem: eating behavior, self-perception, and interactions. Throughout group therapy the patient will keep a diary. Other therapeutic strategies we use are described in detail elsewhere (Vanderlinden, Norré, & Vandereycken, 1992).

Because the majority of the patients are between 20 to 30 years old, most of them are still in the launching stage of their life cycles, even if they are living far away from home. As a consequence, promoting and encouraging independence is a central theme in the treatment. This separation–individuation issue provokes in many patients a lot of ambivalence and tension, resulting sometimes in temporary relapses. Frequent themes in the group sessions are perfectionism, feelings of emptiness and abandonment, fear of intimacy and sexuality, problems in expressing aggressive feelings, and the working through of traumatic experiences. The group therapy or second treatment phase takes on average six months to one year.

Finally, we plan a *follow-up* (up to one year) aimed at the consolidation of the achieved changes and the stimulation of the continuation of these changes. This again takes place on an individual basis and the sessions are progressively spread in time. The clinical importance of this phase is based upon long-term follow-up studies (see Herzog, Deter, & Vandereycken, 1992).

INPATIENT AND DAY-HOSPITAL TREATMENT

In the stream of reports on treatment of bulimic disorders little can be found on failures, relapses, and drop-outs. If outpatient therapy fails, does this mean that inpatient treatment becomes unavoidable? What are the indications for inpatient treatment? There exists consensus about only two criteria: a high risk of suicide and an alarming physical condition. In our experience, there are three other important indications for admitting patients to a specialized inpatient unit or day treatment hospital (Norré & Vandereycken, 1991). (See Table 5.1.)

1. *Multisymptomatic bulimia.* As described in Chapter 3, multisymptomatic or "multi-impulsive" bulimia means that these

TABLE 5.1
Indications for Inpatient Treatment*

- Critical physical condition
- Risk of self-destructive behavior
- Complexity of clinical picture
    chronicity (5 years and more)
    comorbidity (multi-impulsivity)
- Intolerable family situation
- Extreme social isolation
- Failure of outpatient treatment

*Including day hospital treatment

patients do not only show a disturbed eating pattern, but also exhibit problems in impulse control: drug and/or alcohol abuse, self-injury, stealing, obsessive-compulsive rituals, and sexual disinhibition. Frequently we find a personality disorder of the borderline type, a history of sexual or physical abuse and/or the presence of pathological dissociative phenomena. This group of patients requires a more intensive form of treatment, as will be described later.

2. *A disturbed family context.* Some patients live in a family atmosphere of high conflict, which could reinforce the vicious circle between bulimia and interactional conflicts. They are involved in overt or subtle triangulation within the family (for example, divorce battles). Parents may persist in denying the severity of the physical and psychological aspects of the eating disorder. Parental psychopathology (depression, substance abuse) could also lead to an uncollaborative attitude towards the treatment of their daughter.

3. *Social isolation.* The bulimic ritual is a time- and energy-consuming activity. It can become so important that the whole day is planned around the possibility of bingeing and purging. All leisure or "empty" time is dedicated to food. Social contacts and activities gradually diminish or are completely avoided. If the patient lives alone, there is no longer any form of social control over her eating. To keep their eating disorder concealed patients isolate themselves more and more. In this way they create more empty time and occasions for bingeing. The vicious circle is closed and becomes self-supporting.

In these complicating circumstances, first of all, we try to challenge the patient's attitude and motivation. If she wants to continue outpatient therapy she must be prepared for real change in her daily life, give priority to the treatment, and involve a social support system. In view of these conditions, we make a time-limited written contract in which the necessary preparation is formulated in terms of clear changes. We always give the patient the benefit of the doubt and continue outpatient treatment if she can convince us of its usefulness. If not, we stop the therapy and propose inpatient treatment in a specialized unit for eating disorders. Only during treatment do many patients become aware of the severity of their problems and the demands of therapy. So, outpatient treatment can have a motivational function: The patient gains some insight into the meaning and complexity of her bulimic behavior, for which no magic solution exists. The step towards an inpatient treatment then becomes easier. Patients might be able to consider hospitalization not as a failure but as a new chance. It will act as a turning point, allowing her to break through unescapable vicious circles. Within our inpatient unit, the abovementioned principles are translated into an intensive multidimensional treatment program (see Table 5.2).

Use of Medication

As in the case of different forms of psychotherapy, nearly all possible psychotropics have been tested in eating disorders. Often, however, conditions were based only on limited experience or the clinician's personal preference rather than thorough scientific research. Although they were in use until the 1980s, it has never been proved that strong sedatives belonging to the group of so-called *neuroleptics* or "major tranquilizers" are effective in anorexia nervosa.

TABLE 5.2
A Multidimensional Inpatient Treatment

Individual behavioral contract:
   normalizing weight and eating
   regaining self-control
Intensive group psychotherapy
Art and occupational therapy
Body-experience therapy
Involvement of family:
   parent counseling group
   family/marital therapy (when indicated)
   sibling therapy (when indicated)

They are more likely to be used now in patients with borderline features or in cases of impulsive self-injurious behaviors. The same applies to anxiolytic (minor) *tranquilizers,* some of which are also utilized for sleep disturbances. The most discussed group of psychotropics in eating disorders are the *antidepressants,* to which we pay some attention here.

In bulimic patients mood swings occur quite often. Their susceptibility to depressive reactions is possibly biologically determined and partly inherited. Binge eating may be associated in a complex way with such emotional instability: It may be both the cause and the consequence of mood swings. If the bulimia nervosa exists for some months or years, we usually see a vicious circle with no distinct beginning or end.

Therapeutically there are several approaches a therapist may employ to break this circle: dealing with the mood, the eating behavior, or with both. A subgroup of bulimia nervosa patients appears to respond positively to antidepressants, with regard to both mood improvement and decrease of binge-eating frequency. From the group of "classical" antidepressants (the so-called tricyclics) a number of drugs have been tested with varying results. But it should be considered that these medicines may have unpleasant side effects. Particularly in patients with eating disorders, the occurrence of a dry mouth (with a greater inclination to drink) and delayed bowel movements (causing obstipation or constipation) may be particularly disturbing. Fewer side effects are induced by the new generation of serotonergic antidepressants. A major exception, however, is the occurrence of nausea. Apart from the fact that this may incite a patient to stop the intake, for obvious reasons an inclination to vomit is an undesired effect in eating disorder patients.

Among these "new" antidepressants, fluoxetine is most widely researched in bulimia nervosa patients. It has been shown to suppress their urge to eat: The frequency of their binges strikingly decreases. However, we do not know which type of patient will respond favorably. A more important problem has to do with the limited length of improvement: As soon as medication stops, a large group of patients soon relapses. The beneficial effect also gradually disappears or relapse increasingly occurs if the patient takes the remedy continuously for several months. Thus a therapist can expect only a short-term effect from treatment with antidepressants. Further-more, a beneficial effect on binges and mood doesn't mean that all problems associated with bulimia nervosa automatically will be solved. Hence prescription of these medicines should be accompa-nied by psychotherapeutic measures and a few precautions (dis-cussed below) also should be considered. That doesn't alter the fact that a possible beneficial short-term effect—breaking through the bulimic spiral—is a hopeful sign for the patient and may strengthen her effort in further psychotherapy.

In our opinion, psychotropics in eating disorders should always be combined with some form of psychotherapy. The therapeutic effect should be assessed on the basis of the guidelines mentioned at the beginning of this chapter. Furthermore, in prescribing medicines to these patients the therapist should take the following major prob-lems into account.

1. *Compliance.* Because patients with an eating disorder are afraid of gaining weight, they are sceptical about any med-ication that may increase the appetite. Bulimic patients often hope for a magic potion that will suppress their urge to eat. Therefore they frequently take appetite suppressants surrep-titiously or experiment with the dose of a product. In their state of emotional instability they also may "forget" to take the remedy. Others are soon inclined to stop taking the rem-edy if it doesn't provide the desired effect quickly enough. Antidepressants are especially likely to cause problems if pa-tients are impatient, for the side-effects are immediate while the beneficial effects usually take at least ten days.

2. *Impulsiveness.* Because of their mood swings and problems in impulse control, in a moment of disillusionment and despair patients suddenly may throw away all their pills, or they may take an overdose. Such impulsive self-poisoning might be a suicide attempt; certainly in bulimia nervosa this risk should not be underestimated. In case of alcohol abuse, patients are more prone to taking an overdose of drugs, the lethal risk of which is increased through the combination with alcohol.

3. *Vomiting and purging.* Regularly induced vomiting or abuse of laxatives may lead to a serious disturbance in electrolytes (lack of potassium) and, as a consequence, to a perilous disturbance of the heart function. Taking an overdose of antidepressants, particularly the tricyclic drugs, may be life-threatening because these medicines themselves may already disturb the heart function. Besides, the therapist should take into account that vomiting itself may impede or hamper the effects of a medicine: a pill just swallowed may be vomited before it has been sufficiently absorbed into the body.

4. *Addiction and dissociation.* In general people can become easily dependent upon tranquillizing drugs. This risk will be higher for patients with some inclination towards becoming addicted. Abuse of psychotropics will be more likely when combined with serious symptoms of anxiety—for example, nightmares in traumatized patients. Psychotropic drugs also may induce or worsen dissociative experiences, especially depersonalization and amnesia.

GUIDELINES FOR PATIENTS WITH A HISTORY OF TRAUMA, DISSOCIATION, AND/OR IMPULSE DYSCONTROL

The eating disorder patients to whom this book is devoted require additional therapeutic measures. Many have to find a way to regain control over impulsive and self-destructive behaviors. They often are convinced to be out of control, especially when they have been traumatized and/or show the tendency to dissociate. Therefore, a basic treatment goal will be for them to attain sufficient internal control over what they do, think, and feel. We continuously give the message that from the moment the therapy starts, they must take responsibility for their behavior. We stress that nothwithstanding their bad experiences in the past, they can take their lives in their own hands and make their own positive choices.

Of course, a basic condition for this learning process in any therapy will be the establishment of a trusting and safe relationship. Especially in traumatized patients, safety and trust in the therapeutic relationship are the cornerstones of the treatment. In the following sections we want to focus on those therapeutic actions that can help these patients to deal more effectively with the aftermath of trauma, the dissociative episodes, and the maladaptive behaviors that disrupt their lives.

Structure, Education, and Safety

Psychotherapy with these patients requires a clear and explicit treatment contract. In general terms, it is meant to structure the therapeutic relationship into a trustful working alliance. It should be clear for both parties what they expect from each other. The therapist must guarantee certain commitments but the patient will not yet be able to do the same. Although we have to accept that the patient will repeatedly need to test the therapist, we address treatment compliance from the very beginning. We expect two explicit forms of compliance: regular attendance at the therapeutic sessions and completion of assignments (homework) in between sessions. In this way, we emphasize the patient's responsibility before any therapeutic action has started. Furthermore, a written treatment contract usually will stipulate the following basic rules:

- The patient will take care of her physical health and thus avoid any self-harming behaviors (depending on the case, this condition will be specified with regard to eating, drinking, sleeping, self-injurious behaviors, and so on).

- The patient is not allowed to use any drugs or alcohol; psychotropic medication may be used only with the consent of the therapist.

- The patient is not allowed to see another therapist, except by agreement.

In trauma survivors no therapeutic work possibly can succeed if safety has not been adequately secured (Herman, 1992). Some specific therapeutic efforts might help the patient in experiencing the therapist, and gradually the wider social network, as reliable and safe. The therapeutic contract is a first step in this direction. Next, using a direct style of interviewing about the occurrence of "shameful" behaviors (such as vomiting and self-cutting) or "weird" experiences (such as dissociative symptoms) will give the patient the message of acceptance and recognition.

A basic element in the treatment is to educate patients and families about eating disorders, impulse dyscontrol, and dissociation. Many patients believe they are weird (or will be called mad), for instance when they (reveal that they) hear voices in their heads, cut themselves, binge and vomit in secret, and so on. The therapist must inform and reassure patients that their symptoms have some understandable function. Especially with respect to dissociative phenomena we explain that they may belong to everyone's daily experience, but they are only distressing or maladaptive when they can no longer be controlled. Furthermore, we tell patients that dissociation is a well-known way in which children deal with frightening situations.

Exposure to severe threat constitutes a classical conditioning procedure, in which various stages of imminence (triggers) evoke particular states of defense, including dissociative reactions. The latter experiences, including feelings of derealization and memory gaps, are installed to help the patient to cope with a painful, traumatic situation. Hence, the dissociative reaction at first has a positive, protective function. However, on repetition, the triggers associated with the original trauma situation will re-elicit representations of the traumatic event, and by consequence automatically induce dissociative experiences in the patient. In this way, formerly functional defenses against overwhelming traumatic experiences may turn into maladaptive reactions. Specific triggers and situations, probably referring to or associated with patients' traumatic past, will evoke specific emotional states in which patients have the feeling of being out of control. Similar explanations—the learning process of dissociation—are given to family members or other important people with whom the patient lives.

If patients need to be hospitalized for their safety, it is equally important to offer them clear information about the rules and principles of the inpatient treatment. In a transparent therapy the patient knows from the beginning what she can expect. For many patients clear rules will avoid their feeling manipulated ("out of control"). Especially in the case of self-destructive behavior, a plan for future protection must be prepared together with the patient (see next paragraph on management of self-injury). This usually implies some form of a contract, including the possible alternative actions or interventions to be applied in case of emergency, when the patient risks the loss of control over her behavior.

An important step in the establishment of safety may be the involvement in the treatment of meaningful others, such as family members or friends (see Chapter 7). If patients live in social isolation, it is important either to provide a social network or to help the patients to create one, so that they can learn to trust other people and ask for support outside the therapeutic milieu. At the same time they have to find out what type of milieu or person is a potential source of danger (Herman, 1992).

In the case of patients who are still living in an abusive family system, as a general rule we will try to get them out as soon as possible. Moreover—even if they are admitted to the hospital—it is important to consider the need to stop all contact with the family members in question for a while. The therapist must make sure that all possible abusive actions stop. For some patients this might imply that the therapist (or therapeutic team) working with the patient will have no direct contact with the abusive person. If this concerns family members, they can be offered the possibility of seeing another therapist, who is not directly involved in the treatment of the patient. Chapter 7 describes other ways of working with the family.

> Shortly after her admission to our inpatient unit, we realized that Rosalyn, a 28-year-old anorectic with severe episodes of bingeing and vomiting, always became extremely upset and confused after visits from her parents. She was very tense and restless for several hours. As a result, she found it difficult to engage herself in the therapeutic program. Later on we discovered that Rosalyn had been severely sexually abused by her father. We therefore decided to stop the family visits for the following weeks.

To avoid loyalty problems it was announced to the parents that this decision had been made by the team in order to give Rosalyn the opportunity to develop a certain autonomy.

Management of Self-Injury

Our essential treatment goal that each patient should learn to take her life in her own hands implies a serious confrontation with herself: first with her actual daily life and next (to a variable extent) with her past. This principle of "back to reality" is inseparably connected to the basic idea of self-responsibility. First and foremost this concerns a patient's own physical health. The contract we mentioned above includes this basic rule. But this should be based on a critical assessment of the patient's ability to do so. We cannot require a certain degree of self-control if that is exactly what patients are lacking. Therefore this fundamental goal must be linked to the principle of structure and safety in treatment, as discussed in the previous paragraph.

There are many strategies to improve the patient's self-control. We refer, for example, to Linehan's "dialectical behavior therapy" focusing on the emotional dysregulation of patients with a borderline personality disorder. Linehan (1993) showed how her approach can be effective in reducing suicide attempts and self-injurious behaviors ("parasuicidal acts") in these patients. Inspired by this work, as well as by other publications about the management of self-injury (Hawton, 1990; Torem, 1995; Van Moffaert, 1990; Walsh & Rosen, 1988), we stress the following elements in our therapeutic approach.

We expect that therapists or team members realize how their own reactions towards a self-harming patient in general and a concrete self-injurious act in particular will be part of a positive or negative learning process. This becomes crucial in cases of repetitive self-mutilation. Therefore we like to work within the context of *contract management*: a clear agreement is made about what each party (patient and therapist) can expect from the other in case of self-injury.

On the part of the therapist or the team, two basic rules are guiding the concrete management:

1. *Neutral nursing.* Wounds have to be taken care of in a technically appropriate way but without direct comments or questions (except for those that are medically necessary). Once the acute situation is over, and/or at a more appropriate moment (from a few hours to a few days later), the second rule should be applied:

2. *Open communication.* The event should be discussed in a therapeutic context with special attention to the messages expressed by the patient (even just in maladaptive body language). Together with the patient the therapist analyzes the possible functions of the self-injurious behavior (as we have discussed in Chapter 3—see Table 3.8).

On the patient's part the behavioral contract concerning self-injury includes three elements:

1. *Self-monitoring.* Patients are asked to keep a diary in which they describe all problematic situations, systematically recording their thoughts, feelings, and behaviors before and after the event. This self-observation will help to discover particular situations where they are at risk for inducing some form of impulse dyscontrol. Then measures can be taken to stop the chain of reactions in time (stimulus control).

2. *Response prevention.* If patients are faced with dangerous and/or uncontrollable acts, protective measures have to be agreed upon (both at home and in the hospital) so that a strong urge is not followed by a concrete act of self-harm. Related to the previous rule, this could mean some form of time out (escaping from the risky situation); or it may be the application of the third rule.

3. *Alternative abreaction.* Patients learn to use physical exercises (such as running, cycling, or fitness training) to get rid of their tension. The guiding principles in the selection of these exercises are that they should be easily available, harmless (for both the patient and other people), and quickly dis-

charge emotional energy without bringing the patient into a trance-like state.

Identifying Triggers

Throughout treatment, patients continue their self-observation by writing down thoughts, images, feelings, and circumstances that might lead to a loss of control over their behavior. In the following pages we will discuss a series of special triggers often connected to dissociative reactions and/or impulse dyscontrol in traumatized patients.

Situations ("Cues") That Refer, Directly or Indirectly to the Trauma

Patients may become very anxious and tense in the evening. The fact of being alone, combined with the darkness outside, may function as a trigger related to the original trauma situation (when the patient as a young child was often left alone in the house in the evening). In the case of a history of sexual abuse, all kinds of sexual stimuli may be threatening for the patient, varying from hearing people making jokes about sexual issues to the reality of physical contact. Other stimuli may indirectly evoke the fear of sexual assault—for example, asking the patient to undress for physical examination or to be weighed, making a picture or a videotape of the patient, hearing someone else screaming, and so on. Certain dates may also refer to specific moments when a particular traumatic experience took place, for instance the day the patient ran away from home, or when her father left his family after a terrible fight with her mother, or the day a special family member died.

> Marilyn, a 25-year-old anorectic woman, wrote in her diary that every time she took the train back home during the weekends, she became very anxious. She did not understand at all why she felt so bad. By paying close attention, she discovered that her anxiety increased every time the train passed the psychiatric hospital she was admitted to

several years ago. When discussing this issue in therapy, Marilyn was able to identify the trigger: Because of repetitive self-mutilation acts, she had been locked in the seclusion room for several weeks, tied to her bed.

Certain Emotional States

When analyzing the diaries of eating-disordered patients, a therapist may find that the bulimic episodes are preceded by negative feelings, such as loneliness, sadness, fear, anger, emptiness, boredom, guilt, feelings of not being loved or understood, frustration, and so on. But, strange as it might seem, the confrontation with positive feelings also may elicit an urge to binge or harm. Some patients find it extremely difficult to deal with situations in which they receive positive comments or feel appreciated, loved, or cared for. Others may not accept feelings of pleasure or happiness; such feelings make them very uneasy because they don't know how to deal with them. They expect that these feelings will not last long, or they fear to be rejected or disappointed again if they believe in them or get attached to someone. All these stimuli may trigger a dissociative reaction that only reinforces the patient's already existing conviction of not being able to be in control over her own actions and feelings.

Certain Physiological States and Bodily Sensations

In some eating disorder patients, physical hyperactivity or restlessness can result in a state of hyperarousal or trancelike dissociative reaction. Some patients jog or dance till they reach exhaustion. The experience of being physically exhausted can induce a state of derealization. For some patients it means that they don't feel the inner pain anymore. Stories of other patients suggest that sexual arousal itself can provoke a state of dissociation and being out of control (this might be linked to hyperventilation while being aroused).

> Janet always used the same kind of ritual to initiate her bulimia. In the evenings, alone in her flat, she felt lonely and restless, and would go out to a disco. There, she started to drink alcohol and dance for hours. Being an attractive

woman, often dressed conspicuously, many men tried to make contact and invite her to go out with them. So it often happened that she woke up several hours later, finding herself in bed with a stranger without remembering what she had done. Afterwards, as soon as she was again alone in her apartment, she felt dirty and began to binge-eat. Next she vomited and took a shower to clean herself from "all the dirt inside and outside." The whole pattern became almost ritualized, with a "psychological purging" as the ultimate goal—getting rid of negative feelings and thoughts.

This ritual happened on average two to three times a week. Later on in the treatment, Janet disclosed that she had been sexually abused by her uncle and that in those days she became anorectic and very hyperactive. She would then go out riding the bicycle against wind and rain up to the point of feeling so much physical pain that she "forgot" the internal pain that was the result of the sexual abuse.

Some patients become extremely nervous, sad, or confused during their menses. It is often a critical period with a higher risk of binge-eating and other forms of impulse dyscontrol (self-mutilation, kleptomania, drinking). Many eating-disordered patients try to avoid menstruation by keeping their weight below a certain level. Although the fear of menses may have different meanings, in some patients it may be related to a traumatic experience, especially sexual abuse and abortion. We discovered that some patients were abused only when they were menstruating, so they could not become pregnant. For those patients menstruation became the most important trigger for bringing back traumatic memories and feelings.

Certain Foods

Eating disorder patients with histories of abuse may avoid specific foods for reasons unrelated to weight concerns. Certain foods may be closely associated with the original trauma situation. Some patients were given sweets and candies as a way to seduce or reinforce them during or after the sexual abuse. In other cases, the parents gave sweets, chips, and other foods to comfort their children when they were left alone at home. Hence, particular foods may elicit memories and feelings related to the childhood experiences of emotional neglect and/or abuse (Levin & Spauster, 1994). Other patients who have been victim of severe and long-lasting sexual abuse may develop an extreme distaste for meat and become "fanatical vegetarians." Other patients avoid all liquid or semiliquid food (milk, pudding) because they were associated with the memory being forced to perform oral sex and swallow sperma. Some patients develop an aversion for mealtimes or eating with others, because their parents often had terrible fights during meals at the family dinner table. In all these situations we assume that classical conditioning and stimulus generalization resulted in a phobic-like reaction towards certain foods or eating in general.

> Upon admission in our inpatient unit, Carol immediately said that she would refuse to eat any kind of meat. Later on in the treatment, her extreme dislike of meat became meaningful. Carol had been abused by her father, a butcher, on the chopping block where he used to hack his steaks. Even the smell of meat made her feel anxious and out of control.

Stopping the Anorectic/Bulimic Behavior

In patients with eating disorders and a history of abuse, dieting, bingeing and purging, and the desire to be slim may have special meanings. Although the anorectic or bulimic behavior usually can be understood as an anxiety-reducing strategy in response to fears of weight gain, for many abused patients the eating symptoms serve to help escape from sexual abuse and/or its consequences. For instance, anorectic patients with a history of sexual abuse might feel that becoming skinny might function as a way to make their bodies sexually unattractive. Losing weight might also have helped them to have no feelings anymore: The emaciation almost always induces a state of emotional anesthesia. Moreover, when anorectics lose weight their menses will stop and they can have the additional security of knowing that they cannot become pregnant.

Similar motives are found in bulimic patients who have a history of abuse. For many patients the bingeing and purging may have functioned as way to emotionally anesthesize themselves when confronted with fear-related stimuli. Special attention must be given to their purging behavior, which is often therapy-resistant. In patients with eating disorders and a history of abuse, bingeing may be not only a way to reduce weight, it may also represent a cleaning ritual connected to the feeling of being dirty after sexual abuse took place (Levin & Spauster, 1994). Many sexually abused subjects report nausea after sexual abuse, especially oral sex; they feel dirty and also may develop a disgust towards their own bodies. Here we assume that the vomiting may have functioned as a way to reduce the nausea and revulsion. When we ask these patients to stop dieting, bingeing, and purging, this could make them anxious and even trigger a dissociative reaction. Although it is a general rule in our treatments to stop vomiting and laxative abuse as soon as possible, patients with a history of abuse often will need more time and do it very gradually. Of course the triggering factor is often the increasing weight, with all its associated fears (becoming attractive, menstruating again).

Revictimization Experiences

One of the most striking characteristics in trauma patients is the fact that often they will engage in new situations and interactions where the original trauma situation or some parts of it will be repeated. It is as if some patients are trapped in a trauma-prone pattern. Revictimization experiences frequently occur in trauma victims. How can we understand this? One possible explanation might be that most patients did not learn to establish safe and appropriate boundaries in social interactions. Moreover, they perceive themselves as bad, and because of this negative self-image they think that they do not deserve positive things in their lifes.

Another factor that might help to better understand the great risk for revictimization in these patients, is their tendency to dissociate when faced with threat-related situations. When the dissociative reaction mechanism is activated, the patient's ability to escape from the situation or to install safe boundaries will be weakened if not totally inhibited. Thus, the patient will have great difficulty in protecting herself in intimate relationships.

> Laurette, a single woman of 23, was admitted to our eating disorders unit for anorexia nervosa with life-threatening vomiting. Having grown up in a family with an alcoholic father who frequently physically abused her, she became extremely anxious about her father and about all men who abuse alcohol. Nevertheless, during the inpatient treatment Laurette fell in love with a male patient who was hospitalized for alcohol abuse problems. In her psychotherapeutic sessions, we discussed with Laurette the risk that she was not yet ready to establish clear boundaries and enough protection in this relationship. After a few weeks she found out that her new friend had begun to drink again and had become verbally aggressive towards her. We tried to show her how she was getting caught in her old scenario and so in a reenactment of her trauma, but she engaged herself even more in the relationship, hoping to rescue her boyfriend. Only when he became physically aggressive did she realize that this situation was indeed a repetition of the traumatic history in her family of origin. Then the therapeutic team hoped that Laurette would stop the relationship, but she did not want to consider this possibility. The team was convinced that continuing her therapy was useless as long as Laurette maintained her relationship with her abusive friend, and so they decided to stop the treatment. When we confronted Laurette with this decision, she immediately complied with our condition. As a matter of fact, she even said that she was very relieved that we had made the decision for her.

This example demonstrates that in some cases the therapeutic team must set limits. A therapist who is consistent in securing the protective conditions of psychotherapy also conveys a clear message of real care. No one had ever protected Laurette, so for both her and the team the confrontation was a moment of truth, a test of the cornerstone of psychotherapy, mutual trust and commitment.

Patients are expected to keep a detailed diary of their difficult "triggering" moments. In order to facilitate and structure this task, a standard form has been designed (see Exhibit 5.1). In some cases patients are nervous about writing down their experiences (fear of using certain words, of revealing secrets, of betraying others, and so on); it may take time, but it is an important sign of commitment if patients try their best to write at least a few things and then gradually fill out the forms. A complete refusal should always be questioned within the context of the therapeutic working alliance.

EXHIBIT 5.1
Helen's Diary During Her Inpatient Treatment: November 6

TIME PLACE	CONTEXT (activities, feelings, thoughts)
7:00 AM Bathroom	While I was taking a shower and washing my body, I suddenly started to feel numbed in my head. I became anxious and I could not understand why. I felt a very strong urge to wash my hands, and I washed them until it became painful. Afterward I felt some relief.
10:30 AM Body therapy session	When Diana touched my body during a massage exercise, again I became very anxious. I felt totally frozen and I wanted to run away. After this therapy session I went to the cafeteria and I immediately bought some chocolate, and I ate it rapidly in secret.
4:30 PM Bedroom	I finally found the time to read a letter that my mother wrote to me. I am furious. She says that I have to develop more self-discipline and that this way I will solve my problems. I have the feeling that she does not understand me at all.

6:30 PM Bedroom	I feel rejected and misunderstood; a voice in my head orders me not to eat in the evening. I throw the food away. I realize I specially dislike pudding and bread. I already felt some nausea looking at the pudding. I don't understand this reaction at all.
8:00 PM Nurses' room	I went to see the nurse to have a talk. Since it became dark outside I feel totally restless. If I were at home, I probably would have gone outside to buy food and have a binge. Now I feel imprisoned and I don't know what to do.
10:00 PM TV room	When I was watching the movie *Body of Evidence* with Madonna, on the one hand I suddenly became emotionally numbed, and my feelings and behavior changed. On the other hand, I became very anxious when I realized the sudden change in my mind. I thought that I would become crazy. My first idea was to go out for a binge. But then I decided to call my husband, and for a while I had the feeling of returning to my own feelings. I was again able to think normally.

The excerpt from Helen's diary in Exhibit 5.1 shows that she risks the loss of control when:

- she is confronted with her body

- her body is touched

- she gets specific messages from her mother

- she has to eat specific food, such as bread and pudding

- it gets dark

- she watches erotic movies on television

If the patient keeps a detailed diary for several weeks, a list of triggers can be easily identified. Then, the patient is asked to make a hierarchy of these situations according to the degree of threat. On this basis further treatment can be planned as a successive approximation—a gradual exposure to less threatening situations while more difficult ones are temporarily avoided.

The following is Janet's rating of each situation according to the level of threat experienced (10 = maximum):

- I am naked in the bathroom = 8

- I have to undress (to be weighed) = 4

- I watch myself in the mirror = 3

- Other people talk about physical violence = 7

- I am exposed to meat, pudding, or sweets = 9

- I feel alone in the evening = 8

- I watch others drinking alcohol = 6

- I go out to a bar = 4

- Others give positive comments on my appearance = 5

- I am confronted with the topic of sexuality = 9

- My father kisses me during visits = 7

Constructing a New Behavioral Script

Once the patient has identified her most important triggers, alternative and more efficient coping behaviors must be tested and learned. For many patients this part of the treatment will be quite difficult. Because of their long-lasting experience of being out of control, patients find it hard to believe that they can learn to take better control over themselves. Generally speaking, triggers do not provoke immediately and suddenly uncontrollable changes in the patient's behavior, thoughts, and feelings. A trigger is not just an on/off switch, but a careful analysis often reveals a kind of "automatic" scenario. Bulimic episodes, for instance, rarely happen completely unexpectedly. First, the patient has to find food or go out shopping for food. Then she must find a place to be alone or take care that nobody can see her eating. Many patients will not binge if they do not think that they will be able to vomit afterwards. The example shows that if patients describe all the steps in detail it soon becomes clear that the so-called loss of control is a predictable chain of events in an important number of situations or conditions. Now the patient must take responsibility over her actions in these situations: she must ask herself where and how she can break the chain. A list of possible alternatives has to be made and practiced.

In our hospital we offer the patients a list of alternatives to be executed when they are at risk of losing control:

1. *Behavioral strategies*

- Go to the nurse and ask for a talk.

- Don't isolate yourself in your room, but stay in the living room with the other patients.

- Call your husband, brother, sister, friend.

- Go out for jogging with another member of your group (after permission from a nurse).

- Write down in your diary all your feelings and thoughts at this moment.

- Start painting, drawing, knitting, playing music, watching television, and so on.

2. *Emotional/cognitive strategies*

- Listen to your self-hypnosis audiotape.

- Distract your mind and relax by listening to your favorite music.

- Firmly touch an object that symbolizes your "safe place" and concentrate on the feeling.

- Concentrate on the rhythm of your breath.

- Hold ice cubes in your hands and focus on them.

- Write down all negative consequences that would follow if you were to lose self-control right now.

In the beginning of the treatment, we select different alternative strategies to help the patient to cope more effectively with emotional stimuli. The alternatives may be aimed at decreasing tension, distracting attention, or pushing away the threat-related material while not inducing a dissociative state (without losing contact with the here-and-now). The patient must list at least five alternative strategies. These new and realistic scenarios have to be written down on a small piece of paper that the patient always has to carry with her. We further suggest that she reads it over and over again, especially in confrontation with threat-related stimuli. Apart from the self-suggestive influence, it is aimed at reorienting the patient in the here-and-now and emphasizing her self-responsibility.

> Janet chose the following scenario: "When I am confronted with difficult situations and fear that I will lose control, I will immediately take my scenario and read it loudly to myself. I will not isolate myself in my room, but stay in the living room where I will try to read today's newspaper. In case I am still anxious, I will talk to the nurse or a group member. If no one is available I will take my walkman and listen to my favorite music."

As soon as the patient has described her new script, she will be invited to expose herself gradually to the threat-related situations and emotional stimuli, following her treatment plan. It is important to motivate the patient for this often very difficult phase in the treatment and to explain to her why gradual exposure according to the principles of systematic desensitization is necessary. The goal is to extinguish the traumatic reactions (negative feelings, emotions and sensations) through habituation to feared stimuli.

In general, we will start with exposure to the triggers related to the eating symptoms. If the patient reports some phobic-like reactions toward specific foods, she will be asked to make a hierarchical list of forbidden foods (see Vanderlinden, Norré, & Vandereycken, 1992). Next, she will be invited to expose herself gradually to the feared foods. It is important, of course, to make sure that it will not be followed by vomiting or laxative use (principle of "response prevention"). In difficult cases it can be practiced first using hypnosis: after relaxation induction to counter the anxiety response ("reciprocal inhibition"), the patient can be asked to imagine that she is exposed to the fear-related foods (seeing, smelling, and tasting them) and finally she will imagine that she is eating them. When this exposure in fantasy ("in vitro") has been done successfully, a similar procedure can be followed for the exposure in reality ("in vivo").

To discover hidden meanings and to further decrease her anxiety, the patient is asked to discuss her experiences with food and eating as much as possible, both directly (with friends, family members, therapist, and nurse) or indirectly by recording all her feelings and thoughts in her diary. In several cases it might be very helpful to encourage patients to express the emotional significance of food and eating in a painting, drawing, or collage. (In the hospital, we use thematic art therapy.)

Following the same basic procedure, all major triggering situations will be tackled in an hierarchical order. The patient should make the choice of each new step while the therapist must watch the feasibility of the exposure program. Usually the exacerbation of symptoms (or emergence of new maladaptive behaviors) is a warning signal that the patient cannot cope with the situation because it is too difficult or because of shortcomings in the new scenario.

> Alice, a 23-year-old nurse, asked for inpatient treatment because of her suffering from uncontrollable bulimia for several years. She ran away from home at the age of 16 after her parents found out that she was using soft drugs. Shortly afterwards she started to binge-eat and vomit. During all these years she has had almost no contact with

her family. But now that she was in the hospital, her parents insisted on a reconciliation. In the beginning Alice refused all contact, but her parents kept on calling her and writing letters.

Now Alice began to behave rather strangely and often seemed totally absent. Just by accident we found out that she was abusing drugs again and had burned herself with cigarettes. Meanwhile, her attitude toward the therapy program changed dramatically. Suddenly she wanted to leave the hospital against medical advice. When analyzing this situation with Alice, it became clear that she was not ready yet for a confrontation with her parents. We proposed to make special arrangements with the parents, together with a social worker who could act as a go-between in the negotiations. However, the parents refused this and insisted upon direct contact with their daughter without any outsider involved. Soon after this loyalty crisis—choosing between therapy or family—Alice left the hospital and returned to her parents' home. A few weeks later she was admitted to an emergency unit because of a serious suicide attempt. . . .

In patients with dissociative reactions, a basic element of their back-to-reality script is learning strategies to *reorient themselves in the here-and-now situation.* While they are in a dissociative state, patients find it difficult to realize where they are, what time it is, what they are actually doing, and so on. Moreover, they may be overwhelmed with all kinds of negative emotions and thoughts they cannot understand or explain. The ability to evaluate the actual situation realistically is often also decreased at moments of impulse dyscontrol, including binges. Recent research seems to support this assumption of cognitive inhibition in bulimics. Waller, Quinton, and Watson (1995) found that women with strong bulimic tendencies were slower in their response to threatening information than to neutral words, while there was not such an effect for women with less pronounced bulimic attitudes. A simple technique to help dissociative patients stay in touch with reality is to make an audiotape with a short self-description that the patient can listen to, for example using a walk-man, whenever it is appropriate (Van der Hart, 1991).

> My name is Judith Vanderbild. I am 32 years old and I am staying in the hospital at Kortenberg. I decided to take care for myself and to enroll myself in this therapeutic program. When I recorded this, it was the 16th of November, 1995. Listening to this tape, I realize that I want to take my life into my own hands. I am here to learn how I can protect myself against self-harm. As an adult woman of 32 years I want to take responsibility for what I do, feel, and think. Here, I can feel safe. People are here to protect me; no one is going to hurt me here. Whenever I feel in danger or fear that I will lose self-control, I will take the little paper out of my back pocket and read the alternative scenario I have proposed to myself. I will read it right now, to make sure. . . .

Many alternatives from the list of new strategies described above can be used to reorient patients in the here-and-now. It may be something very simple, like touching a familiar object or a symbol of safety. In one case the patient's own technique was discovered by accident.

> Janice was a middle-aged woman with a history of severe incestuous abuse. She had been in outpatient treatment for more than a year when it was discovered that after each session she went to the local bookshop. One day she said how distressed she had felt after last session, because the bookshop in the village had been closed that day. She explained that going to this bookshop and reading the date on the newspapers had helped her to become aware again of time and place. Only then was she able to drive home safely.

What should be done with severe or frequent dissociative reactions during therapy sessions or on the ward? Our general rule is that we don't allow patients to escape into dissociation. They have to be brought back to the reality of here and now as soon as possible. Otherwise, the therapist indirectly reinforces this dysfunctional reaction to emotional stimuli. When it happens the first time, the therapist immediately should try to reorient the patient with a clear and loud voice, and if necessary use such nonthreatening tactile stimuli as touching or even firmly shaking the patient's shoulder. Afterwards the therapist explains why he or she has done so. Now it will be up to the patient to make proposals on how to cope with these dissociative reactions in the future—to come up with a new scenario.

Cognitive Reprocessing

The theory of information processing (Resick & Snicke, 1992, 1993) forms the basis of a therapeutic approach recently introduced in our treatment package. This information is also presented to our patients. A mechanism of information processing has been proposed to explain the development and maintenance of posttraumatic reactions. Information processing theory describes the way in which information is encoded and recalled in memory (for a review of the literature see Resick & Snicke, 1992). Human beings process a considerable amount of information every day. One way of organizing and processing this information is through the development of cognitive schemata.

A *cognitive schema* is a stored body of knowledge that interacts with the incoming information and influences how that information is encoded, comprehended, and retrieved (Resick & Snicke, 1993). Especially when the subject is confronted with an unpredictable and uncontrollable situation, as is the case in a traumatic event, new information must be processed. When a child is abused, for instance, this experience may stand in great contrast with the generally accepted view that people, especially parents and other caretakers, are nice and kind. In the case of sexual abuse, the child is confronted with two different, opposite messages.

Resick and Snicke (1988) suggest that when an individual encounters new information that is inconsistent with pre-existing beliefs or schemata, two different things can happen: assimilation or accommodation. In the case of *assimilation*, the subject will alter or distort the new information to fit or assimilate into the existing schemata. In the process of *accommodation*, people who are subjected to traumatic situations—for instance, rape victims—will develop new cognitive schemata. They will replace or change the existing schemata to accept new, incompatible information. The goal in cognitive processing therapy is to assist the patient in refraining from assimilating (distorting the event to fit prior beliefs) but instead to help her to accommodate new cognitive schemata to explain the new information. To reach this goal, cognitive processing therapy consists of a specific treatment package that follows the basic principle of exposing patients to the traumatic memory, and at the same time training them to challenge their maladaptive beliefs. In the description of the phases of cognitive processing therapy as applied in our treatment program we will focus only on misconceptions related to a history of traumatization.

Step 1

As outlined earlier, the patient is asked to write her most important and significant feelings, thoughts, and activities of the day in her diary. This way she can start to identify and trace irrational conceptions and ideas, not only those related to the eating disorder, but especially those misconceptions related to the traumatic situation. The patient will be instructed to identify conflicting or strong negative beliefs that create unpleasant emotions and dysfunctional or unhealthy behaviors. We further explain how certain irrational beliefs or misconceptions can make therapeutic progress very difficult, if not impossible, if they keep on existing in the patient's mind. For instance, misconceptions and irrational beliefs may be related to food, body image, perfectionism, and responsibility.

Some common misbeliefs:

- You cannot trust men.

- Men always want sex.

- I was abused because I was a bad person.

- I am guilty of being abused.

- Things only happen when you want them to happen.

- I cannot keep myself under control.

- My childhood was a mess, and so will my whole life.

- I have a disgusting body.

Step 2

Once the most important misconceptions are identified, the patient will be asked to analyze these beliefs with the well-known A-B-C procedure used in rational emotive therapy: (A) the situation (what happened?), (B) the beliefs (what were you thinking?), and (C) the consequences (what did you feel or do afterwards?).

An example of rape:

A (situation): My boyfriend used physical force to make me have sex with him.

B (interprctation): I scduccd him and it was his right to havc sex with me because I lived with him and he truly loved me.

C (consequences): I felt very frightened at first, later I became totally frozen; I felt guilty that I didn't comply from the beginning. I secretly had a binge and vomited afterwards.

Step 3

The patient is asked to write about the traumatic event several times in as much detail as possible, and to write down everything she remembers. She should not only note the facts, but also the feelings, sensory details, and thoughts she had during the incident. Next, she will be instructed to read the account again and again. Patients will find it very difficult to do so and will try to avoid it at all costs. Many keep on idealizing the abuser. Writing and reading the story repeatedly exposes the patient to all cognitive, emotional and sensory elements of the traumatic event. It can be a first step to extinct these negative experiences and to re-interpret the event.

Step 4

Once the traumatic event has been described in detail and discussed in the therapy sessions, the patient will be asked to go over it again and to start to formulate some thoughts that challenge the original beliefs. A sheet with challenging questions will be offered to the patient (Resick & Snicke, 1993). For example:

- What is the evidence for and against this belief?

- Are you confusing a habit with a fact?

- Are you thinking in all-or-nothing terms?

- Are you taking selected examples out of context?

- Are your judgments based on feelings or on facts?

Meanwhile, the therapist can try to identify faulty thinking patterns in the patient's story (Resick & Snicke, 1993). The patient may, for instance:

- draw definitive conclusions when evidence is lacking;

- practice mind-reading, assuming that people think negative about her although there is no reasonable argument for it;

- exaggerate or minimize the meaning of an event or of certain aspects of the traumatic situation;

- disregard important aspects of the situation;

- oversimplify things by thinking in all-or-nothing terms;

- base conclusions on feelings rather than on facts (use emotional reasoning).

Using this method, exposure techniques and principles of cognitive restructuring are combined throughout the therapy sessions.

Special attention must be given to beliefs regarding responsibility for the traumatic situation. Many patients are convinced that they are responsible for the abuse. Or even worse, they often feel guilty for the abuse, as if it were their fault that it happened. A necessary step toward therapeutic progress is that the patient no longer takes responsibility for the abuse. This is very difficult when the patient still has contact with the abuser (for example, the abuser may be a family member).

> Kate, a 23-year-old anorectic, developed her eating problems soon after she decided to live with her boyfriend. It soon became clear that bingeing and vomiting often happened after sexual intercourse. Further on in therapy Kate confessed that the sexual contacts were happening against her will. She explained that her boyfriend often "convinced" her to have sex with him and that she allowed him to do with her whatever he wanted. "Out of love" Kate had been both sexually and physically abused by her boyfriend. He often had tied her up in bed and abused her; he also forced her to have sex with other men. Though she started to disclose her abuse history, Kate was still convinced that she was responsible for what happened. The following misbeliefs were identified: he is my friend, therefore he has the right to have sex with me; being nice means agreeing to have sex; I was 20 years old, so I could have reacted and left him, and so my decision to stay with him means that I must have wanted it.
>
> Especially highly confusing to Kate was the sexual arousal she sometimes experienced during the rape. Therefore, she developed the strong belief that "she must have wanted it, otherwise it would have been impossible to have positive sexual feelings." We explained to her that the body can be sexually aroused, even if you don't want it, when specific parts are stimulated.
>
> Kate agreed to write down her story of the events: "I don't know where I have to begin. . . . One evening he was sitting in the bathroom and shouting at me that I had to come. I knew what was going to happen. I was scared, but

felt forced to go. He undressed me quickly and he immediately put his penis between my legs. I asked him not to
proceed too quickly, since I was feeling an enormous pain.
The more I reacted, the more he became sexually
aroused. So I had no choice but to let him do it. I always
thought that it was his right to have sex with me. After a
while, I was able to switch off all my feelings."

Writing down the story of the abuse and discussing it in
the therapy sessions was the first step in developing a new
cognitive schema for Kate: The former belief: "I must have
wanted it, I am responsible for what happened" was re-
placed with the new cognitive schema: "I have not wanted
this, my friend abused me and he didn't have the right to
do so. I am not a bad person." When Kate started to look
at the traumatic events in this new way, she burst out in
tears, and for the first time she expressed all the pain inside her. She decided to write her boyfriend a letter to tell
him how much he had abused her love and how much suffering he had caused her.

The question of whether a therapist would go along with the patient's taking action against the abuser (as in the last example)
should always be evaluated against the background of the treatment
goals. Especially in cases of intrafamilial abuse this might be a very
delicate issue, as discussed in Chapter 7.

6

Using Hypnotherapeutic Techniques

The findings of our research on hypnotizability in anorectic and bulimic patients (see Vanderlinden, 1993; Vanderlinden, Spinhoven, Van Dyck, & Vandereycken, 1995) have confirmed what we already knew from clinical experience: Many eating disorder patients can benefit from the use of hypnosis. Binge-eating patients in particular have good to excellent hypnotic capacities. Only the very emaciated anorexia nervosa patients with serious concentration problems and physical restlessness find it very difficult to relax and/or respond to a classical hypnosis induction.

The rationale for using hypnosis is to provide an alternative coping behavior for the eating symptoms, especially in those situations that might trigger bulimic behavior. Hypnosis can also be used to alter the negative images, messages, and suggestions commonly present in patients with a history of childhood trauma. We often remark that these patients seem to be stuck in a state of self-hypnosis, focusing on negative thoughts and feelings. As soon as the patient has regained some self-control over her eating behavior and other impulse-like reactions, hypnosis can be employed to explore the underlying dynamics of the bulimic symptoms. Here, we want to stress that hypno-explorative techniques should be used only after careful evaluation of the pitfalls of trauma exploration as described in Chapters 4 and 8.

In this chapter an overview of the different hypnotherapeutic techniques will be given, and each will be illustrated with a case example. Although the therapeutic process has to be shaped according to each individual's personal needs, treatment usually passes through different phases or stages, each with more or less specific strategies and interventions (see Chapter 5). First we will describe the various hypnotherapeutic techniques that can be integrated in the beginning phase of the treatment, where self-control issues are the main therapeutic goal. Next, a description of how hypnosis can be used to explore and manage the presence of traumatic experiences and/or dissociative phenomena is given.

SELF-CONTROL

Hypnosis as a Relaxation Technique

The regaining of self-control over the eating behavior and other impulse-like behaviors deserves absolute priority in the treatment. Self-hypnosis is taught to the patient to allow her to relax and experience some safety and self-control in her life. In the first session obvious misconceptions and prejudices concerning hypnosis should be corrected. Because there still are many myths and fantasies about this technique, nowadays we rarely call our method hypnosis. Instead we ask the patients if they are interested in learning a relaxation and/or concentration exercise that might help them to feel comfortable and calm in future moments of crisis. To further motivate the patients, we explain to them that the technique we use can easily be learned by anyone with or without an eating disorder (except for severely emaciated anorectics).

For patients with a traumatic history the physical setting for hypnotic induction needs special attention. For many patients, lying down on a couch might trigger traumatic memories. We therefore ask patients to sit in a comfortable chair, keeping both legs on the ground. This way patients will experience more self-control and safety.

When we started to work with *classical hypnosis* in the mid-eighties, we generally offered the patient a formal hypnosis induction, for which we used the following four steps:

1. *Induction* with eye fixation technique (choosing a focus). The patient is asked to choose a spot upon which to focus. Meanwhile, suggestions are given that her eyelids will become heavier as her eyes focus on that spot, and after a while in many cases her eyes then will close automatically.

> Make yourself as comfortable as you can in your chair. And when you have the feeling of sitting comfortably in your chair, I would like to ask you to choose an object and to stare at it. You can continue to focus all your attention to it . . . You may notice that your eyelids will become heavier . . . and heavier. Your eyelids will become so heavy that they will want to close by themselves . . . that they will close automatically . . . while you keep on focusing on the object of your choice . . . And when your eyelids become heavier and heavier, they can become so heavy, so tired, that they start to flutter all by themselves . . . The eyelids can close just by themselves when they are ready to close . . . The idea that your eyelids will close very soon may help you right now to become more and more relaxed . . .

2. Next a *deepening* technique is offered. Speaking to bulimia patients, we may suggest descending a staircase, or concentrating on the rhythm of their breath; in the case of anorexia nervosa, we suggest going up a staircase, counting from one to ten, meanwhile suggesting feelings of lightness. In general, eating disorder patients do not like to become heavy or to experience heavy-like sensations. Hence we prefer to give the suggestion that they will become lighter and fly through the air.

> And now that your eyelids are closed, I just want to ask you to focus your attention on the rhythm of your breath . . . And when you are breathing out, you may have the feeling of becoming lighter and lighter, you may have the feeling that your body is becoming so light that it can fly

through the air . . . Perhaps you can imagine that you are at the bottom of a staircase, a solid staircase covered with a beautiful carpet . . . you may notice right now the color of the woolen carpet on the staircase, you might feel yourself standing on the carpet, and soon, as I count from 1 to 10, you can imagine yourself going up the staircase . . . and on top of the staircase you will find yourself in a unique, safe place for yourself, a place where you can hide yourself, where you can be yourself, and feel safe . . . and with every step you take, you might feel more and more relaxed. As you go up the staircase you will be able to relax . . . deeper and deeper . . . I will start to count from 1 to 10, perhaps you can count with me: *1* while you hold your hand to the bannister, you become more and more relaxed, *2* feel lighter and lighter, *3* your body can become even more lighter, while you are going up the staircase, *4* further and further up, *5* you may feel more and more comfortable, *6* and more and more relaxed, *7* as you are going up the staircase, *8* following your own rhythm, you will perhaps feel more and more concentrated on this stair, on the carpet, on its colors . . . and now that you are almost at the top, you may already observe this particular space for you, where you will feel relaxed and at ease, *9* feeling ever more lighter and lighter, *10* going up to this wonderful state of deep relaxation, feeling calm and at ease . . .

3. When the patient is able to experience some feelings of relaxation and calmness, the therapist will suggest that she imagine that she finds herself in a safe place and/or environment (*guided imagery*). Especially in patients with a history of trauma, the therapist must carefully discuss this place and/or scene in detail and make sure the patient will feel safe when she imagines being in this particular situation. Therefore, before the hypnosis induction the therapist should ask about a situation in which the patient might feel comfortable and relaxed right now. In our experience, many eating disorder patients, especially when they have been traumatized, have no idea at all of such a safe place and are not able to imagine such a situation.

The therapist can therefore suggest some situations, such as lying and walking on a lovely beach, resting in a familiar room where nobody can enter, and so on.

> You can already observe this safe spot in your house, your sleeping room, a private space of your own . . . I wonder if you can see it already now, maybe some sounds might remind you how good it is to be there . . . And while you enter this unique private space, you feel its calmness, your body may feel lighter and lighter, a wonderful experience, becoming more and more relaxed . . . There you can sit in a comfortable chair, or do whatever you like to do right now . . . listening to your favorite music . . . and feeling deeply relaxed and comfortable . . .

4. Finally, here is the *awakening* phase. To terminate the exercise, the therapist suggests that the patient herself can decide whenever she wants to end the exercise by silently counting slowly backwards from three to one. Most patients will awaken without any difficulty. We routinely add to the wording that the patient will bring back with herself from the hypnosis exercise only those memories, feelings, and thoughts that she can face in the waking state.

> . . . and when you are ready for it, you may decide to end this exercise and count back from 3 to 1. And you will bring back with you only those experiences, feelings, thoughts, and images you are able to face once you are again in the waking state. And while you count back from 3 to 1 you will be fully awake, back in the here and now . . .

When confronted with increasing numbers of complex ("multi-impulsive") or traumatized eating disorder patients, we were more and more inclined to use *indirect hypnotic techniques* (so-called "Ericksonian" approach). An interesting new technique is that of "active alert hypnosis" developed by Banyai and colleagues at the University of Budapest (Banyai, Zseni, & Tury, 1993). In this form of hypnosis induction the patient rides a bicycle ergometer (also called a home-trainer) and keeps her eyes open throughout the entire hypnotic session. While bicyling, the patient is asked to concentrate on the automatic pedalling of her legs, and next suggestions are given to enhance her alertness and attentiveness, and to give her a feeling of freshness. This technique has inspired us to experiment with a kind of active hypnotic procedure: Instead of actively pedalling on the home-trainer, the patient is asked to imagine that she is doing her favorite physical activity. The fact that many eating disorder patients are strongly preoccupied with physical activity and training is now uscd as an casily acccptcd cntrancc to thc patient's experiential world, and from there we induce a hypnotic state.

First the patient is asked to write a story about her favorite activity, something she would like to do or perform right now. She can choose whatever she likes, but it is important that the preferred activity can help her to feel good, safe, and calm. This way, the therapist gets the necessary information to introduce a state of relaxation. During the exercise the patient will be asked to imagine herself performing the kind of activity she likes most. The patient can imagine, for instance, that she is jogging, and slowly her body will become more and more relaxed, tired, and in need of some rest. Now she can be invited to take this rest in a safe place, for instance on a lovely beach.

To start or introduce this hypnotic exercise we now generally use a standard procedure. We ask the patient if she is able to open her eyes when she inhales and close them when exhaling. Most patients have no problem doing this. Repeatedly opening and closing the eyes, in coordination with the rhythm of breathing, is at the same time an induction and a deepening technique. It is suggested to the patient that each time she opens and closes her eyes she will feel more and more relaxed. After this brief starting technique, the patient is invited to imagine her favorite activity as explained above. To end the exercise the same procedure is employed as it is in classical hypnosis.

> Stella, a 26-year-old, extremely emaciated patient, became
> very tense when we used a classical induction technique.
> Because of her bad physical condition, she was not able to
> concentrate on a spot and just became more anxious and

irritated. We therefore asked her what kind of activity could help her to feel a bit more relaxed. She said that the only activity she liked was jogging, particularily when it's rainy and windy. Hence we invited her to write down how jogging could help her to feel better and more relaxed.

"And now that you are sitting in this comfortable chair, I would like to ask you to open your eyes when you breath in, and next while breating out, just to close your eyes again. Perhaps you will notice, while you repeat this exercise, that your eyelids will become more and more tired every time you breathe out . . . opening your eyes will become more and more difficult, your eyelids may become heavier and heavier, and you may start to feel more and more at ease, comfortable, and calm, maybe your eyes will just remain closed, while they are getting more and more tired, you will become more and more interested in when your eyelids will close, and you discover how you can become more and more relaxed as your eyelids close . . . and now your eyelids are closed . . .

(*guided imagery*) . . . you can imagine that you are preparing yourself for jogging. Maybe you can see now what clothes you are wearing . . . or you can concentrate on the weather, maybe it is a lovely, sunny day . . . When you feel ready to start jogging, when everything is done that needs to be done, you can start right away . . . Please try to find a stable rhythm, not too fast, not too slow, your body can tell you what is good for you . . . Very soon you might become interested in your surroundings, you may start to enjoy the neighborhood and the beauty of the surroundings . . . You may feel yourself becoming more and more relaxed, while jogging you can free yourself from tensions in your body, tensions perhaps you are not aware of . . . I wonder what you can see now, and which experiences can help you to become more and more relaxed . . . With every step you take . . . *1* you become more and more relaxed, *2* and perhaps you will enter that warm, glowing state, that is so typical of jogging, *3* all your muscles are moving, and while you are breathing in and out,

4 your blood brings new energy and power to help you to go on with this relaxing activity, *5* becoming more and more relaxed, *6* you may notice how your body starts to sweat, *7* freeing yourself this way of tensions . . . *8* your muscles becoming more and more relaxed, *9* with very step you take, *10* deeper and deeper relaxed . . . Now every body has its own language, and so has yours. Every body needs to rest after a while, I wonder how your body can signal or communicate to you at this particular moment that it needs some rest, maybe your heart is beating very fast, or you're sweating very much. You may feel that you have less energy and strength to go on . . . I wonder how your body can tell you to have some rest now, and to enjoy even more the experience of jogging when you will be resting, relaxing in this particular place . . ."

Gradually, Stella told us that she felt her heart beating and that she was feeling weak, and next she decided to start walking instead of jogging. In the beginning, it was impossible for her to imagine a place for relaxing and resting. After a few weeks, she was able to imagine that after jogging she could have a deep rest while lying on the beach and enjoying a sunset.

This basic exercise is always recorded on an audiocassette, and patients are asked to practice with it at home every day (preferably at fixed times and places). In this way patients are trained in self-hypnosis as a relaxation exercise. After completing the exercise each time, the patient is asked to judge the depth of her relaxation on a 10-point scale (0=absence of relaxation, 10=deepest relaxation) and to write this in the diary. This way the therapist can get a clear overview of the progress the patient is making.

Hypnosis for Self-Control over the Eating Behavior

The first and most important step in the beginning phase is always the gradual regaining of self-control over the eating behavior, weight, and other disturbing behaviors. The basic therapeutic principles and guidelines are explained in Chapter 5. It is a general rule in our treatment plan to give all responsibility concerning food, eating behavior, and weight to the patient herself. For this purpose techniques from behavior and cognitive therapy can easily be combined with a hypnotherapeutic approach.

In case of anorexia nervosa, direct suggestions of reexperiencing appetite and hunger and starting to eat again are not recommended at all. This direct approach has the risk of making the fear of changing and gaining weight even stronger. Instead we recommend an indirect approach, where the eating behavior is anchored or connected with a favorite activity. During the hypnotic trance the patient is told that eating might help her to perform better in her favorite activity—ballet dancing, studying, sports, and so on.

> When therapy began, Dora, a 20-year-old ballerina with severe anorexia nervosa, was no longer able to perform or dance, which made her feel very depressed. Although physically exhausted, she was extremely anxious about eating and had eaten almost nothing at all for some weeks. Dora was asked to imagine that she was sitting at a table and starting to eat her favorite dish, because this was the only way she could regain the physical strength and force that she needed so badly for dancing. Here the eating was connected with an activity that the patient liked very much.

Another way to deal with the fear of putting on weight is by asking the patient to imagine, during an hypnosis exercise, making a short trip into the future (guided imagery) and trying to observe her body in detail, now that she gained a little weight. We can also invite the patient to rediscover the smell and taste of food, again detouring attention from the eating itself and focusing on all kind of physical sensations.

We have described how anorectic patients can learn to relax by imagining that they are engaged in a pleasurable activity such as jogging. This exercise also can be useful in gradually reducing a patient's hyperactivity, as the therapist can suggest that after jogging the body can become tired and will need some rest. Of course these exercises will not be sufficient to promote weight gain in anorexia nervosa patients, but they may help the patient to comply with the treatment contract concerning her eating behavior and weight (see Chapter 5).

A patient with bulimia nervosa is asked to write in her diary daily about the circumstances in which the bingeing and purging take place, together with accompanying feelings, thoughts and images. Now, during the basic hypnosis exercise, the therapist may suggest that the patient will choose a moment each day to write in her diary and that this will bring her comfort and release. Hypnosis can also be used to teach patients to resume a regular and normal eating pattern (to stop the bingeing–purging cycle) and to become more conscious of feelings of hunger and satiety. Hypnosis can be introduced: (a) to concentrate on hunger and satiety cues; (b) to eat slowly and concentrate on tasting and smelling the food; (c) to learn to relax after the meal by reading an exciting book, watching a movie, or having a pleasant daydream.

> Imagine yourself waking up in the morning. You might still be a little bit sleepy. At this time, most people take a shower. I wonder if you will do so? Taking a shower might help you to wake up and to relax . . . This way, indeed, many people become very relaxed, and start to realize that they are hungry. I don't know if this is also your experience, if you are becoming relaxed or just starting to realize that you are hungry, and that a breakfast will give you new energy, necessary to do the things that are important right now in your life . . . Imagine now that you are already sitting at the breakfast table. I don't know if you are listening to some of your favorite music. I am wondering if you are already becoming aware of the nice smell of the fresh bread and the coffee, or are you drinking tea? Do you like fresh orange juice? I don't know what you are actually eating and tasting and it really doesn't matter at all that I don't know it . . . all that matters is that you enjoy rediscovering how it feels to smell and taste again . . . And after a while, I wonder what kind of body signals or physical sensations you will feel, in your stomach for example,

to tell you that you have eaten enough. Will you feel that your stomach is full? Or do you just have the feeling of being satisfied and relaxed? You might well want to relax now, by reading a favorite book or just calling your friend to tell him that you had a nice breakfast.

Most bulimic patients begin therapy with one goal: Finding a magic means to stop bingeing for the rest of their lives. Stopping the bulimic episodes and vomiting suddenly is often not a realistic goal (see Chapter 5). Only gradually stopping the bingeing-vomiting cycle is recommended. Meanwhile, alternative behaviors to cope with the situations that trigger the eating symptoms must be learned. The patient may be asked to plan one or more binges a week at a fixed time, and with a specific kind of food (if possible not a favorite food). This procedure may help the patient to reexperience for the first time in quite a while some control over her bingeing. She now still binges, but not "suddenly" at unexpected moments: now she decides when to binge and on what kind of food. Patients may be surprised to learn about this procedure, which urges them to plan their binges and to stop vomiting, first with the help of hypnosis. Although some patients refuse to do so, most patients comply with this proposal.

The patient is asked to remember the last time she binged, and to describe it in her diary. Next, after hypnosis induction, the patient is asked to imagine that she is having a binge, but that afterwards she has to refrain from vomiting. In behavior therapy terms, this procedure is called *exposure with response prevention*. The patient must elicit a bulimic urge to eat a certain amount of binge food, but she is not allowed to vomit afterwards. Although quite threatening to the patient, it might help her to discover about crucial influences in the bingeing-vomiting cycle.

> After hypnosis induction, Laura, a 25-year-old bulimic, imagines that she is at home, resting on her bed. She feels very calm and almost has the feeling of falling asleep. Next, the therapist asks her to switch on the television screen in her room and to watch the videorecording of her last binge (she was too much afraid to experience it

directly). She is told that she can stop this videotape whenever she wants to, or go fastforward in case she prefers to
avoid certain parts. With a finger signal, she indicates that
the videotape is running, and very soon she becomes
tense. The therapist gives the suggestion that she can talk
to him about what is happening at that moment, and
Laura tells she now realizes—while carefully watching her
behavior—the state of agitation and despair she always
feels before she starts to binge. She decides to fastforward
the videotape and stop when the binge is finished. Now
she observes that the tension disappeared—this way she
discovers how bingeing helped her to get rid of her negative feelings, but now she becomes afraid of putting on
weight and wants to vomit.

Here the therapist asks Laura to stop the videotape for
a while and discusses with her the possibility of an alternative activity that is incompatible with vomiting—perhaps reading a book, going outside for a walk, or phoning
a friend. Laura prefers to walk. She continues watching
her videotape and then she ends the session with a walk
outside as she gradually calms down. At the end of the session the therapist proposes that she try out this alternative
each time she has the urge to vomit.

Enhancing Motivation for Change

Besides self-monitoring (diary) and self-control techniques (pre-
scribed bingeing with nonfavorite food at fixed times and places),
we often introduce another strategy to enhance motivation for
change, the strategy of positive and negative consequences (Wright
& Wright, 1987). Patients are asked to imagine a future without an
eating disorder and to list all positive changes that may happen in
their bulimia- or anorexia-free lives. Next, they are asked to specify
all negative consequences if they continue to binge, purge, and/or
fast. This information can be used in a hypnosis exercise. When we
started we regularly used the negative consequences. But since we
realized that in many patients the eating disorder might be a way of

punishing themselves or of dealing with feelings of guilt associated with a history of trauma, we prefer to work with the positive consequences and even overaccentuate them during the hypnosis exercise. Often, patients might find it very difficult to imagine a future without bulimia or anorexia, and in these cases we try to work on a more methaphorical level.

> Seventeen-year-old Sylvia had already started to fast by the time she was 14. At that time there were many problems in her family; frequent fights between her alcoholic father and her mother, who was quite depressed, had forced Sylvia to take over the daily care of her younger brother and sister. When we ask her if she could imagine an anorexia-free life, she became tense and said that it would be impossible for her to do so. Next, we introduced hypnosis and asked her to make an imaginary trip into the future toward a life without anorexia. Suddenly, Sylvia explained that she found herself in front of a high mountain but she was afraid to climb it. Nonetheless she felt somehow familiar with this strange situation. We used this image: "At this particular moment you are physically too weak to climb this mountain. You will need more strength and energy. Gaining some weight will probably help you."

Correcting Irrational Conceptions

Eating disorder patients continually put negative labels on themselves: I am weak, inferior, ugly, stupid, ridiculous, childish, immature, dependent, and so on. In addition, patients with a trauma history are often convinced they are bad, worthless, or dirty, and usually believe that they deserve punishment for having been abused. In many cases these negative labels have been put on the patients, directly or indirectly, by other family members. Therefore, we have the impression that most trauma patients are stuck in a state of negative self-hypnosis, continuously repeating all kind of negative suggestions and messages to themselves. Through this process of "monoideistic fixation" (Kaffman, 1981, 1991; Kaffman & Sadeh,

1989) the negative self-image and the interrelated eating disorder symptoms (as well as other disturbed behaviors) are maintained as a kind of negative self-fulfilling prophecy. When such negativism becomes part of the anorectic or bulimic identity, it may impede therapy, with the patient believing "I don't deserve treatment" or "It won't work with me."

In the patient's diary, the therapist can detect these irrational and therapy-inhibiting self-perceptions, thoughts, images, and suggestions. The most rigid conceptions often deal with negative feelings and thoughts about their own bodies, and when there has been abuse with feelings of guilt for what happened in the past. Hypnosis can then be combined with cognitive restructuring techniques in order to question and change these thoughts. We often start to challenge the negative self-perceptions that are related to the eating disorder; later on trauma-related misconceptions can be dealt with (see cognitive reprocessing in Chapter 5). Here, we recommend the use of guided-imagery exercises—patients will be invited to make an imaginary trip into the future while trying to concentrate on positive images, thoughts, feelings, and experiences in their lives.

> Although extremely emaciated, 27-year-old Peggy hates her body: "It's so fat and ugly, especially my thighs and belly." She avoids looking in mirrors and continuously repeats to herself how disgusting her body is. Daily she does specific gymnastic exercises compulsively to bring her body into the ideal shape. She also perceives herself as weak, childish, and inferior. In order to positively change her body experience, the therapists suggest to Peggy that she watch herself in a mirror while she is in a hypnotic trance. Peggy is asked to observe her body in detail and to express her feelings and thoughts.
>
> In the beginning, Peggy is afraid to look in the mirror, and only after a while can she look at the parts of her body with which she is pleased—for instance, her eyes and ears. After an interruption we ask her to make a short trip into

the future and to imagine that she has put on four pounds. Now she discovers that this weight increase does not provoke the disaster she was fearing. She even realizes that she can wear some new clothes she likes very much and that she might gain more energy and strength.

Several patients may become anxious or even confused when the therapist starts to challenge their negative self-beliefs. In these cases the origin of the rigidly defended convictions needs to be explored first. Often their roots can be found in a history of sexual or physical abuse.

DEALING WITH TRAUMATIC AND DISSOCIATIVE EXPERIENCES

As explained in Chapter 1, both traumatic and dissociative experiences may be linked to more severe problems with binge-eating and purging. We assume that the eating pathology may function in the subgroup of patients who have suffered such abuse as a survival mechanism to escape from the emotional damage of overwhelming trauma. Bulimic behaviors may block awareness or even induce a kind of freezing state that allows patients to avoid memories and feelings related to the trauma experience. The bingeing-purging ritual thus becomes part of a dissociative state, and both the ritual and the state are maladaptive ways of coping with the emotional aftermaths of sexual/physical abuse or other traumatic experiences. In this subgroup of eating disorder patients (especially those with bulimia nervosa of the purging type and anorexia nervosa of the bingeing/purging type), hypnotherapeutic techniques can be employed to deal with the trauma experience, from exploration to integration in the patient's life (Vanderlinden & Vandereycken, 1988, 1990). Before we describe different therapeutic techniques, we first want to pay tribute to the pioneering work done about a century ago by the French physician and psychologist Pierre Janet.

The Pioneering Work of Pierre Janet

The idea that dissociated traumatic memories may lie at the roots of such eating disorders as anorexia and bulimia nervosa, and that these memories therefore should be involved in the treatment of these disorders, was introduced and defended by Pierre Janet at the end of the 19th century (see Pope, Hudson, & Mialet, 1985). According to Janet, dissociation implies the escape of a particular fixed idea (*idée fixe*)—or even a complex whole of conceptions with accompanying feelings—from the control and sometimes even the knowledge of the personal conscious mind. The escaped or dissociated idea begins to lead an independent existence on a subconscious level. This causes the anorectic patient, for instance, to refuse voluntarily and obstinately all food during the day, but makes her be overwhelmed by the urge to binge and vomit at night. The underlying conception manifested by the refusal of food and the bingeing-vomiting in many cases can be seen as a secondary idée fixe, but on further consideration it appears to be related to a dissociated traumatic recollection, a primary idée fixe. Janet has repeatedly emphasized that in order for the complaints associated with the secondary idée fixe to disappear, the primary one must be resolved as well. In other words, the traumatic experiences underlying the complaints should be dealt with and integrated. A clear illustration of this approach is shown by Janet's patient Isabella (Janet, 1901, 1911).

> Isabella arrived in Salpêtrière Hospital in Paris in deplorable physical condition, having refused all food for the past six weeks. Food introduced through a nasal tube was never thrown up but instead was perfectly digested. Hence, it seemed obvious to the physicians to make the diagnosis of purely mental anorexia. However, exhortations, pleas, and threats all proved unsuccesful in making the patient eat: Isabella did try, but at the very first bite she spit the food out and rejected all the rest of it with aversion. According to Janet, an idée fixe was involved, but it seemed impossible to discover its origin. Indeed, Isabella had been questioned by many people in various ways; she did not seem to dissimulate and under pressure she con-

fessed to much more serious things that she had kept secret for various reasons.

"I can assure you," she said, "I am not all obsessed by the idea of not eating; I even have the impression that I should like to. But whenever I start eating I feel myself grow anxious, I loathe it and I can't. Why? I do not know. In any case I can assure you that I do not wish to die. I even become afraid of the idea. But in spite of all my attempts to force myself to eat, something inside prevents me from doing so."

"If we leave it at that," Janet continues, "we cannot understand the patient at all and we risk letting her die of starvation. On the other hand, if we examine her during all of her subconscious states (during sleep, in somnambulant states, with automatic writings, and so on), we always hear the same story. Her deceased mother appears to her, accusing and condemning her for an error Isabella had once committed. Her mother also tells her that Isabella is unworthy of life, that she is to join her in heaven and for that reason commands her not to eat."

Isabella has frequent "fits" of this kind, with vivid images of her mother. These hallucinations (as Janet calls them) are connected with a whole series of preceding events, making it clear to Janet that this idea alone does not cause the disorder. However, the hallucination does determine the anorectic symptoms, because altering the hallucination is enough to make the anorexia disappear. Once she is back in the state of wakefulness, Isabella is amazed that she is able to eat without knowing what had prevented her from doing so. "It is true, of course," Janet concludes, "that the anorexia reappears after the following fit, because the hallucination turns up again and has subsisted as a subconscious suggestion. The patient needs treatment for this subconscious delirium" (Janet, 1911, p. 248).

Here Janet identified an extended secondary idée fixe in the form of a dissociated ego-state, an introject of Isabella's mother, who accused her and tried to drive her to suicide by starvation. Janet realized that this ego-state was hidden by a primary idée fixe, which had to be identified and treated. Isabella herself sometimes gave indications of this fixed idea, but she was only conscious of the emotional component and not of the whole complex. In other words, it concerned a partial dissociation.

"For about a week she is dejected and sad, she hides and refuses to speak to anyone. It takes great effort to make her utter a few words that she pronounces very softly, with downcast eyes. 'I am not worthy of talking to other people . . . I am so deeply ashamed, I suffocate under a heavy burden, a horrible remorse that is gnawing at me . . .' 'Remorse about what?' 'Ah! I have been trying to find out day and night. Whatever have I done wrong in the past weeks? Tell me frankly, did I do something wicked last week? Before I did not feel like I do now.' " As one can see, there is no concrete action involved, but a feeling, an overall emotional state that Isabella interprets as remorse. However, she is unable to understand or phrase the idée fixe that underlines this feeling. Through automatic writing, hypnotic exploration, and observing Isabella during her fits, Janet was able to chart a "very complicated dream" in which Isabella believed that she murdered her sister, who actually died some time ago (Janet, 1911, p. 249–250).

Only when the patient has gained sufficient control over her eating pattern and when a favorable development is noticeable with regard to the other symptoms (see Chapter 5) may the therapist begin to explore the traumatic memories and experiences, and then only if there are no clear contraindications (see Chapter 8) and if the basic rules for trauma exploration are met (see Chapter 4). Once again we want to stress that we do not believe in catharsis—the emotional purging of the traumatic experience—as the alpha and omega of therapy. Against the background of these principles, different hypnotherapeutic techniques will be described and illustrated with case examples. For more technical information we recommend *Hypnotherapy and Hypnoanalysis* by Brown and Fromm (1986) and *Trauma, Trance, and Transformation* by Edelstein (1982).

Direct Age Regression

Using this hypnotic technique, the therapist can, for instance, count backwards from 20 to 1 while suggesting that the patient become younger and younger. Usually it is suggested that the patient go back in time to a specific moment or situation that could have special significance.

> Dominique, a 23-year-old bulimic patient, asked for therapeutic help to stop her daily binges. For a year she lived with a man whom she really loved. But soon after she moved in with him, her bulimia started. After about five months of outpatient treatment, the binge frequency was strongly reduced: Dominique now had only two bingeing episodes at a fixed time and place every week. However, she was not able stop the bulimia completely. Moreover, she still felt very insecure and inferior, and consequently lived very much isolated socially. She kept on saying that she was not enjoying her life and that "something inside herself" was sabotaging the therapeutic progress. A direct cognitive attempt to change her negative beliefs remained unsuccessful. Therefore, we proposed hypnosis.
>
> After hypnosis induction, Dominique was asked to imagine herself in a place where she felt safe. Only when she was able to imagine this situation and experience safety did we ask her to travel back in time, more specifically toward the situation where her negative ideas originated. The therapist suggested that Dominique imagine that she was becoming younger and younger and counted from 20 to 1, suggesting to Dominique that she might find herself suddenly in a specific place or situation that could give her more insight into the origins of her block in therapy.
>
> After a while, Dominique began to tremble. We asked her what was happening and she whispered in French: "Maman, ma mort" [Mother, my death]. We asked her where and with whom she was. Dominique saw herself sitting at the table with her mother. She said she was about

six or seven years old now. She was very frightened, because her mother was very angry and was shouting at her. A further exploration revealed that the following messages were often given to Dominique by her mother: "You are a bad girl"; "Since you were born, I have never been happy"; "I don't love you, I don't want you"; "You don't have the right to exist"; "You will never be happy." As a result, Domininique felt deeply inferior, convinced that she was unwanted and deserved not to be loved. She had no right to be happy!

After this age-regression exercise Dominique realized why a part of her was still sabotaging the therapeutic attempts to change her negative self-perceptions. In order to tackle these unrealistic ideas, we changed the old scenario and invited Dominique, who was then 23 years old, to explain to her mother (while still in trance) that she had her own life now, and she had the right and the power to be happy.

Indirect Age Regression

The previous technique, bringing the patient directly back to the past, might be too confrontational and, therefore, too threatening for some patients. In recent years, more often we make use of the video technique as an indirect age-regression method. It is at the same time very simple and offers the patient a maximum of safety. Once the patient, during hypnosis, feels that she is in a safe place, she has to imagine that she is watching a videotape on which all the important events in her life have been recorded. She can hold the remote control in her hands and decide when to start, and—even more important—when to stop at the moments when she is confronted with images that are too painful to watch then. In this technique, the patient is not asked to regress in age. Instead, she remains in the here-and-now as she watches pictures from her past.

Two years ago Rosita, who was 35 years old, was treated for long-lasting anorexia nervosa at our inpatient unit. She first showed clear improvements in her eating disorder but gradually marital tensions surfaced, especially because she no longer wanted to have sex with her husband. He became very angry and even mentioned the possibility of divorce, if the sexual relationship did not improve. Rosita herself could not understand why she was now refusing sexual contact with her husband: "Something in myself prevents me from giving and receiving sexual pleasure . . . I don't understand why and perhaps with some hypnosis I can gain more insight in this problem." She believed that something must have happened in her life, during her childhood or adolescence, that was likely to have provoked these antisexual feelings. After careful evaluation of all contraindications of trauma exploration (explained in Chapters 4 and 8), the video-technique was proposed to Rosita.

After hypnosis induction, Rosita imagined that she was lying on top of a hollow in the dunes. Here she could feel very safe; she had a fantastic view of the landscape and she could hide herself whenever necessary. We then addressed ourselves to Rosita's inner world as if it concerned another person: "Did something happen in Rosita's life, something she is not aware of, something that might help her to better understand her sexual problems? Has Rosita enough inner strength to deal with these memories? Will Rosita's problems get better when she gains more insight in the origins of her problems?" All these questions were answered positively by means of finger-signaling, as described in the next section. Then we asked Rosita to start the videotape and wind it backwards, and suggested that the videotape would stop automatically when something important was shown. Whenever she wanted to stop the videotape, she could decide to do so for any reason. The tape stopped when Rosita was about three years old. She saw herself sitting in the corner of her bedroom, alone and sad, while her mother was playing with the other children. Rosita then spontaneously wound the tape forward and described different situations where the same experience was repeated. Two traumatic situations that occurred when she was 10 and 12 were shown on the videotape. First, Rosita began to weep very loudly and next she described how her mother was also crying in her little brother's bedroom; her brother was dead on his bed. Rosita then said, "I was so angry at my mother that again she was giving all her attention to my deceased brother . . . I wanted to say to her: 'But, you can still take me in your arms, I am still alive and also need your attention.' "

After this situation, the videotape stopped again when another brother died, this time in a car accident. Rosita was about 12 years old, and she described how she had to take care of the other children while her parents were in the hospital (her brother was in coma for several weeks before he died). Again she felt very lonely but at the same time something inside said that it was not fair that she had to substitute for her parents. When she described this situation she suddenly had the feeling that something hard inside her was starting to grow—a hard feeling that could help her to distance herself from others and make her less vulnerable to emotional pain. "I believe that I must have decided there already never to give to others what I had not received myself." Through this exercise Rosita became more aware of the neglect she had experienced in her family of origin and, later, the unfulfilled needs in her marriage. For a long time these feelings had been hidden by the anorexia; after therapy she could not avoid them any longer.

Le Cron's Seven Questions

Another way of indirect exploration is the ideomotor questioning technique with finger signaling developed by Le Cron (Cheeck & Le Cron, 1968; Wright & Wright, 1987). In this technique, patients are told that their inner world (their unconscious or subconscious mind) will reveal information about their problems that had been unaccessible before. The inner world can then answer questions by spontaneous finger responses indicating "yes," "no," or "stop"—this is finger signaling. Especially for trauma patients, defining a clear stop signal is extremely important. In this way the therapist creates a safe milieu for exploration; the patient is assured that no event, memory, or feeling will come to the surface if she is not ready to deal with at that point in the therapy. After having defined finger signals, the patients have to signal when there is something in their inner world that blocks them. A further analysis makes use of Le Cron's seven questions:

1. Does the problem serve a purpose; is something pleasant achieved or something annoying avoided by it?

2. Is it the result of an inner conflict, of something you would like but cannot or may not do?

3. Is the problem caused by a trauma, a nasty event from the past?

4. Is the problem caused by a feeling of guilt and the need to be punished for it?

5. Is it a result of identification with someone else?

6. Is it a result of your imagination or of a remark made about you while you were in a responsive emotional state?

7. Is the problem a result of body language, as if you wanted to express something psychological on a physical level, such as headache when somebody is "bugging you" or vomiting because something is "lying heavy on your stomach"?

Once she has regained some control over her bulimia, 27-year-old Veronica became depressed and had frequent flashbacks to traumatic situations. When she was 15 years old she was raped by a friend, and from that moment on she started to behave as "a whore," she said. Because we assumed a relationship between the bulimia and these traumatic memories, we invited her to explore the meanings of her eating disorder through Le Cron's seven questions. Unexpectedly, she answered only one question positively: "Is the problem caused by a remark made about you while you were in a responsive emotional state?" Further exploration revealed that when she was 15, Veronica felt that she was in love for the first time, very much against her mother's wishes. One evening, while Veronica was almost asleep, her mother came to her bed and shouted that she was a whore. Later on, Veronica's mother repeated this sentence several times. Apparently the bulimic behavior helped Veronica to forget all the bad feelings that were connected to this past.

Ego State

As was indicated in Janet's description of Isabella's case, some anorexia nervosa patients state that an inner voice commands them to refuse all food. On the other hand, many bulimics state that during bingeing they have the feeling that they are undergoing a change of personality: "It is as if someone else was bingeing; Some strange power forced me to binge; I am continually engaged in a fight against myself; I don't remember the binge and only after vomiting do I get the feeling that I should wake up again." In other words, the patients describe their bulimic episodes as if some part or so-called "ego state" took control over their behavior. According to Watkins and Watkins (1982), an ego state is an organized complex of behaviors, thoughts, feelings, and experiences, whose elements are bound together by some common principle but separated from another ego state by boundaries that are more or less permeable. Each ego state constitutes a kind of "subself" with more or less individual autonomy in relation to other states and to the entire personality. Ego states may be created and split off from the conscious mind when the patient is confronted by a traumatic experience. Hence the ego state may even escape control from the conscious mind. When such an ego state is split off or dissociated from the conscious mind, the boundaries between the different ego states are no longer permeable—they become rigid. Hypnosis can be used to explore and activate these ego states. Such an *ego state therapy* runs in different phases:

1. When the therapist presumes—for instance on the basis of the description of the bingeing or fasting by the patient— that a dissociated ego state is present, he or she first will ask the permission of the patient's inner world or subconscious mind to explore the hidden ego state that provokes the bingeing or fasting.

2. Next the patient is asked to imagine having a binge and to concentrate on the bulimic or anorectic part inside. It is explained that this might help the patient to come in touch with that unknown part. The therapist then asks the bulimic or anorectic part to make itself known.

3. As soon as that part has made itself known, the therapist thanks it for its appearance and asks: "What is your name?" or "Who are you?" [We no longer proceed this way but rather suggest that "some feeling" can show up]. In many cases a feeling will then come to the surface, for instance sadness or anger.

4. Now the therapist will try to find out how old the patient was when that part or feeling first manifested itself and what its intention was. We often observe that the bulimic or anorectic part pursued a specific goal, such as protection, comfort, or punishment.

5. At this stage, the therapist positively reformulates the purpose of the bulimic/anorectic part and asks if it wants to collaborate to find new, more effective ways to achieve similar goals. This leads to a negotiation process about a different and constructive approach.

6. Finally, the bulimic/anorectic part is asked to try out this new approach during the following week and it is thanked for its cooperation.

It is often discovered that a dissociated ego state essentially exercises a favorable, protective function for the patient. In case of bingeing, purging, or fasting, one or more of the following functions may be detected (Root & Fallon, 1989):

1. It is a way to anesthesize such intense negative feelings (perhaps associated with a trauma) as anger, pain, anxiety, and powerlessness.

2. It is a means for a patient to cleanse herself in a symbolic manner of negative sexual experiences.

3. It is the patient's expression of her anger and feelings of hatred.

4. It is a way to air the feelings of inferiority or guilt that frequently occur in traumatized patients (see Janet's example of Isabella).

5. It is the patient's attempt, in a very concrete manner, to render her body unattractive (sexually less vulnerable) so as to construct a psychological and physical barrier or to protect her intimacy against intruders.

6. It is a way to relax and calm down when particular traumatic events with accompanying feelings are relived.

By the time we proposed to Laura that we explore the underlying dynamics of her bingeing, we had already been working for three months to achieve some self-control over the bulimic episodes. At the beginning of the therapy, Laura was bingeing three to five times a day and followed it with self-induced vomiting. She gradually reduced the frequency to three episodes a week. More and more she became convinced that her bulimia had special meaning. After hypnosis induction (and having arranged the finger signaling), the following interaction took place:

[Therapist] "And while you are enjoying your trance state, you can come in touch with that part or feeling inside you that forces you to binge and to vomit. And that feeling can present itself and make itself known to us and communicate with us through Laura's voice."

For the first minutes nothing happened, but after a while Laura's index finger ("yes") moved up and down

[Therapist] "Is that part willing to communicate through Laura's voice?"

Laura's "no" finger moved and she started to weep a little bit.

[Therapist] "I notice some tears in your eyes. I therefore wonder if this feeling or perhaps also some other feelings can come to the surface?"

Laura's "yes" finger responded.

[Therapist] "Are there several feelings involved?"

Again reaction from the "yes" finger.

Next the therapist asked what kind of feelings were involved, and they came to the surface—shame, anger, despair, sadness, and later on anger. Further exploration revealed that these feelings started to exist when Laura was seven (when it is likely that Laura had been sexually abused by her father).

Dorina came into therapy because she was overweight, caused by daily binge eating. Self-control techniques did not help to limit the number of binges. "Every time I try to change my eating pattern, it is as if a strong irresistible force is sabotaging me and forces me to binge even more than ever before." Then we applied hypnosis and began the following exploration:

[Therapist] "Does Dorina's inner world want to collaborate in exploring Dorina's bingeing?"

Dorina's "yes" finger moved.

[Therapist] "Is there a part in Dorina that is afraid of losing weight?"

Again a "yes" signal.

[Therapist] "Does this part force Dorina to eat and even overeat from time to time?"

A "yes" response.

[Therapist] "Does this part, that is afraid of losing weight, want to communicate with us today by means of Dorina's voice?"

Dorina's "no" finger reacts.

[Therapist] "Is this part willing to communicate with finger signaling?"

Now the "yes" finger is clearly going up and down.

[Therapist] "Is Dorina strong enough to deal with the information that will be revealed?"

Again a "yes" answer.

[Therapist] "Will Dorina be better off if she gets in contact with that part of her that forces her to binge?"

The "yes" finger was moving.

Affect Bridge

Watkins' (1971) affect bridge technique is one of the best ways to produce age regression and uncover memories and fantasies associated with a particular affect. In this procedure, a specific emotion (such as anxiety, agitation, or depression) preceding the problematic behavior (for example, binge eating or vomiting) is used as a bridge to the past, to one or more situations where that feeling was comprehensible and explicable. The affect bridge will be effective only when the intensity of the emotion is strong enough. Therefore, during the exercise suggestions to amplify the feeling can be given. But when the intensity of the feeling becomes too strong, the therapist must stop the exercise and calm down the patient.

> Suzy was admitted to our specialized unit for severe bulimia nervosa, with daily binges, vomiting, and laxative abuse. Except for her work, she lived a very isolated life. Once in her appartment in the evening, she commonly became scared and felt unsafe, even to a state of panic. Then a bulimic episode would follow during which she had the feeling that she no longer existed, as if her mind were totally paralyzed. Next she would go to the bathroom and painfully force herself to vomit. In a state of exhaustion she would go to sleep . . . Although in the treatment Suzy learned to regain control over her eating behavior, the anxiety episodes did not cease. After having learned self-hypnosis for the purpose of relaxation, Suzy herself asked for more in-depth hypnotherapeutic work, so we decided to explore these negative feelings using the affect bridge technique.
>
> Suzy had to concentrate on her anxiety and amplify it so that it could function as a bridge toward the past. She became very tense, her arms and hands trembled, and she said that she wanted to run away. Because we feared that the emotions were becoming too intense, we suggested to her that she was no longer in that situation but that she could watch what happened on a video screen. Suzy described the following situation: She saw herself as a girl of 11, visiting her handicapped uncle. She was alone with him when he suddenly opened his trousers. She ran away to the balcony, locked herself outside, and felt that she could not move anymore. Posthypnotic suggestions are given that no material that she could not deal with at that time in the therapy would be remembered after the end of the hypnosis exercise.

Implosive Desensitization

This hypnotic technique, described by Edelstein (1982), can be used to decrease the intense feelings that are associated with a traumatic event. This way the trauma experience can be better integrated in the patient's personal history. Implosive desensitization is a mild flooding technique in which the patient, while in a trance, is gradually exposed to the original trauma situation. Time and again, the patient has to relive the feelings associated with the traumatic experience, each time including a short pause to rest. After every exposure exercise, the patient can be asked to rate the degree of anxiety experienced during the procedure. The therapist can go on with the exposure until the feelings of anxiety have decreased sufficiently. The therapist will extend the duration of the imagination exercise for as long as the patient can tolerate it. We recommend this technique only when no complex trauma histories are present—for example, when it concerns one specific event, such as rape.

> At the age of 16 Sophie (a 19-year-old bulimic) was raped by a man. In therapy she could describe the event in detail without any emotional reaction. It was because she employed partial dissociation: she had a vivid descriptive memory of the event while the associated feelings seemed to be dissociated. However, at night she often woke up with terrible nightmares. In recent years she became extremely avoidant toward men and developed a severe bulimia nervosa.
>
> After she had been carefully evaluated, Sophie was invited to relive the situation again under hypnosis. First, we asked her to describe all the details of the rape. Next, she was exposed again to every detail, now described by the therapist. Then, gradually, she began to experience again feelings of anger, anxiety, powerlesness, and especially guilt. During a one-and-a-half hour session, Sophie was exposed to the rape situation eight times, and after every exposure she was guided back to a state of deep relaxation. The anxiety scores decreased from 8 (very high) to 2 (very low).

After this session Sophie slept much better, and the next week she asked to go back again to the rape situation under hypnosis. She wanted "to do more" with it. In the two following sessions, she totally changed the rape scenario: She imagined that she could defend herself against the abuser and that she finaly could escape. Shortly afterwards she disclosed the rape to a good friend and was very pleased that she had had the courage to do so.

CONCLUSION

If carefully chosen and adequately applied, hypnotic techniques can be very useful tools in treatment. Although controlled research is still scarce, recent data point to the efficacy of a hypnobehavioral approach in eating disorders (Griffiths, 1995; Griffiths, Hadzi-Pavlovic, & Channon-Little, 1994, 1996). The incorporation of hypnotherapeutic techniques into the treatment of these patients may have some important advantages with respect to dissociative experiences and trauma histories:

- Hypnosis may help the patient to find the necessary mental strength and emotional safety necessary to deal with a traumatic past.

- Hypnotic techniques facilitate the exploration and assimilation as well as the integration of dissociative and traumatic experiences.

- Hypnosis can induce or enhance the process of developing a more positive self-image and a balanced appraisal of daily life situations.

- In addition, using hypnotic techniques patients may get in touch with parts of their psychological life that have been dissociated in a maladaptive way.

But the cost–benefit balance of hypnosis also should take into account the possibly negative side effects in these patients, especially
with regard to the therapeutic relationship, the problem of
(over)suggestibility, and the dangers of trauma exploration (see
Chapter 8). Hypnotherapeutic techniques are not magic tricks, but
only creative instruments in a multidimensional treatment (Vanderlinden & Vandereycken, 1990). The following more extensive case
example will illustrate this, with special emphasis on therapeutic
flexibility within an evolving treatment process.

> Rosalinde, a 28-year-old single woman, had a history of
> anorexia nervosa since she was 14, but up to a year before
> she had refused any professional help. For the last 10
> years her weight had not been conspicuously low because
> of regular bulimic episodes, so she had managed to con-
> ceal her problems from the outside world (including her
> family of origin). Rosalinde had a very low self-esteem,
> lived completely on her own, and was afraid to become at-
> tached to anyone. Sexuality was nonexistent for her. Her
> relationship with her parents was quite ambivalent. She
> had frequent contact with them and felt too dependent
> on them, but at other times she was very angry at them
> without knowing why.
>   Her reason for asking help had nothing to do with the
> eating disorder, but with "strange experiences" that were
> more and more troubling to her at her secretarial job. In
> the office she regularly had "blackouts"; at noon she
> sometimes could not remember what she did in the morn-
> ing. A few times she suddenly found herself somewhere
> (in a restaurant, for instance) without remembering how
> she got there. These experiences frightened her greatly.
> Sometimes she even thought that she was going com-
> pletely crazy. Here, we will summarize her treatment
> (which took two years, a total of 45 sessions) with special
> attention to the use of hypnotherapeutic techniques.
>   In the first phase of the treatment, we attempted to
> teach Rosalinde better control over her eating pattern.
> She noted in her diary that "one side" was willing to do so,

while "another side" seemed to sabotage it. Either an irresistible power drove her to binge and vomit, or she felt forced to fast for several days. Although she showed great mood fluctuations, the recurrent feeling underneath was emptiness. She agreed to examine this feeling more closely under hypnosis. Via the ego state technique she told, in a childish voice, that she was scared and furious. It is this part inside—anxiety and anger—that makes Rosalinde binge or fast. She calls it fury, and says that it began when she was around six or seven years old. During this first hypno-exploration, Rosalinde trembled all over her body, cold shivers ran up and down, and at moments her arms and legs felt like they were paralyzed.

The next hypnotic sessions revealed a history of sexual abuse by an uncle and, later on, by a neighbor. These men seduced her mostly with candies and sweets; these "goodies" apparently induced a sort of anesthesia during the abuse. Rosalinde could not believe that she had forgotten those experiences; the only vivid memory she had of her young childhood was about the candies she got from her uncle and the man next door. Talking about the sexual abuse, she recalled her first sexual contact of her own free will, when she was 15, with a boy with whom she was in love. During intercourse she became very anxious and was suddenly overwhelmed by a strong urge for sweets.

Six months before this event she had started a strict diet because she felt "too fat" to be attractive to boys. In fact, it was the beginning of an anorectic lifestyle that after one year was complicated increasingly by bingeing. Thinking back, she realized that in the following years the attempts to diet were a way to render her body sexually unattractive, and that through bingeing and vomiting, she got rid of a deep-rooted anger and fury that were caused by the sexual abuse.

During the hypnotic exercises Rosalinde expressed mainly feelings of guilt about what happened; she dared not to criticize her uncle and neighbor. When we proposed that she expose herself through hypnosis to the abuse experiences, she refused to do so. The next week she cut her arms (something she had never done before). We viewed this as a warning signal; we had probably gone too fast or proceeded in too confrontational a way. We therefore chose to focus the next hypnotic sessions on ego-strengthening suggestions. We tried a new confrontation after a few weeks, using the indirect videotape technique. Rosalinde was told that she could look at a screen to see how she expressed her anger directly toward her uncle and her neighbor, without having to feel guilty about it. The exercise was repeated several times, until she indicated that her fury had sufficiently decreased in intensity.

Further therapeutic progress began to move very quickly. Rosalinde refrained completely from fasting, and her binges diminished in frequency. In the meantime she started a relationship with an older man, to whom she revealed her whole story. She felt very safe with him, and after half a year, at her initiative, they had sexual intercourse. Afterwards she felt "like a real woman again." We planned a few follow-up sessions, and despite some short episodes of sadness, she appeared to do so well that we were able to stop our treatment.

7

The Place of the Family

In Chapter 2 we discussed the link between physical and/or sexual abuse in childhood and dissociative phenomena. Therefore it is logical to expect that theoretical and therapeutic models for dissociative disorders would take into account at least the family context in which the patient has been raised. But the literature shows a striking neglect of this area, except from a few articles (e.g., Benjamin & Benjamin, 1992; Porter, Kelly, & Grama, 1993; Sachs, Frischolz, & Wood, 1988; Williams, 1991) and the studies we have mentioned in Chapter 2. This is remarkable in view of the fact that a family approach may have great preventive significance with regard to possibly transgenerational influences (Oliver, 1993).

In cases of dissociative disorders, the involvement of the family in treatment might be indicated for at least two reasons: (1) it is plausible that family tensions lead to an increase of the disorder, and (2) family members are faced with unpredictable consequences of the patient's symptoms, which they do not understand (De Wachter & Lange, 1996). In this chapter we will discuss some special family issues—our family approach to eating disorders in general has been described in detail elsewhere (Vandereycken, Kog, & Vanderlinden, 1989).

A CONSTRUCTIVE FAMILY APPROACH

Dealing with the family does not automatically mean applying family therapy. Moreover, the following *contraindications* for conjoint family therapy must be taken in consideration (Vandereycken, 1995):

- When the parents are divorced or separated. Family therapy might reinforce the idea that the family could be reunited, a fantasy or wish of many anorectics.

- When a parent displays severe psychopathology (for example manic depressive psychosis). In that case, the parent's individual vulnerability needs some protection.

- When a parent has physically and/or sexually abused the partner or a child. In that situation, the victim must be protected and kept from confronting dilemmas of loyalty.

- When family interactions are highly negative or destructive. This increases the risk that direct confrontations in the presence of an "important other" (the therapist) might lead to more disruption.

Of course, these situations do not exclude the use of family therapy if it is conducted by experienced therapists and/or counterbalanced by other therapeutic measures. In fact, in most specialized centers for the treatment of eating disorders, family therapy is seen as just one component in a multidimensional approach. Therefore, the issue of family therapy probably is much more a question of therapeutic attitude than of therapeutic technique. We plead for a *constructive and flexible family approach* to eating disorders. Its concrete form may range from parent counseling groups to classical family therapy, from some informal meetings to marital therapy for the parents, depending on the functional analysis of the eating disorder within the family context and the willingness of family members to engage in therapy.

More important than the therapeutic methods are the following principles or guidelines for a family-oriented approach (Vandereycken, 1995):

- A family *crisis* does not mean family pathology. Start with the assumption that the parents did their best, but were lacking essential problem-solving capacities.

- All kinds of family problems or disturbed interactions can be both *cause and consequence* of the eating disorder. Hence, consider the patient to be at the same time victim and architect of the situation.

- Do not consider parents to be guilty but rather *co-responsible* for the development of the eating disorder. This implies that their cooperation is quite valuable in the treatment.

- Involve brothers and sisters in the treatment, not just because they may be neglected co-patients but also because *siblings* can act as reliable consultants and excellent cotherapists (Vandereycken & Van Vreckem, 1992).

In adolescent anorectics or bulimics, the most difficult, if not critical, point in the course of the treatment arises when the therapist attempts to deal with the separation-individuation issue, which practically always lies at the heart of the eating disorder. In a sense, the therapist may look at anorexia or bulimia nervosa as a maladaptive reaction to a critical phase in the evolving family life cycle, or as an escape from it. The fact that the eating disorder itself can be the stagnating factor in the developmental process of the adolescent implies indirectly that it hampers healthy evolution in the family life cycle. Hence, the treatment of an anorectic or bulimic adolescent cannot but affect the family in one sense or another. Often the parents fear the loss of their child, while overlooking that they already have lost contact due to the disorder. The inevitable crisis during therapy will be overcome when everyone realizes that at the end of treatment all parties involved will have gained from it (Vandereycken, 1995).

THE PATIENT'S FAMILY DIAGNOSIS

Usually a family diagnosis is made by clinicians or therapists from their outsider's viewpoint. Although it is quite valuable from a research perspective, we think that it should be complemented by the insider's viewpoint of the patient. Especially when traumatic events (are presumed to) have occurred in the family, we prefer to start by looking through the patient's eyes at her family.

First, to gain more insight in the patient's *actual relationships* she has to explore her present-day interactions with parents, family members, spouse or boyfriend, and other meaningful others. In many cases a more authentic family picture will be revealed if the patient uses nonverbal expression. Patients are invited to make a family portrait in a drawing, painting, or collage. If an idealization of the family or a minimization of conflicts can be expected (as is the case for many anorectics), the nonverbal expression can be indirect: the family members should be portrayed, for example, in the form of different animals or trees. Another way is to ask patients to make two family portraits, one showing how they actually experience their family life, and another expressing their ideal family. Once they are finished, the portraits are discussed either in individual or in group psychotherapy, and the following questions are discussed:

- What differences do you observe between the two family portraits?

- Which things would you like to see changed in your family?

- Which family member stands closest to you?

- If there is a problem in the family, who cares first?

- What are the happiest and saddest moments in the family?

It is important to note which figures from the larger family system (such as grandparents) are included or excluded. The next task can be to situate the family portrait in a broader social network: The patient has to indicate for each family member one important person who does not live in the same house.

Of course, group therapy has many advantages here. Each family portrait may mirror aspects of other patients' families. To better feel and understand the position of the patient in her family, it might be helpful to have the group enact the family portrait. This exercise may range from a "family sculpture" to a role-played family scene. The patient will be encouraged to express her ideas and feelings towards family members in the safe and supportive environment of the group. The techniques of family portrait, family sculpting, and role play can also be seen as a way to bring to the surface both positive and negative family myths (cf. cognitive reprocessing in Chapter 5). Finally, traumatic experiences within the family may be revealed in the group. But they should not be dug out too soon; patients may feel trapped by the group (or by the therapist) in betraying or accusing their families. Once the family portrait is finished (eventually corrected after discussion), it may be presented by the patient in a family session.

To help the patient make a family diagnosis with emphasis on abusive experiences we also use a form of bibliotherapy. Patients are asked to read the book *Toxic Parents* by Susan Forward and Craig Buck (1989). (Fortunately, the Dutch translation has a more constructive title: *Finally, I Have My Own Life.*) This book describes all kinds of ways in which parents make serious mistakes in the education of their children. Special attention is paid to addicted parents and different forms of abuse (psychological, verbal, physical, and sexual). It then discusses means of coping with a negative past and starting a new life. Patients are asked to read the whole book, chapter after chapter, and to make notes about the things they recognize. These notes are discussed with the therapist and other group members.

After a period of resistance ("Nothing is wrong in my family") and guilty feelings ("I don't want to accuse my parents"), this task can become so confrontational that a period of reduced contact with the family must be instituted. Sometimes, even complete separation from the family is necessary. This is usually the case with very intrusive or overcontrolling parents and/or very vulnerable, weak and unassertive patients. If the patient is convinced of the importance of distance, she writes a short letter to her parents explaining that she needs some time without direct contact with them. During this period parents may contact another therapist or a clinician who works closely with the principal therapist (during inpatient treatment this will be a team member). Parents are also invited to join the parent counseling group that meets every two weeks.

A gradual confrontation with negative family experiences through bibliotherapy and discussion in group therapy usually takes the following steps:

- *Denial.* "This book is not for me." The theme of loyality is an important one at this stage. We emphasize that we are not putting parents on trial as if we were judges; it should be stressed that most probably the parents' intentions were good but nevertheless they may have made mistakes or caused pain.

- *Self-criticism.* "It was all my fault." At this point it can be helpful for a patient to make contact with their inner hidden child. She is asked to bring pictures of herself as a young child. Neutral questions (what she liked to do at this age, whom she liked to be with, what she preferred to do at school . . .) bring her back into the experiential world of the little child. Additional cognitive restructuring can be done by circular questioning: "Do you know a little child of six years old? Imagine that she comes to you, starts crying, and tells you about a problem with her parents. Would you blame her for doing so?"

- *Shame.* Some patients may have difficulties in revealing serious events in a direct way. They are invited to write it in a secret diary or express it in some art form. They can do this in private and show it to the therapist when they feel ready to do so. In group therapy we never force patients to reveal things, but we reinforce everyone who has the courage to do so (modelling).

- *Anger.* When they start realizing what happened to them, patients often feel angry. They are encouraged to bring this out instead of repressing, denying, or acting it out against others or themselves. They will be invited to learn how to express and get rid of aggressive feelings in a healthy way (preferably by means of physical exercises: see management of self-injury in Chapter 5).

- *Grief.* Patients now realize what they have missed, how different life could have been if harmful things hadn't happened to them. Now, self-soothing techniques are encouraged, such as the image of the inner child who, when hurt, may cry and ask to be soothed.

- *Preparing for the future.* As they read, patients write down their feelings in their diaries. When they have finished reading the book they should come to some conclusion. At this stage they are asked to prepare a letter to their parents or to the significant people with whom they have had negative experiences. Here patients formulate the pain of the past (traumatic experiences are no longer concealed but described in clear terms). At the same time, realistic plans for the future are formulated. The patient explicitly states what she expects from the other people to improve relationships or even to make further contact possible. This letter eventually will be used in the family confrontation session.

Claire developed bulimia shortly after she ran away from home at the age of 18. For several years, her parents didn't know where she was. One day she showed up again, but her parents refused any further contact. Several attempts to meet her parents resulted only in a firm rejection—they acted as if she were no longer their daughter. In therapy Claire told about the severe physical abuse she experienced as a child from her alcoholic father and about the lack of support from her depressed mother. At the beginning of her therapy Claire felt greatly ashamed and she apologized for the way her parents had behaved, blaming it on the poverty in which her family lived becuse her father was often unemployed. Gradually Claire began to express anger, despair, and especially feelings of grief for the things she had missed as a child. Finally she decided to write a letter to her parents, with whom she had had no contact for more than ten years.

Mom and Dad,
Here's a letter from Claire. I find it difficult to begin. Anyway, writing this letter is a part of the therapy I have been in for several months now. I was admitted to a hospital for the treatment of severe bulimia (bingeing and vomiting). These eating problems have existed for many years. It started when I was 15 years old. Nobody has ever known this. Everything happened in secret. Everyone told me that I was ugly, and fat, a complete failure; so I tried to comfort myself with sweets and cookies that I secretly bought. Then the vomiting began, but nevertheless I did put on weight all the time.

Later, other problems surfaced. I felt stupid and worthless. I thought I was a bad child: father beat me so often without any clear reason and mother never intervened or comforted me afterwards. I never saw that you loved me, that you were proud of me. None of the things I did was good. I felt a lot of sorrow and pain. You have never made time for me, you were always busy with other things. When we were sitting at the table, we were not allowed to talk. I felt like a robot. And when I got pregnant at 17 you have forced me to have an abortion. I was guilty and this was my punishment. From the moment I ran away, I felt free. Free as a bird but still with a lot of pain inside. I couldn't trust people anymore. I felt ugly and lonely. More and more I had sexual relationships with different men; they seemed to give me the affection and love I never received from you. After a while I became a drug addict; it eased the pain inside.

Luckily someone convinced me to change my life and go into therapy. Here I have learned to express my feelings, to get a more positive view of myself. Part of the therapy is this letter; it is a relief from all the emotions I have bottled up for so many years. And it will be the start of a new life. My own life, even without parents!

FAMILY CONFRONTATION

Once the family portrait or the letter is ready, a meeting between the patient and her parents can be arranged. This can happen only when there are no contraindications (as mentioned above), when the session has been carefully prepared and announced to the parents (or the other people involved), and when the parents are willing to collaborate in a constructive way. The session is led by a neutral therapist who is not directly involved in the patient's therapy; the patient may be accompanied by her principal therapist.

The patient explains the portrait or reads the letter in front of the parents, who are asked not to interrupt her but to react afterwards. Often it is a dramatic session for all parties involved. If the parents do not try to defend themselves but are willing to listen and understand their daughter's feelings, it may be the turning point toward a new style of communication and a more constructive relationship. In other cases, however, parents appear to be deaf to the message and are only concerned about their own feelings of being wrongly accused, and then they often induce feelings of guilt in their "ungrateful" daughter. Sometimes parents even counterattack. If the patient is not well prepared for this, or if she is not strongly supported afterwards, the old vicious circle of negative interactions will continue.

Confrontation sessions should be avoided (or at least postponed) in the following situations:

- The patient is psychologically too vulnerable (for example, she has insufficient self-control over self-damaging behavior);

- The parents are not ready to accept responsibility for their actions (Friedrich, 1990);

- There are known histories of long-lasting and severe physical/sexual abuse by parents;

- There is a highly negative relationship between the parties involved.

In these situations parents certainly will keep on denying everything, and thus they will become even more defensive. The disclosure also may catapult the family into crisis and shock (Solin, 1986). Parents may then respond defensively by displacing anger onto the therapist, the patient, or both.

MARRIED PATIENTS

Many adult patients have to deal with two family systems, their family of origin and the one newly created through marriage. We will briefly mention some issues specific to this patient group. (see also Van den Broucke, Vandereycken, & Norré, 1977).

Psychoeducation. The husband (and the children if they are old enough) should be involved in the treatment, but the treatment need not take the form of marital therapy. The most important need to be met is for education. In case of dissociative disorders, for example, the spouse (Panos, Panos, & Alfred, 1990) and—to an extent depending upon their age—the children (Benjamin & Benjamin, 1993) are informed about the clinical picture, the possible causes, and ways in which to cope with the patient's sometimes incomprehensible behavior.

Care for the children. The therapist must evaluate how great a burden the problem behaviors have put on the children. How much have they suffered? What questions do they have? Do they need support or perhaps therapy themselves? Do they feel safe in the family environment? Have they been involved in traumatic events? We recommend that the therapist sees the children separately and gives them the opportunity to tell their own stories and to express their worries, frustrations, and anxieties. There is a significant risk that a child has taken over some parental responsibilities ("parentification"). In other cases children have been neglected emotionally and sometimes even physically.

Triggers at home. After the spouse is told how specific triggers may provoke out of control behaviors, he can be asked to pay attention to such situations. Physical intimacy and sexual contact, in particular, may be very threatening. Therefore, an agreement can be made to abstain from sexual contact for a certain period of time. Next, it is important to discuss how the spouse can react when the patient loses control, but the therapist must keep in mind the principle of self-reponsibility (see also Chapter 5).

Marital interaction. The husband may have functioned for a long period as a kind of parental figure or even as therapist. He may have searched for refuge in his professional career or engaged in an extramarital relationship. As soon as the patient becomes more self-assured, new tensions may arise in the relationship because the husband may have difficulties in accepting these changes.

Sexual relationship. Most couples will need specific therapeutic guidance to cope with their sexual problems. Sometimes these difficulties only surface when the eating disorder or dissociative disorder has improved. We advise many couples to stop all sexual interaction for some time. Next, the steps towards renewed sexual contact should be made according to the principles of gradual exposure or systematic desensitization. All steps should be agreed upon beforehand and the patient should use a clear stop sign whenever she feels uncomfortable. This way the patient may feel safer and in control over what might happen to her. For some couples the treatment may reveal that the husband himself has sexual problems that had been concealed by the patient's disorder.

Mary was the mother of three boys (ages 7, 9, and 12), and their education always was her responsibility because of her husband's extremely busy work schedule. Her main reason for seeking help was her overweight (230 pounds); she binged almost daily, without any purging. She had tried every possible diet but the result always was the same: she put on even more weight than before. Through our standard assessment (including the Dissociation Questionnaire—see Chapter 4) we noticed that Mary had frequent memory gaps; she often realized that she was in a place without knowing how she got there or what she was supposed to do there. She also reported having been sexually abused in her family of origin. So, beside the binge eating disorder, she suffered from dissociative amnesia that might have been related to a trauma history. Finally, she admitted to being very dissatisfied with her marriage.

Though the husband, John, first voiced practical objections to his involvement in the outpatient treatment, we agreed to have a marital therapy session once a fortnight, while Mary also had a weekly session of individual psychotherapy. (Both therapists work in the same clinic and discuss their cases regularly.)

The most important information that came from the marital therapy session is as follows:

Psychoeducation. It was explained to the couple how a dissociative coping style became part of Mary's life. The partners frequently quarrelled about her forgetfulness; John, who was very meticulous in his work, could not understand her absent-mindedness. He often had the feeling of being married to two "different" women. The explanation that Mary lacked conscious control helped him to look at it in a less criticizing way.

Identifying triggers. It was made clear to the couple that specific situations associated with a traumatic childhood can induce dissociative reactions (feelings of depersonalization, derealization, and memory gaps). John could then help his wife in detecting those critical stimuli. The following situations were identified:

- the children were sleeping and John was not home;

- fights between the children;

- quarrels between John and Mary;

- when he saw her naked;

- during sexual intercourse;

- when she visited her parents.

They decided that they would try to avoid these situations for a while, and that he would phone home every day at least once to check on how things were going. Whenever she felt tense or had an urge to binge, they decided, she would go to the study and listen to her favorite music or read a book. Every day she would also cycle on the home-trainer for at least half an hour.

Care for the children. Despite her problems, Mary seemed to behave adequately in her relationship with the children, but she sometimes was overprotective with the youngest child. Her basic goal became giving to her children what she had missed during her childhood. John also noticed that Mary had too strong a bond with her oldest son despite his sometimes difficult behavior. They agreed to discuss the children's education more often; John also arranged to have at least half a day per week to spend with the children, while Mary would do something else.

Marital interaction. Several of the previously mentioned actions had immediate consequences for the couple's relationship. Then Mary felt clear understanding and support from John. A crucial event was her decision to stop visiting her parents for as long as they were not willing to discuss the past. She wrote them a letter about what happened to her as a child. To her great surprise, John signed the letter: for Mary this was an important proof of his loyalty.

Sexual relationship. John accepted the proposal that they abstain from sexual contact for the next months with surprising ease. In fact he too felt uncomfortable in intimate contacts: Mary was mostly distant, which reminded him of his cool mother; when he tried to be nice and gentle to her, it reminded her of the seducing sweetness of her father! It was explained to them that they did not know how to have fun together. Therefore, they were to spend at least one evening a week outside the house while the children were looked after by a babysitter. The activity was to include something physical, such as dancing, swimming, or jogging. In fact, they would have to go back in time at least 15 years to when they first met and start all over again. They liked the idea, seeing it as a kind of adventure. The therapy really opened the doors to "going backwards into the future" . . .

8

Risks, Complications, and Pitfalls

Psychotherapy with the patients described in this book is often complex and demanding, not only for the patients but also for the therapist. As Herman (1992, p. 140) stated: "Trauma is contagious." In general therapists are not prepared to deal with serious abuse. We ourselves have to admit that many times we have had great difficulty listening to and accepting our patients' tragic if not shocking stories. Many times we have been overwhelmed with feelings of disgust, anger, and helplessness; and often we have felt incompetent to respond to the patients' needs and questions. Repeated exposure to stories of human cruelty challenges the therapist's basic belief system as well as his or her personal vulnerability (Herman, 1992). The risk of narrowing the psychological world of patients to one of trauma and survival is considerable. Therefore, we will first discuss the contraindications of trauma exploration itself. Next, we will address the possible complications and pitfalls therapists can encounter in their work with trauma patients. Finally, we offer some suggestions are can help to protect therapists, in both their professional and their personal lives.

157

WHEN TO AVOID TRAUMA EXPLORATION

For a long time many therapists thought that bringing the traumatic past "alive" again was an essential if not crucial element of the "corrective emotional experience" needed in successful psychotherapeutic work with trauma victims. Patients' confrontation with the thoughts and feelings linked to the trauma experience was assumed to be a *sine qua non* in the therapeutic process, a necessary step toward the integration of these experiences (both emotionally and cognitively) into the patient's current life history. In recent decades, more and more therapists used hypnosis to explore traumatic experiences in childhood and to let patients re-experience the trauma.

After a period of (over)optimism about this approach, an important and dramatic change in the treatment of trauma victims has taken place in the last few years. Trauma therapy, especially in the form of extreme emotional catharsis, had been misused by well-meaning but naive therapists who taught that their therapeutic "surgery"—their removal of old "abscesses"—could lead only toward recovery. But for many patients the cure was worse than the disease. Trauma therapy can become a kind of revictimization experience for the patient. In other cases therapists encouraged their patients—directly or indirectly—to take action against the alleged perpetrators. And even when this was based upon reliable information, the action itself—for example a public accusation or a law suit—might have damaged the patient more than the traumatic event in question. Furthermore, many therapists felt compelled to act as detectives checking the facts, lawyers defending their client, attorneys blaming the perpetrators, or judges searching for the ultimate truth. Not only did they fall into the trap of role confusion, but often they neglected the basic rights of the other people who became involved in these actions. Finally, some therapists overlooked the highly influential role they play in the lives—both in fantasy and in reality—of their patients. Therefore, once again, we would like to stress the necessity of a clear therapeutic role within an ethically well-circumscribed context (as outlined in Chapter 4) before proceeding.

But all these warnings could lead to an equally big mistake: avoidance of the trauma issue on the part of the therapist. In many cases, trauma exploration and integration are crucial elements in treatment. Helping patients tell their story is a work of reconstruction that may actually transform the traumatic memory itself, so that it can be integrated into the survivor's life story (Herman, 1992). In other words, from the viewpoint of cognitive behavioral therapy, re-experiencing the trauma in the safe treatment environment can be considered as a kind of gradual process of exposure and desensitization of terrifying feelings and memories. In the following section we discuss some important issues for a therapist to take into consideration when trauma exploration becomes a serious option in treatment.

Ongoing Abuse

Some patients continue to be abused even while they are in therapy, sometimes the abuse continues even when the perpetrator knows that the victim is in therapy. Safety is a basic condition for the therapeutic work with trauma victims, and so measures must be taken to ensure that the abuse cannot continue. For some patients, hospitalization in a psychiatric ward could be a necessary way to stop the abuse, but even for them inpatient treatment weekend visits must be planned with special care, because even in this situation the risk for continuing abuse still exists.

> Judith, a 25-year-old divorced women, was admitted to our inpatient unit for several reasons. She had a serious anorexia nervosa, with daily bingeing and vomiting, and told us a story of severe physical and sexual abuse in both her family of origin and her ex-marriage. Because of the complexity of her problems and her extreme social isolation, we decided to admit her in the hospital. But we also assumed that the abuse in her family of origin hadn't stopped yet. We therefore asked Judith not to visit her parents for some time. However, she did not follow our advice, and after a weekend visit to her parents' house she came back with a severely burned thigh. Judith told us that she felt guilty for not visiting her parents and that

"something inside her" forced her to do so. During this visit her father tried to touch her on her thigh and she became totally frozen. Afterwards she felt dirty and to clean her body she burned herself. She also had a binge followed by vomiting and laxative abuse "to clean the inside as well."

Limited Coping Abilities

The patient's lack of coping abilities and problem-solving capacities may (temporarily) impede an unavoidably stressful trauma confrontation. Therefore, middle-aged and older patients are probably better off with a supportive therapeutic contact aimed at symptom stabilization and ego strengthening. Similar limitations are to be considered in pregnant women and mothers of newborn or very demanding children. For similar reasons, a therapist should be careful in treating mentally retarded people or patients with a seriously disabling or life-threatening somatic condition.

> Helen, a mother of three young children, was searching for help for a bulimic problem. Now that she was confronted with the education of her children, several bad memories from her own childhood came to the surface. The confrontation with her young children probably functioned as a trigger, bringing back all kinds of traumatic memories and feelings. She felt very lonely, not loved by her husband, and during these moments she binged and vomited. She began to realize, day after day, how she was expected to give love and care to her children, something she had never received herself in her family of origin. We decided to help Helen first to deal with these feelings in the here-and-now, to teach her how to be a "good-enough" mother, instead of exploring her history of trauma. If that exploration, however, had been the only way to help her at this moment, then special measures would have been taken to relieve her; otherwise the

combined emotional burden of child care and therapy would have been too much for her.

Psychogenic Amnesia

In some patients we find serious forms of "psychogenic amnesia" (exemplified by sometimes extremely high scores on both the total DIS-Q score and its amnesia subscale). When asked to describe some important events from their childhoods, some patients seem not to remember anything in particular before a certain age. They may describe their childhoods as "a black hole," or feel as if everything from their childhood has been swept away. Besides the amnesia toward past experiences, they often complain about memory gaps in their current daily lives. During the day they may become aware that they did something (for instance, they discover that they bought some clothes) without remembering when and how they did this.

Striking memory lacunae between the age of 5 and 12 years might reflect to serious abusive experiences in childhood. The amnesia could have functioned to help the victim to cope with traumatic events; or, in other words, it may be forgetting as a psychological survival mechanism ("what's out of my mind doesn't mind me anymore"). In these cases, we prefer to respect the amnestic barrier and not to use (hypno)therapeutic techniques to evoke images or feelings related to the apparently traumatic past. The controversy around recovered memory therapy has been a serious warning (Pope & Hudson, 1996). Therapists should not forget that there always exists the danger of filling the failing memory with new material suggested by the current therapeutic context!

> Sue, an emaciated adolescent, had already told us during the intake interview that "she didn't remember any special event from her childhood." She couldn't explain this and felt embarrassed when asked to concentrate strongly on her years in primary school: she said "her mind remained totally blank." We didn't push her in this matter, in part because we knew that she had already been in outpatient treatment elsewhere, but suddenly dropped out

when the therapist began to use hypnotherapeutic techniques to explore her past.

Nature of the Trauma

Several authors (see Brown & Fromm, 1986; Terr, 1991) make a distinction between two kinds of trauma experiences: events that only happened once (referred to as type 1 trauma), and more complex, long-lasting trauma experiences (type 2). Type 1 traumas include rape, being witness to a bank robbery, losing a meaningful person. In these cases exploration of the trauma experience seems much more indicated than in type 2 trauma experiences, which often show a history of repetitive abuse or revictimization. In type 2 traumas the therapist must consider very carefully the possibly negative and damaging consequences of trauma exploration. The costs may be just too high. Examples include long-lasting, sadistic abuse during childhood or a situation where the victim has been forced to abuse others and hence become a perpetrator him or herself. In these situations, a realistic therapeutic goal may be to teach the patient to gain more control over symptomatic behaviors such as bingeing, self-mutilation, substance abuse, and dissociative episodes (see Chapter 5). The following example shows that trauma exploration would be not only useless but also very misleading when a patient is not ready for it, physiologically and psychologically.

> Julia, a 35-year-old anorectic, was admitted to our inpatient unit on her request because of her complete social isolation and bad physical condition. In the beginning phase of treatment, she reported some negative experiences in her childhood that could be categorized as "emotional neglect." Probably due to extreme emaciation, she seemed to be indifferent, as if she didn't have any emotional reactions. Later on, when she started to put on weight, Julia got more in touch with her inner feelings; she became severely depressed and started to speak about other negative childhood experiences, especially emotional abuse. When she reached her target weight and

menstruated again—for the first time in several years—
Julia disclosed several adverse sexual experiences. In her
case, the weight restoration was the necessary condition to
bring her emotions "alive" again.

Social Support

Trauma exploration paradoxically requires not only a certain
strength—sufficient psychological health—on the part of the patient, but also the presence of a reliable support system outside the
therapeutic milieu. Hence, it is contraindicated in patients who live
in social isolation or lack a trustful relationship with important people other than the therapist(s). For married patients the husband's
collaboration is a priority, except when there are serious marital
conflicts and, *a fortiori*, in cases of intramarital abuse. The same applies to family members; here we prefer to work with siblings and
not to involve the parents too closely because eating disorder patients usually have ambivalent relations and/or separation problems
with their parents (see Chapter 7). When there is no meaningful
support outside the therapeutic system, patients may become too
dependent upon the therapist. Although group therapy may consti-
tute a (temporarily important) surrogate support, patients should
not become too dependent upon each other. Therefore, establishing a good support system in normal life should be given priority as
a therapeutic goal.

> Joan, a married woman, was treated on an outpatient basis
> for a long-lasting bulimia combined with extreme over-
> weight (115 kg; height 1m65). After her weight began to
> decrease, for the first time she reported a series of inces-
> tuous experiences with her father. She became more anx-
> ious, especially during sexual intercourse with her
> husband. In other situations, when her husband touched
> her she suddenly ran away and hid herself for several
> hours somewhere outside the home. Joan's husband was
> then seen by the therapist, who gave him some informa-
> tion about his wife's problems and the importance of his

being closely involved in the treatment. For Joan it was a relief to be able to talk with her husband about her experiences after each therapy session.

Comorbidity

Many traumatized patients show a cluster of psychiatric disorders (see Chapter 3). The presence of several comorbid behaviors should make the therapist cautious in planning any kind of trauma exploration. The same applies to a borderline or antisocial personality disorder. As a general rule, before a therapist attempts confrontational therapy the patient first must regain sufficient self-control. If necessary, the patient should be helped to find a safe environment (see Chapter 5).

> Annie, 18 years old, was admitted to our inpatient unit for bulimia nervosa combined with depression and serious abuse of alcohol and soft drugs. A physical examination revealed several scars, both old and recent, due to self-mutilation (cutting herself with a knife and burning herself with cigarettes). On a self-report questionnaire she admitted to regularly stealing food in supermarkets. We knew that she had lived in a family with a lot of violence centered around father's alcoholism. Although we assumed that she might have been the victim of physical abuse, we did not explore this then. Instead our first treatment goal was to help Annie to regain self-control and to take good care of herself.

RISKS AND COMPLICATIONS FOR THE THERAPIST

The Therapist as Detective

Although our society has gradually become aware of the high frequency of physical violence, emotional neglect, and sexual abuse in and outside families, this has become more than ever before a controversial issue in our professional field. A large number of therapists believe that most stories rely on fantasy or must be considered as "ia-trogenic in nature," mostly suggested by the (hypno)therapist. Especially with regard to allegations of sexual abuse, it is noticeable that the psychotherapeutic field is split into two irreconcilable camps, believers and nonbelievers. One important reason for this sceptical attitude may be the flood of reported cases of sexual abuse in the United States; from 6,000 cases in 1976 to 300,000 in 1993 is a 55-fold increase (Ney, 1995). It is no wonder that in recent years the history of sexual abuse has become an area of great tension between recognition and backlash (Wooley, 1993). As a consequence, therapists often feel forced to investigate the validity of the patient's stories, and, acting like detectives or judges, their main concern may be to find out the "one and only truth." Therefore, we endorse the following suggestions made by Loftus and Yapko (1995, pp. 187–189).

- Do not jump quickly to the conclusion that abuse occurred simply because it is plausible.

- Do not use therapy, especially hypnosis, in order to confirm or disconfirm a suspicion of abuse.

- Do not assume that repression is in force if the person seems not to remember much from his or her childhood.

Whenever therapists feel compelled—primarily for ethical reasons—to validate the patient's stories and the information revealed to them, we recommend that the therapist refer the patient to another health care professional (see also Chapter 4 on assessment) who:

- avoids becoming emotionally and therapeutically involved with the patient;

- evaluates the information on its factual reality;

- engages other parties when and where needed, without violating the rights of the patient or significant others;

- discusses these actions and all their implications with the patient (gets the patient's informed consent).

In this way the therapist will not assume the role of a detective or attorney but will continue to work with the patient's "narrative truth"—instead of the "factual truth"—within an ethically appropriate therapeutic relationship of mutual trust.

The Therapist as Victim

Many mental health care professionals may have been trauma victims themselves. However, a therapist cannot solve his or her own victimization through the therapy of other victims (Friedrich, 1990). A trap for therapists may be that the therapist projects his or her own story of a victimization onto the patient. In other cases, a therapist's unresolved history will be activated by the patient's reports of similar trauma. These therapists should realize that their own background makes them incapable of giving adequate professional help to traumatized patients.

Aside from the revictimization experienced by therapists who have traumatic pasts, everyone working with trauma patients runs an important risk of developing symptoms of *secondary traumatic stress* (STS). This refers to the emotional impact and psychological sequelae of being confronted with the traumatic events and experiences of patients. STS in mental health professionals has also been called vicarious traumatization, traumatic countertransference, and compassion fatigue (Figley, 1995; Herman, 1992). Indicators may include feeling distressing emotions, suffering intrusive imagery from the patient's traumatic material, numbing or avoidance of efforts to elicit material from the patient, somatic complaints such as sleeping disorders, headaches, heart palpitations and gastrointestinal distress (for example, poor appetite), and addictive or compulsive behaviors including workaholism (Dutton & Rubinstein, 1995). Therapists suffering from STS also show impairments in their professional and personal life: they may cancel appointments, decrease the use of supervision or consultation, have more problems with intimate relationships, and feel lonely and alienated from normal social life. A typical sign is the gradually changing view of the world, which becomes more cruel or unsafe, because everyone is a possible perpetrator. Hence, such therapists become increasingly cynical about the motives of others and pessimistic about the human condition.

Detachment or Overidentification

Two common responses therapists may show toward trauma victims are detachment and overidentification (Courtois, 1988; Herman, 1992). One way for a therapist to protect against the emotional impact of trauma histories can be to develop a distant attitude toward the patient. The therapist's detachment may result in an identification with the offender, thus he or she may blame the patient for what happened. Diagnostic labels (especially personality disorders) or psychological speculations keep the patient at a distance emotionally. The therapist may also tend to minimize, negate, or invalidate certain aspects of the patient's experience. Other forms of detachment may include adopting a personal and emotional distance during the sessions, often being late, and frequently cancelling or postponing appointments (Dutton & Rubinstein, 1995).

The opposite reponse, overidentification with the trauma victim, is another common error. The therapist may become so empathic that he or she starts to mourn (Herman, 1992) or becomes overwhelmed by feelings of anger, helplessness, and shame. A typical reaction, then, is the attempt to rescue the patient and take excessive responsibility for the patient's life. The rescuer will make him or herself so much available—"I'm always there for you"—that the patient even may intrude into the therapist's private life. Another frequent consequence of overidentification is giving the patient a special position among the other patients. In that case, therapist and patient will establish special rules and exceptions to general therapeutic principles. In our experience it is a golden rule not to make exceptions on general therapeutic rules and principles "because the patient is a trauma survivor."

A combination of detached and overidentifying therapists may be found in some teams. This will lead to serious splitting between the believers and the sceptics. This kind of splitting in the therapeutic team often reflects the internal process in the patient, who may experience an inner fight between "good" and "bad" parts of herself. Needless to say, the therapeutic process will be undermined if the patient is allowed to become a "therapy victim."

CARING FOR THE THERAPIST

Doing psychotherapeutic work inevitably puts the therapist in an emotionally vulnerable situation. Faced with special types of psychiatric problems, such as eating disorders, the burden of this work may be a serious test of the therapist's own psychological strength (Vandereycken, 1993b). The strain would be even higher in the subgroup of patients described in this book. The following guidelines, therefore, can be considered as preventive measures for the sake of the therapists involved.

Define Realistic Therapeutic Goals

Realistic treatment goals should be delineated, depending on a careful analysis of both the patient's problems and the therapist's expertise. Time and again we have emphasized in this book that a therapist should start by helping the patient to have greater self-control over her maladaptive behaviors. Hence, a great deal of the therapy will focus mainly on symptom reduction and stabilization. Even in very obvious cases of traumatization, it is still a serious question if confrontation and so-called psychological integration of the traumatic past would be beneficial. Especially at risk are therapists who like the dramatic aspects of their work but forget that the drama will end in a tragedy for the patient! So, being realistic also applies to the qualities of the therapist. There is always the danger of the therapist dreaming of omnipotence or rescue fantasies, seducing the therapist to treat every kind of patient, regardless of the diagnosis, or to handle an increasing number of patients (Cerney, 1995). Others believe that they must be supertherapists, who can operate at peak competence at all times with all patients. Solo work should be avoided or at least combined with the next guideline.

Plan Regular Supervision

Regular supervision of the therapist must be considered an essential protective factor in the therapeutic work with trauma patients. Therapists need extra support and understanding, and they must be aware of such antitherapeutic reactions as overidentification and detachment. In supervision, the therapist can be watched for secondary traumatic stress reactions or symptoms of burnout. Therapists who themselves have had traumatic pasts should be very careful in this work, starting at the beginning with a stringent selection of their patients. Finally, regular contacts with colleagues or supervisors can provide a crucial opportunity for therapists to debrief their own feelings and reactions to their patients' stories.

Establish a Balance Between Personal and Professional Life

Establishing a good balance between personal and professional life is not an easy task (Cerney, 1995). For many therapists the first step will be to reduce the number of patients they see. Installing a clear boundary between professional and personal life is another important step. For instance, a therapist cannot be on call for 24 hours a days, seven days a week. If a therapist considers this form of availability to be necessary for the patient, something is going wrong: A therapist must never become a patient's only significant other. In psychotherapy the therapist should start with the axiom that both parties need a social support system outside the treatment situation. The therapist's personal life should be emotionally rich and psychologically strong enough to nourish his or her professional life, and not the reverse!

APPENDIX A

AN OUTCOME STUDY

This appendix presents the results of a follow-up study carried out at our treatment center. The goal of the investigation was to systematically assess the (changing) presence of dissociative symptoms over time: at admission in our specialized inpatient unit, and then after 6 months and 1 year. Because we are not aware of similar follow-up studies on dissociative pathology, we considered ours as primarily exploratory in nature, without clear-cut hypotheses but focusing on the following issues:

1. Considering the discussion of whether dissociative experiences are to be considered a trait or state characteristic, we wanted to study how dissociative symptoms evolve (stay stable or change) after an intensive treatment and at follow-up 1 year after admission.

2. Based on previous research findings (see Chapter 1), a higher level of dissociative symptoms was expected in those patients who had a bulimic component and a history of childhood trauma. Do eating disorder subgroups—for instance, restricting anorectics versus bulimics—and patients with a history of childhood trauma evolve differently as to the reporting of dissociative symptoms at the three measurement moments? Is there a relationship between the reporting of dissociative symptoms and the patient's general functioning at follow-up?

3. Finally, we wanted to study the possibly predictive value of eating disorder features with respect to the outcome of dissociative symptoms and vice versa.

METHOD

Subjects

A total of 62 female patients took part in the study at the three measurement points (admission, after 6 months, and after 1 year). According to DSM-IV criteria, 38 (61%) were categorized with anorexia nervosa of the restricting type (mean Body Mass Index or BMI was 14.1), 13 patients (21%) with anorexia nervosa of the binge eating/purging or "mixed" type (mean BMI 17.6), and 11 patients (18%) with bulimia nervosa of the purging type (mean BMI 20.3). The average age of the sample at admission was 21.6 years; the duration of illness averaged 5.8 years. Eleven patients (18%) were married or lived together with a partner, but the largest number (n=30 or 49%) were still living within their family of origin.

The patient characteristics of the subjects who participated in the study were compared with those of the patients who dropped out of the study at the follow-up assessments (N=23). The drop-out group showed a higher age and a longer duration of illness; these features are known to be generally related to a poorer outcome (see Herzog, Deter, & Vandereycken, 1992). So we may assume that the patients for whom we have follow-up data are doing better in general than the drop-outs. Hence, our findings should not be viewed as representative for the whole sample.

All patients were admitted at the eating disorder unit of the University Center St. Jozef in Kortenberg (Belgium) where they participated in a directive and eclectic group therapy program (described in Chapter 5; see also Vanderlinden, Norré, & Vandereycken, 1992). Because of Belgium's generous health insurance system, there are practically no financial barriers against hospitalizing any patient for several months (in our program there is a maximum six-months hospital stay).

Measures

Subjects completed a series of self-report questionnaires at the three assessment points (for more details see Chapter 4):

- Eating Disorder Inventory (EDI).

- Eating Disorder Evaluation Scale (EDES). (The total score on the scale is used as a measure of general functioning. For this study, we also calculated a so-called "comorbidity score" that combined scores on nervousness, sleeplessness, anxiety, depression, suicide attempts or serious bodily self-harm, abuse of alcohol, and drug use. Contrary to the other instruments used in this study, a lower score on the EDES points in the direction of more pathology.)

- Body Attitude Test (BAT).

- Dissociation Questionnaire (DIS-Q).

- Traumatic Experiences Questionnaire (TEQ); (only filled out at admission and not repeated at follow-up assessments).

Data Analysis

To compare the DIS-Q scores at the three assessment points, ANOVAs were carried out on the total DIS-Q score and four subscale scores separately (first for the total sample of eating disorders, next for the eating disorder subgroups separately). Whenever the ANOVA was significant, post-hoc Tukey LSD tests were used. To compare patients with and without a history of trauma, a series of two-way ANOVAs (trauma vs nontrauma x time point) have been conducted on the total DIS-Q score and the four subscales separately. To study the variables related to the DIS-Q scores at follow-up, linear regression analysis was employed (forward stepwise).

RESULTS

General Outcome

The EDES total score was used as a measure of general functioning. A minimum score of 55 has been suggested to identify subjects who are functioning in the normal range on different aspects: eating problems, psychosocial adaptataion, and sexuality (Vandereycken, 1993a). The total EDES score showed that at the first follow-up (6 months after admission) 55% of the eating disorder sample was functioning in the range of normality; approximately the same proportion (50%) was showing a favorable outcome after 1 year. However, there were important differences between the different eating disorder subgroups at 1-year follow-up: 52% of the restrictive anorectics, 70% of the bulimia nervosa patients, but only 18% of the mixed anorectics scored within normal range.

How Do Dissociative Symptoms Evolve in Eating Disorders?

ANOVA showed a significant effect of time on the total DIS-Q score and the subscales identity confusion, loss of control, and absorption (Fs (2)= 4.13–7.19; p<.02–.001). Post-hoc tests (Tukey LSD; see Table A.1), compared with the DIS-Q scores at admission, indicated a significant decrease for the total DIS-Q scores and the subscales identity confusion, loss of control at the two follow-up assessments, and for the subscale absorption only at the first follow-up.

The evolution of the DIS-Q scores of the different eating disorder subgroups were evaluated at the three assessment points. ANOVA showed that only restricting anorectics and bulimics report a significant decrease in dissociative symptoms, while the DIS-Q scores in mixed anorectics remained unchanged (see Table A.2).

In restricting anorectics, ANOVA showed a significant effect of time on the total DIS-Q score and subscales identity confusion and loss of control (Fs(df1,2)=5.43–6.20; p=.006–.003). Post-hoc tests (Tukey LSD; see Table A.2) showed that 6 months after admission restricting anorectics reported significantly fewer dissociative symptoms on the total DIS-Q score (p=.003) and on the subscales identity confusion (p=.003) and loss of control (p<.01). At 1 year follow-up, compared to the scores at admission, restricting anorectics report still fewer dissociative symptoms on the total DIS-Q score (p<.04), while the scores on the subscales identity confusion and loss of control approach statistical significance (p=.06).

In bulimia nervosa, ANOVA showed a significant effect of time on

TABLE A.1

Mean DIS-Q Scores in Eating Disorder Patients (n=62)
at Admission and at Follow-Up (6 Months and 1 Year)

	Admission	6 Months	1 Year	ANOVA
Total	2.11 (.54)	1.86 (.59)**	1.90 (.62)*	.001
DIS-Q1	2.23 (.75)	1.89 (.78)**	1.95 (.80)**	.002
DIS-Q2	2.27 (.59)	2.02 (.61)**	2.04 (.62)**	.001
DIS-Q3	1.49 (.41)	1.41 (.41)	1.39 (.49)	.12
DIS-Q4	2.62 (.74)	2.37 (.78)*	2.41 (.85)	.02

DIS-Q1 = identity confusion/fragmentation; DIS-Q2 = loss of
control; DIS-Q3 = amnesia; DIS-Q4 = absorption
* p<.005; ** p<.02 (compared to admission)

TABLE A.2

DIS-Q Scores in Subgroups of Eating Disorders at Admission and Follow-Up

	Admission	6 months	1 year	ANOVA
ANR (n=38)				
Total	2.09 (.51)	1.76 (.48)***	1.86 (.58)*	.003
DIS-Q1	2.26 (.75)	1.77 (.64)***	1.93 (.80)	.003
DIS-Q2	2.20 (.57)	1.90 (.54)***	1.98 (.58)	.01
DIS-Q3	1.46 (.35)	1.34 (.32)	1.38 (.40)	NS
DIS-Q4	2.63 (.73)	2.34 (.70)	2.35 (.85)	NS
ANMIX (n=13)				
Total	2.17 (.46)	2.15 (.68)	2.12 (.73)	NS
DIS-Q1	2.26 (.62)	2.18 (.84)	2.10 (.86)	NS
DIS-Q2	2.31 (.46)	2.40 (.69)	2.32 (.75)	NS
DIS-Q3	1.55 (.54)	1.65 (.60)	1.63 (.74)	NS
DIS-Q4	2.72 (.72)	2.37 (.89)	2.70 (.80)	NS
BN (n=11)				
Total	2.12 (.75)	1.88 (.77)	1.78 (.60)**	.01
DIS-Q1	2.10 (.96)	1.96 (1.0)	1.85 (.78)	NS
DIS-Q2	2.46 (.81)	1.97 (.65)#	1.91 (.59)#	.0002
DIS-Q3	1.53 (.45)	1.35 (.34)*	1.27 (.34)**	.005
DIS-Q4	2.50 (.85)	2.47 (.99)	2.27 (.92)	.33

*=p<.05; **=p<.01; ***=p<.005; #=p<.0001 (compared with scores at admission)

the total DIS-Q score and subscales loss of control and amnesia (Fs(df1,2)=6.16–12.66; p<.01–.0003). Post-hoc tests (Tukey LSD; see Table A.2) showed that 6 months after admission normal-weight bulimics report significantly fewer dissociative symptoms on the subscales loss of control (p<.001) and amnesia (p<.04). At 1 year follow-up, compared to the scores at admission, bulimics report still fewer dissociative symptoms on the total DIS-Q score (p<.01), and the subscales loss of control (p<.001) and amnesia (p<.005). As for the results in mixed anorectics, remarkably enough, the DIS-Q scores stayed rather stable over time.

The Influence of Traumatic Experiences on the General Outcome

Because of the small number of patients and the fact that patients reported a combination of several kinds of trauma (for instance sexual and emotional abuse), the whole trauma group was compared with the nontrauma sample. Traumatic experiences included sexual abuse, physical abuse, and severe emotional neglect/abuse. Using this definition, 26 patients (42%) reported a history of trauma at first assessment. Again we used the EDES total score as a measure of general functioning. At the 6 months and 1 year follow-up no significant differences were found between the trauma and nontrauma sample when average scores on the EDES were compared. However, when the EDES cutoff score was used (>55 = within normal range) we found striking differences in the proportion of normally functioning patients: in the nontrauma sample the proportion decreased from 67% to 53%, whereas in the trauma group it increased from 35% to 47%. These data seem to suggest that, generally speaking, trauma patients need more time to evolve positively.

To further elaborate on this finding, we also compared the scores on the other questionnaires (EDI, DIS-Q, BAT). Interestingly enough, no differences were found between the trauma and nontrauma sample after 6 months. At the second follow-up trauma patients scored significantly higher on the total BAT score (p>.05) and its subscales lack of familiarity with one's own body (p<.05) and general body dissatisfaction (p<.01). They also reported significantly more dissociative experiences (total DIS-Q score, p<.05; amnesia, p<.05). These data suggest that trauma experiences must not be considered as a risk factor for the typical eating symptomatology, but have an impact on the presence of dissociative symptoms and negative body experiences.

A two-way ANOVA (trauma/nontrauma X time point) indicated a significant overall effect of trauma on the subscale amnesia (df=2; F=4.02; p<.02; see Table A.3). Post-hoc Tukey tests showed that at 1 year follow-up, the trauma group reported significantly more amnesia compared to the nontrauma sample (p<.0001). Next, we evaluated the DIS-Q scores for the two groups separately on the three time points. In the nontrauma group, ANOVA showed significant effect of time on the total DIS-Q score (F(df1,2)=11.04; p<.0001), and its subscales identity confusion (F(df1,2)=7.65; p<.001), loss of control (F(df1,2)=10.6; p<.0001) and amnesia (F(df1,2)=10.38; p<.0001). Post-hoc Tukey tests compared with the scores at admission showed significant decreases in total DIS-Q scores (p<.005–.0001) and scores for identity confusion, loss of control, and amnesia (p<.005–.0001) at both 6 months and 1 year follow-up. However, ANOVA showed no significant effect of time on the DIS-Q scores in the trauma group. Hence, the scores for this group did not change significantly. Compared with the 6 months follow-up, DIS-Q scores are even higher after 1 year.

Prediction of Dissociative Experiences at Follow-up

To study the relationship between typical eating disorder characteristics and follow-up DIS-Q scores, the following factors have been included in the initial regression analyses as independent variables: duration of illness, age, total score on the EDI, total EDES score, EDES comorbidity scale, and total BAT score. The total DIS-Q at 6 months and 1 year follow-up were separately fed into the regression analysis as dependent variables. The results showed that only one variable of the initial assessment was a strong predictor of the DIS-Q scores at discharge, the total BAT score (F=11.9; p<.001), which accounted for 41% of the variance. The EDES comorbidity factor almost reached significance (F=2.33; p<.13). Next, regression analyses were carried out to study the relationship between initial assessments and the DIS-Q scores at the 1 year follow-up. The forward re-

TABLE A.3
DIS-Q Scores in Trauma Versus Nontrauma
Patients at Admission and Follow-up

	Nontrauma	Trauma	ANOVA	
			F	P
Total				
A	2.07 (.55)	2.18 (.53)	1.34	.26
B	1.80 (.54)	1.96 (.64)		
C	1.76 (.57)	2.10 (.65)		
DIS-Q1				
A	2.16 (.79)	2.34 (.71)	.43	.65
B	1.78 (.71)	2.04 (.86)		
C	1.80 (.77)	2.16 (.80)		
DIS-Q2				
A	2.24 (.57)	2.32 (.63)	1.02	.36
B	1.96 (.57)	2.11 (.67)		
C	1.92 (.58)	2.21 (.65)		
DIS-Q3				
A	1.45 (.37)	1.54 (.45)	4.02	.02
B	1.35 (.35)	1.48 (.48)		
C	1.24 (.31)	1.60 (.60)		
DIS-Q4				
A	2.62 (.81)	2.63 (.64)	1.47	.23
B	2.42 (.83)	2.42 (.73)		
C	2.33 (.88)	2.33 (.81)		

A – at admission; B = after 6 months; C = after 1 year
Two-way ANOVA (trauma/nontrauma X time)

gression analysis showed that none of the independent factors were significantly related to the total DIS-Q score at 1 year follow-up.

DISCUSSION

This study reported the first prospective follow-up data on dissociative symptoms in a sample of eating-disordered patients. Compared with the scores at admission, the total sample reported significantly fewer dissociative symptoms after inpatient treatment, especially with experiences referring to identity confusion (DIS-Q subscale 1) and loss of control (DIS-Q subscale 2). Hence the data show that the treatment had a favorable outcome on the DIS-Q, at least for the total sample. When comparing different eating disorder subgroups with one another, only restricting anorectics and normal-weight bulimics reported significantly fewer dissociative experiences after intensive treatment, while DIS-Q scores of "mixed" anorectics (who also binge and/or purge) stayed rather stable over time. Hence in this subgroup our treatment program has little or no influence on the presence of dissociative symptoms. How can this finding be understood?

One possible explanation may be the fact that this group is known to show a poor long-term outcome, probably related to a longer duration of illness and more comorbidity (Herzog, Deter, & Vandereycken, 1992). Moreover, previous studies carried out at our center (see Chapter 1) also have demonstrated that the prevalence of sexual abuse is highest in the subgroup of mixed anorectics. Therefore, we assume that these patients keep on using a dissociative coping style to deal with both the memories and the feelings associated with their childhood trauma experiences.

This hypothesis is partially supported by the finding that dissociative symptoms do not decrease in eating disorder patients with a history of trauma at the follow-up assessments. Hence, in patients with a history of trauma, dissociative symptoms seem to be rather resistant to therapy, at least in our treatment program and after a follow-up of only 1 year. This finding is also supported by our clinical experience: patients with a history of severe childhood sexual abuse often need longer and more intensive treatment before any significant therapeutic progress can be expected. It takes time before patients will discuss their trauma experiences. Moreover, at the moment the patient is willing to disclose a trauma history, an important increase in dissociative experiences may be expected.

When the impact of traumatic childhood experiences on the DIS-Q scores was studied, the only significant effect found was on the subscale amnesia. This result confirms the findings from other studies, suggesting that psychogenic amnesia is probably the most specific dissociative symptom that can differentiate trauma patients from nontrauma patients, not only in eating disorders but also in the general population (Vanderlinden, 1993).

Finally, the way patients perceive and experience their body (BAT) appeared to be a strong predictor of DIS-Q scores at follow-up. The data suggest a close association between dissociative symptoms and negative body experiences in eating disorders. It is possible that these negative body experiences may function as a specific mediating factor between the trauma experience (input) and the development of the eating disorder and/or dissociative symptoms (output). Overall, the findings underline the importance of a therapeutic approach focusing on positively changing and/or influencing the way patients experience and evaluate their bodies. Further research is needed to study whether a therapeutic approach aimed at positively changing the patient's body experience may also result in a decrease of dissociative symptoms in eating disorders.

APPENDIX B

DISSOCIATION QUESTIONNAIRE (DIS-Q)*

PART 1

Name:

Date:

Your age: _____ years

Your sex:

☐ male
☐ female

Your marital status:

☐ Single
☐ Married
☐ Living together
☐ Divorced
☐ Widower/Widow

Your educational background/training:

☐ Elementary School
☐ High School
☐ Higher nonuniversity training
☐ University training

Do you remember having experienced severely damaging, life-threatening, or traumatic events?

☐ No
☐ Yes (please specify):
    ☐ severe bodily injury
    ☐ physical abuse
    ☐ state of war
    ☐ sexual abuse by family members
    ☐ sexual abuse by others (nonfamily members)
    ☐ emotional maltreatment
    ☐ other (please specify):

---

*Permission to use this questionnaire, together with an easy scoring form, may be obtained from Johan Vanderlinden, Ph.D., University Center St.-Jozef, 3070 Kortenberg, Belgium.

PART 2

You are now asked to indicate to what extent the following experiences apply to you. The experiences mentioned in the questionnaire may have occurred when you were under the influence of alcohol, drugs, or medication. But this questionnaire concerns your condition when you are free of such substances. You are asked to react to the statements by circling the number (from 1 to 5) that applies to you. Any answer is good, as long as it reflects your own view. Please react to all of the statements.

> 1 = *not at all* applicable to me
> 2 = *a little bit* applicable to me
> 3 = *moderately* applicable to me
> 4 = *quite a bit* applicable to me
> 5 = *extremely* applicable to me

1. At times I have the feeling that I am dreaming.   1 2 3 4 5

2. I often have the feeling that everything is unreal.   1 2 3 4 5

3. At times I feel that I have lost contact with my body.   1 2 3 4 5

4. I gorge myself with food without thinking about it.   1 2 3 4 5

5. While I am driving and/or bicycling, I suddenly realize that I cannot remember what happened on the way.   1 2 3 4 5

6. I burst out laughing or crying without any reason and without wanting to.   1 2 3 4 5

7. I have the feeling that I am somebody else.   1 2 3 4 5

8. While I am listening to someone I suddenly realize that I have not heard anything.   1 2 3 4 5

9. When I am tired, it seems as if a strange power from outside takes possession of me and decides what to do for me.   1 2 3 4 5

10. I get into situations that I do not want
    to be in.   1 2 3 4 5

11. At times I feel a great distance between
    myself and the things I think and do.   1 2 3 4 5

12. At times I wonder exactly who I am.   1 2 3 4 5

13. Sometimes I find new articles among my
    things without being able to remember
    ever having purchased them.   1 2 3 4 5

14. I regularly feel an urge to eat something,
    even when I am not hungry.   1 2 3 4 5

15. Sometimes I get angry without wanting to
    be at all.   1 2 3 4 5

16. Sometimes I am determined to do something,
    but my body acts quite differently against my
    own will.   1 2 3 4 5

17. Sometimes I feel confused.   1 2 3 4 5

18. Sometimes I cannot remember where I
    was the day (or days) before.   1 2 3 4 5

19. Sometimes I am told that I act as if friends
    or family members were strangers.   1 2 3 4 5

20. In particular situations, I experience myself
    as a split personality.   1 2 3 4 5

21. Sometimes I cannot remember anything
    about certain important events in my life, such
    as my final examinations or my own wedding. 1 2 3 4 5

22. Sometimes I am about to say something,
    but then something quite different crosses
    my lips.   1 2 3 4 5

23. Sometimes my mood changes suddenly
    and completely.   1 2 3 4 5

24. Sometimes I do something without
    thinking about it.   1 2 3 4 5

25. I immediately forget what other people tell me.   1 2 3 4 5

26. Sometimes while I am doing something I am suddenly struck by a blackout.   1 2 3 4 5

27. I look at myself in the mirror without recognizing myself.   1 2 3 4 5

28. I get the feeling that my body is changing.   1 2 3 4 5

29. I have the feeling that other people, other things, and the world surrounding me are not real.   1 2 3 4 5

30. I have the feeling that my body is not really mine.   1 2 3 4 5

31. When I watch television, I do not notice anything that goes on around me.   1 2 3 4 5

32. Entire blocks of time vanish, and I cannot remember what I did then.   1 2 3 4 5

33. I can remember so vividly something that happened in the past that I have the feeling that I am reliving it.   1 2 3 4 5

34. It seems as if someone else inside me decides what to do.   1 2 3 4 5

35. Sometimes I discover that I have done something without remembering anything about it.   1 2 3 4 5

36. I wonder how I can prevent myself from doing certain things.   1 2 3 4 5

37. Sometimes I suddenly notice that I find myself in a place that is unknown to me, without knowing how I got there.   1 2 3 4 5

38. I am not sure whether certain memories have really taken place, or if I merely dreamed about them.   1 2 3 4 5

39. I find myself in a place I know well but that appears strange and unknown to me.   1 2 3 4 5

40. I have the feeling that I do certain things
    without knowing why.   1   2   3   4   5

41. I think or do something against my liking
    in a way that does not suit me at all.   1   2   3   4   5

42. I notice that I watch myself closely in
    everything I do.   1   2   3   4   5

43. I can enclose myself in fantasies or
    daydreams so much that what I imagine
    really seems to be happening.   1   2   3   4   5

44. I stare aimlessly, without thinking
    about anything.   1   2   3   4   5

45. I often think about nothing.   1   2   3   4   5

46. I find it very hard to resist bad habits.   1   2   3   4   5

47. I forget where I put things.   1   2   3   4   5

48. Sometimes I eat without thinking about it.   1   2   3   4   5

49. I catch myself daydreaming.   1   2   3   4   5

50. I wish I had more control of myself.   1   2   3   4   5

51. When I walk, I am aware of each step I take.   1   2   3   4   5

52. In particular situations, I notice that I
    am able to do certain things with the
    greatest ease, things that I find very hard
    to do in other situations.   1   2   3   4   5

53. When I eat, I am aware of every bite I take.   1   2   3   4   5

54. I lose all sense of time.   1   2   3   4   5

55. I cannot remember whether I have really
    done something or if I merely planned it.   1   2   3   4   5

56. I want to do two things at the same time,
    and I notice that I am arguing the pros
    and cons with myself.   1   2   3   4   5

57. I have the feeling that my mind is split up.   1   2   3   4   5

58. I find notes, drawings, or annotations
    that I have made but I cannot remember
    ever having made them.   1 2 3 4 5

59. I have the feeling that I am made up of
    two (or more) people.   1 2 3 4 5

60. I often do something without thinking
    about it.   1 2 3 4 5

61. I hear voices in my head telling me what I
    am to do or making comment on what I
    am doing.   1 2 3 4 5

62. I see myself differently from the way other
    people see me.   1 2 3 4 5

63. I feel that I am looking at the world through
    a haze so that the people and things
    surrounding me appear remote or vague.   1 2 3 4 5

Use and Interpretation of the DIS-Q

The DIS-Q is a self-reporting questionnaire for the measurement of dissociative experiences (see Chapter 4). Along with a total score, there are four subscales: (1) identity confusion and fragmentation; (2) loss of control; (3) amnesia; (4) absorption. All scores are means. The mean total score in a normal population sample is 1.5 (SD 0.4). The normal means for each subscale are as follows: identity confusion 1.4 (SD 0.4), loss of control 1.7 (SD 0.5), amnesia 1.4 (SD 0.4), and absorption 1.9 (SD 0.6). (See Table B.1.)

In order to select patients with a dissociative disorder, a cutoff score was calculated by comparing the total DIS-Q scores of the normal population sample (N=378) with the scores of a patient group with dissociative disorders (N=100). A cutoff score of 2.5 for the total score yielded 91% sensitivity (ability to correctly identify the true positive cases or subjects with a dissociative disorder) and 97% specificity (the ability to correctly identify the number of true negative cases or subjects without dissociative disorder). With a total DIS-Q score above 2.5, the subject seems to show dissociative experiences within the range of abnormality. To diagnose a dissociative disorder, however, a good interview is necessary (for example, the SCID-D by Steinberg et al., 1990; see Chapter 4). After evaluating the total DIS-Q score by means of the cutoff, a comparison with the scores of different psychiatric patient groups is recommended. This comparison will enable the clinician or researcher to evaluate the subject's DIS-Q scores with different psychiatric samples.

TABLE B.1
DIS-Q Scores in a General Population Sample (n=750) and in Psychiatric Patients (n=450)

		Total		DIS-Q1		DIS-Q2		DIS-Q3		DIS-Q4	
	N	X	SD	X	SD	X	SD	X	SD	X	SD
Normals	750	1.5	0.4	1.4	0.4	1.7	0.5	1.4	0.4	1.9	0.6
OCD	40	2.0	0.5	2.0	0.8	2.1	0.5	1.5	0.4	2.4	0.7
Schizo	40	2.0	0.6	2.0	0.7	2.1	0.6	1.9	0.6	2.5	0.8
Eating	200	2.2	0.5	2.4	0.6	2.4	0.6	1.6	0.5	2.7	0.7
PTSD	20	2.7	0.6	2.7	0.9	3.0	0.7	2.3	0.4	2.4	0.4
BPD	40	2.8	0.6	2.8	0.8	3.1	0.6	2.2	0.8	2.8	0.6
DDNOS	30	2.9	0.6	3.0	0.8	3.1	0.7	2.5	0.8	2.7	0.9
DID	80	3.5	0.4	3.8	0.5	3.2	0.5	3.3	0.6	3.1	0.5

DIS-Q1 = identity confusion; DIS-Q2 = loss of control; DIS-Q3 = amnesia; DIS-Q = absorption; OCD = obsessive compulsive disorder; Schizo = schizophrenia; Eating = eating disorder; PTSD = posttraumatic stress disorder; BPD = borderline personality disorder; DDNOS = dissociative disorder not otherwise specified; DID = dissociative identity disorder

APPENDIX C

The following questions may be difficult to answer because they concern matters normally not disclosed, but we do hope that you will answer them as honestly as possible. We assure you that your answers will remain confidential (they are bound by professional secrecy).

We know from experience that patients with eating disorders such as anorexia nervosa or bulimia nervosa often take things that actually do not belong to them. In fact it is a kind of stealing, although the word theft sounds a bit harsh when it concerns, for instance, money from your parents, food from a friend's refrigerator, or an object of little value from a department store. This stealing may have happened just once, or it could happen frequently. Sometimes you may experience an urge to steal that is difficult to resist, and only afterward do you suffer from a guilty conscience.

Because too little is known about this behavior and because we want to be able to provide better help to patients struggling with it, the information we ask for is of great use to us. Therefore, please try to answer as honestly as possible.

By using the words *stealing* or *theft* in the next pages we mean the taking of any object or goods, regardless of their value, which do not belong to you. As far as your own home or family (parents, brothers, sisters) is concerned, taking food, drink, or sweets on the sly is *not* considered to be stealing; taking money or other objects, however, is.

Please make an *X* by the correct answer in the space provided. If there are several possible answers, you may mark more than one.

Thank you for your cooperation

1. Did you ever steal anything?

   ☐ YES (please go to question 3)
   ☐ NO (please go to question 2)

2. Did you ever feel the inclination or urge to steal anything without actually doing so?

☐ NO (please go to question 20)
☐ YES:

   • When did this happen most recently?

   • Had this anything to do with your eating disorder? If so, how?

   • Did you ever have such an inclination before? yes/no

   • How did you restrain this inclination?

   • Do you have an explanation for such an inclination to steal?

   • Are you afraid of committing theft one day and why?

Please go to question 20.

3. When did you steal something for the first time (approximate year or your age at that time)?

4. When did this happen most recently (date)?

5. How often did it occur in total?

☐ once
☐ fewer than 5 times
☐ 5 or more times

6. How often did it occur in the last 12 months?

☐ not once
☐ once
☐ fewer than 5 times
☐ 5 to 10 times
☐ at least once a month
☐ at least once a week
☐ more than once a week

7. If this happened several times last year, how often did it occur?

☐ several times in succession
☐ with long periods of time between each theft
☐ very irregularly

8. What kind of things do you usually take?

☐ money
☐ food
☐ alcoholic drinks
☐ tobacco products
☐ cosmetics
☐ clothing
☐ other (specify):

9. What do you do with the stolen goods?

☐ use them
☐ keep them without using them
☐ give them away
☐ throw them away
☐ return them to the owner
☐ other (specify):

10. From where do you take things?

☐ from a small shop
☐ from a big department store
☐ from home
☐ from relatives, friends, acquaintances
☐ from strangers
☐ from work or school
☐ from another place (specify):

11. To what extent has the theft been planned?

    ☐ not at all
    ☐ more or less planned
    ☐ well considered and planned

12. In the following boxes indicate your feelings concerning stealing:

	Before	During	After
tense	☐	☐	☐
afraid	☐	☐	☐
dejected	☐	☐	☐
excited	☐	☐	☐
calm	☐	☐	☐
guilty	☐	☐	☐
ashamed	☐	☐	☐
confused	☐	☐	☐
angry	☐	☐	☐

Did other feelings occur at the moment of stealing?

    before:
    during:
    afterwards:

13. Have you ever been caught stealing?

    ☐ no
    ☐ yes:
        • How often?
        • Where, when, and by whom?
        • Were you fined or prosecuted by the police?
        • Which of your family or friends knows about this?

14. While stealing were you afraid of being caught?

    ☐ not at all

☐ a bit or sometimes
☐ very much

15. Did you ever speak to someone about your stealing?

☐ no:
  • Why did you conceal this until now?
  ☐ from shame
  ☐ for fear that others will be told
  ☐ for fear of being prosecuted (police)
  ☐ because people would not understand it anyway
  ☐ because it's no one's business
  ☐ other reason (specify):

☐ yes:
  • Who is informed about it?
  ☐ partner/husband
  ☐ parents
  ☐ brother or sister
  ☐ friend or girlfriend
  ☐ another member of the family or good acquaintance
  ☐ professional (doctor, therapist, social worker)
  ☐ priest or mental/moral guide
  ☐ other (specify):

16. Do you think you will ever steal again in the future?

☐ never
☐ probably not
☐ possibly
☐ probably
☐ I don't know

17. Suppose that in the future you get the urge to steal again. What will you do to restrain it?

☐ I won't go shopping alone.
☐ I'll distract myself.

☐ I'll take some friend, family member, or good acquaintance into my confidence.
☐ I'll seek help from a doctor, therapist, or social worker.
☐ I don't know.
☐ other (specify):

18. Do you know yourself why you stole?

☐ I don't know.
☐ from lack of money
☐ for fun, tension, kicks
☐ from miserliness (to save own money)
☐ to get hold of some food
☐ an irresistible urge, a "sick" inclination
☐ from protest, anger, to avenge myself
☐ other reason (specify):

19. Do you think that this subject should be discussed or get special attention during the treatment/therapy of an eating disorder?

☐ It is very important; it should be discussed.
☐ It is important; discussing it might be useful.
☐ It is not essential; it should not be discussed.
☐ It is of no importance; discussing it is useless.
☐ I don't know.

20. Do you think that stealing (or the urge to steal) has anything to do with an eating disorder (anorexia/bulimia)?

☐ I don't know.
☐ No, it has nothing to do with it.
☐ This might be possible.
☐ Definitely (explain why):

Any comments or remarks concerning this questionnaire:

APPENDIX D

SELF-INJURY QUESTIONNAIRE (SIQ)

When people are tense, they try to work off the tension several ways. You may do this by one or more of the following acts. Please answer each question by detailing whether you have done any of those things during the last six months.

Circle one number on each line.

> 1 = never
> 2 = now and then
> 3 = regularly
> 4 = very often

What do you do when you are very tense?

1. I jog or walk.	1	2	3	4
2. I tire myself out with something.	1	2	3	4
3. I eat sweets.	1	2	3	4
4. I drink alcohol.	1	2	3	4
5. I take a sedative pill.	1	2	3	4
6. I bite my nails.	1	2	3	4
7. I pick the skin around my nails.	1	2	3	4
8. I pull out my hair.	1	2	3	4
9. I scratch myself.	1	2	3	4
10. I squeeze pimples.	1	2	3	4
11. I scratch my skin with an object.	1	2	3	4
12. I cut myself.	1	2	3	4
13. I prick myself with a needle.	1	2	3	4

14. I pinch myself until I bleed.	1	2	3	4
15. I burn myself with a cigarette.	1	2	3	4
16. I beat my head against the wall.	1	2	3	4
17. I beat or hit myself.	1	2	3	4
18. I punch something.	1	2	3	4
19. I throw something.	1	2	3	4
20. I beat or punch someone else.	1	2	3	4

Reactions or habits

Check whether the following applied to you during the last six months.

> 1 = not applicable to me
> 2 = a little or sometimes applicable
> 3 = often or regularly applicable
> 4 = very applicable to me

21. When I have a superficial wound some-where, I can hardly keep my hands away from it.	1	2	3	4
22. When a sharp object is in the vicinity, I feel the inclination to cut or scratch myself.	1	2	3	4
23. When I feel angry, I am inclined to work this feeling off on myself.	1	2	3	4
24. I cannot stand a scab or a lump on my skin so I scratch it.	1	2	3	4
25. When I am nervous, I collide with or bump easily into things.	1	2	3	4
26. When I am in a hurry, I often cut or hurt myself but unintentionally.	1	2	3	4

27. When I am furious, I feel like causing someone an injury.   1   2   3   4

28. I may lose my temper or become angry for something trivial.   1   2   3   4

29. I feel the need to punish myself.   1   2   3   4

30. When I feel pain, I think that I should learn to bear it.   1   2   3   4

31. I may intentionally torment myself physically to punish myself.   1   2   3   4

32. Tormenting myself physically may offer satisfaction or enjoyment.   1   2   3   4

33. I hurt myself to show others that something is wrong.   1   2   3   4

34. I hide some scars to avoid explaining this to others.   1   2   3   4

Intentional self-injury

Did you do one of the following things over the last 12 months?

1. Pulling out hair:

☐ NO
☐ YES

Number of times:
_____ a day   or   _____ a week   or   _____ a month

Is it painful?

☐ not at all   ☐ slightly   ☐ moderately   ☐ extremely

When does it occur?

☐ when I am nervous
☐ when I am bored
☐ when I am angry

☐ when I am dejected
☐ when I am afraid
☐ when I am/feel (specify):

2. *Scratching myself until it bleeds:*

☐ NO
☐ YES

Number of times:

_____ a day   or   _____ a week   or   _____ a month

Is it painful?

☐ not at all   ☐ slightly   ☐ moderately   ☐ extremely

When does it occur?

☐ when I am nervous
☐ when I am bored
☐ when I am angry
☐ when I am dejected
☐ when I am afraid
☐ when I am/feel (specify):

3. *Bruising myself intentionally (bruises, bumps)*

☐ NO
☐ YES

Number of times:

_____ a day   or   _____ a week   or   _____ a month

Is it painful?

☐ not at all   ☐ slightly   ☐ moderately   ☐ extremely

When does it occur?

☐ when I am nervous
☐ when I am bored

☐ when I am angry
☐ when I am dejected
☐ when I am afraid
☐ when I am/feel (specify):

4. *Cutting or prodding myself intentionally:*

☐ NO
☐ YES

Number of times:

_____ a day   or   _____ a week   or   _____ a month

Is it painful?

☐ not at all   ☐ slightly   ☐ moderately   ☐ extremely

When does it occur?

☐ when I am nervous
☐ when I am bored
☐ when I am angry
☐ when I am dejected
☐ when I am afraid
☐ when I am/feel (specify):

5. *Burning myself intentionally:*

☐ NO
☐ YES

Number of times:

_____ a day   or   _____ a week   or   _____ a month

Is it painful?

☐ not at all   ☐ slightly   ☐ moderately   ☐ extremely

When does it occur?

☐ when I am nervous
☐ when I am bored

☐ when I am angry
☐ when I am dejected
☐ when I am afraid
☐ when I am/feel (specify):

If you have answered YES to one or more of the previous five questions, please also answer the following:

How long has this self-injury been going on?

☐ less than a month
☐ between 1 and 6 months
☐ between 6 months and 1 year
☐ between 1 and 5 years
☐ more than 5 years

How old were you when it occurred for the first time?

I was _____ years old

Which parts of the body have been hurt most?

☐ head, throat, neck
☐ arms, hands
☐ trunk, belly, buttocks
☐ legs, feet
☐ genitals, breasts

When self-injury occurs, how does it happen?

☐ suddenly, unexpectedly
☐ like an urge I cannot restrain
☐ like something I have planned
☐ I do not know afterwards how it happened

References and Readings

LIST I: TRAUMA, DISSOCIATION, AND HYPNOSIS IN EATING DISORDERS

Abramson, E.E., & Lucido, G.M. (1991). Childhood sexual experiences and bulimia. *Addictive Behaviors, 16,* 529–532.

Andrews, B., Valentine, E.R., & Valentine, J.D. (1995). Depression and eating disorders following abuse in childhood in two generations of women. *British Journal of Clinical Psychology, 34,* 37–52.

Bailey, C.A., & Gibbons, S.J. (1989). Physical victimization and bulimic-like symptoms: Is there a relationship? *Deviant Behavior, 10,* 335–352.

Baker, E.L., & Nash, M.R. (1987). Applications of hypnosis in the treatment of anorexia nervosa. *American Journal of Clinical Hypnosis, 29,* 185–193.

Barabasz, M. (1991). Hypnotizability in bulimia. *International Journal of Eating Disorders, 10,* 117–120.

Beckman, K.A., & Burns, G.L. (1990). Relation of sexual abuse and bulimia in college women. *International Journal of Eating Disorders, 5,* 487–492.

Berger, D., Ono, Y., Saito, S., Tezuka, I., Takahashi, Y., Uno, M., Ishikawa, Y., Kuboki, T., Asai, M., & Suematsu, H. (1995). Relationship of parental bonding to child abuse and dissociation in eating disorders in Japan. *Acta Psychiatrica Scandinavica, 91,* 278–282.

Berger, D., Saito, S., Ono, Y., Tezuka, I., Shirahase, J., Kuboki, T., & Sue-matsu, H. (1994). Dissociation and child abuse histories in an eating disorder cohort in Japan. *Acta Psychiatrica Scandinavica, 90,* 274–280.

Birnie, C.R. (1936). Anorexia nervosa treated by hypnosis in outpatient practice. *Lancet, 2,* 1331.

Brenman, M., & Knight, P. (1945). Self-starvation and compulsive hopping with paradoxical reaction to hypnosis. *American Journal of Orthopsychiatry, 15,* 65.

Bulik, C.M., Sullivan, P.F., & Rorty, (1989). Childhood sexual abuse in women with bulimia. *Journal of Clinical Psychiatry, 50,* 460–464.

Calam, R. D., & Slade, P.D. (1987). Eating problems and sexual experience: Some relationships. *British Review of Bulimia and Anorexia Nervosa, 2,* 37–43.

Calam, R.D., & Slade, P. (1989). Sexual experiences and eating problems in female undergraduates. *International Journal of Eating Disorders, 8,* 391–397.

Calam, R., & Slade, P. (1994). Eating patterns and unwanted sexual experiences. In B. Dolan & I. Gitzinger (Eds.), *Why women? Gender issues and eating disorders* (pp. 101–109). London: Athlone Press.

Calof, D.L. (1986). Brief hypnotherapy in a case of bulimia nervosa. In E.T. Dowd & J.M. Healy (Eds.), *Case studies in hypnotherapy* (pp. 147–165). New York: Guilford Press.

Chandarana, P., & Malla, A. (1989). Bulimia and dissociative states: A case report. *Canadian Journal of Psychiatry, 34,* 137–139.

Channon, L.D. (1981). Modification of the affect-bridge technique in weight control. *Australian Journal of Clinical and Experimental Hypnosis, 9,* 42–43.

Collins, J.K. (1985). Hypnosis, body image, and weight control. In S.W. Touyz & P.J.V. Beumont (Eds.), *Eating disorders: Prevalence and treatment* (pp. 105–116). Sydney: Williams & Wilkins.

Coman, G.J. (1992). Hypnosis in the treatment of bulimia: A review of the literature. *Australian Journal of Clinical and Experimental Hypnosis, 20,* 89–104.

Coman, G.J., & Evans, B.J. (1995). Clinical update on eating disorders and obesity: Implications for treatment with hypnosis. *Australian Journal of Clinical and Experimental Hypnosis, 23,* 1–13.

Connors, M.E., & Morse, W. (1993). Sexual abuse and eating disorders. *International Journal of Eating Disorders, 13,* 1–11.

Council, J.R. (1986). Exploring the interface of personality and health: Anorexia nervosa, bulimia, and hypnotic susceptibility. *Behavioral Medicine Abstracts, 7,* 165–168.

Covino, N.A., Jimerson, D.C., Wolfe, B.E., Franko, D.L., & Frankel, F.H. (1994). Hypnotizability, dissociation, and bulimia nervosa. *Journal of Abnormal Psychology, 103*, 455–459.

Dalle Grave, R., Rigamonti, R., & Todisco, P. (1995). Trauma and dissociative experiences in eating disorders. Paper presented at the Fifth Annual Spring Conference of the International Society for the Study of Dissociation, Amsterdam.

Damlouji, N.F., & Ferguson, J.M. (1985). Three cases of post-traumatic anorexia nervosa. *American Journal of Psychiatry, 142*, 362–363.

Davis, H.K. (1961). Anorexia nervosa treatment with hypnosis and ECT. *Diseases of the Nervous System, 22*, 627–631.

DeGroot, J.M., Kennedy, S., Rodin, G., & McVey, G. (1992). Correlates of sexual abuse in women with anorexia nervosa and bulimia nervosa. *Canadian Journal of Psychiatry, 37*, 516–518.

Delay, J. (1949). La narco-analyse d'une anorexie mentale [Narco-analysis in a case of anorexia nervosa]. *La Presse Médicale, 59*, 577.

Demitrack, M.A., Putnam, F.W., Brewerton, T.D., Brandt, H.A., & Gold, P.W. (1990). Relation of clinical variables to dissociative phenomena in eating disorders. *American Journal of Psychiatry, 147*, 1184–1188.

Douzinas, N., Fornari, V., Goodman, B., Sitnick, T., & Packman, L. (1994). Eating disorders and abuse. *Child and Adolescent Psychiatric Clinics of North America, 3*, 777–798.

Erickson, M. (1985). The case of Barbie: An Ericksonian approach to the treatment of anorexia nervosa. *Transactional Analysis Journal, 15*, 85–92. (Reprinted from *A teaching seminar with Milton H. Erickson*, J. K. Zeig, Ed., 1980, New York: Brunner/Mazel.)

Erickson, M.H., & Rossi, E.L. (1979). Anorexia nervosa: Paradox and double bind. In M.H. Erickson & E.L. Rossi, *Hypnotherapy: An exploratory casebook* (pp. 268–281). New York: John Wiley.

Everill, T.J., & Waller, G. (1995). Dissociation and bulimia: Research and theory. *European Eating Disorders Review, 3*, 129–147.

Everill, T. J., Waller, G., & Macdonald, W. (1995). Dissociation in bulimic and non-eating-disordered women. *International Journal of Eating Disorders, 17*, 127–134.

Fallon, B.A., Sadik, C., Saoud, J.B., & Garfinkel, R.S. (1994). Childhood abuse, family environment, and outcome in bulimia nervosa. *Journal of Clinical Psychiatry, 55*, 424–428.

Favaro, A., & Santonastaso, P. (1995). Dissociative experiences, trauma and eating disorders in a female college sample. *European Eating Disorders Review, 3*, 196–200.

Finn, S., Hartman, M., Leon, G., & Lawson, L. (1986). Eating disorders and sexual abuse: Lack of confirmation for a clinical hypothesis. *International Journal of Eating Disorders, 5*, 1051–1060.

Folsom, V., Krahn, D., Nairn, K., Gold, L., Demitrack, M.A., & Silk, K.R. (1993). The impact of sexual abuse and physical abuse on eating disordered and psychiatric symptoms: A comparison of eating disordered and psychiatric inpatients. *International Journal of Eating Disorders, 13*, 249–257.

Fullerton, D.T., Wonderlich, S.A., & Gosnell, B.A. (1995). Clinical characteristics of eating disorder patients who report sexual or physical abuse. *International Journal of Eating Disorders, 17*, 243–249.

Georgiou, E. (1995). Hypnotherapy in the treatment of anorexia tardive. *Australian Journal of Clinical and Experimental Hypnosis, 23*, 14–24.

Gleaves, D.H., & Eberenz, K.P. (1994). Sexual abuse histories among treatment-resistant bulimia nervosa patients. *International Journal of Eating Disorders, 15*, 227–231.

Godfrey, J.M. (1992). Eating disorder and childhood sexual abuse [Letter to the editor]. *British Journal of Psychiatry, 160*, 563 (reply by G. Waller, p. 564).

Goldfarb, L. (1987). Sexual abuse antecedent to anorexia nervosa, bulimia and compulsive overeating: Three case reports. *International Journal of Eating Disorders, 6*, 675–680.

Goldner, E.M., Cockhill, L.A., Bakan, R., & Birmingham, C.L. (1991). Dissociative experiences in eating disorders. *American Journal of Psychiatry, 148*, 1274–1275.

Goodwin, J.M., & Attias, R. (1993). Eating disorders in survivors of multimodal childhood abuse. In R.P. Kluft & C.G. Fine (Eds.), *Clinical perspectives on multiple personality disorder* (pp. 327–341). Washington, D.C.: American Psychiatric Press.

Gotterfeld, B., & Novaes, A. (1945). Narco-analysis and subshock insulin in the treatment of anorexia nervosa. *Digest of Neurology and Psychiatry, 13*, 486–494.

Greenes, D., Fava, M., Cioffi, J., & Herzog, D. (1993). The relationship of depression to dissociation in patients with bulimia nervosa. *Journal of Psychiatric Research, 27*, 133–137.

Griffiths, R.A. (1995). Hypnobehavioural treatment for bulimia nervosa: A treatment manual. *Australian Journal of Clinical and Experimental Hypnosis, 23*, 25–40.

Griffiths, R.A. (1989). Hypnobehavioral treatment of bulimia nervosa: Preliminary findings. *Australian Journal of Clinical and Experimental Hypnosis, 17*, 79–87.

Griffiths, R.A., & Channon-Little, L.D. (1995). Dissociation, dieting disorders and hypnosis: A review. *European Eating Disorders Review, 3,* 148–159.

Griffiths, R.A., Hadzi-Pavlovic, D., & Channon-Little, L. (1994). A controlled evaluation of hypnobehavioural treatment for bulimia nervosa: Immediate pre-post treatment effects. *European Eating Disorders Review, 2,* 202–220.

Griffiths, R.A., Hadzi-Pavlovic, D., & Channon-Little, L. (1996). The short-term follow-up effects of hypnobehavioural and cognitive behavioural treatment for bulimia nervosa. *European Eating Disorders Review, 4,* 12–31.

Gross, M. (1982a). Hypnosis in the treatment of anorexia nervosa [abstract]. *International Journal of Clinical and Experimental Hypnosis, 30,* 332.

Gross, M. (1982b). Hypnotherapy in anorexia nervosa. In M. Gross (Ed.), *Anorexia nervosa: A comprehensive approach* (pp. 119–127). Lexington, MA: Collamore Press.

Gross, M. (1983a). Hypnoanalytic approach to bulimia. *Medical Hypno-Analysis, 4,* 77–82.

Gross, M. (1983b). Correcting perceptual abnormalities, anorexia nervosa and obesity by use of hypnosis. *Journal of the American Society of Psychosomatic Dentistry and Medicine, 30,* 142–150.

Gross, M. (1984). Hypnosis in the therapy of anorexia nervosa. *American Journal of Clinical Hypnosis, 26,* 175–181.

Gross, M. (1986). Use of hypnosis in eating disorders. In F.E.F. Larocca (Ed.), *Eating disorders* (pp. 109–118). San Francisco: Jossey-Bass.

Groth-Marnat, G., & Schumaker, J.F. (1990). Hypnotizability, attitudes towards eating, and concern with body size in a female college population. *American Journal of Clinical Hypnosis, 32,* 194–200.

Gutwill, S. (1994). Eating problems in patients with multiple personality disorder. In C. Bloom, A. Gitter, S. Gutwill, L. Kogel, & L. Zaphiropoulos (Eds.), *Eating problems. A feminist psychoanalytic treatment model* (pp. 227–242). New York: Basic Books.

Gutwill, S., & Gitter, A. (1994a). Eating problems and sexual abuse: Theoretical considerations. In C. Bloom, A. Gitter, S. Gutwill, L. Kogel, & L. Zaphiropoulos (Eds.), *Eating problems. A feminist psychoanalytic treatment model* (pp. 184–204). New York: Basic Books.

Gutwill, S., & Gitter, A. (1994b). Eating problems and sexual abuse: Treatment considerations. In C. Bloom, A. Gitter, S. Gutwill, L. Kogel, & L. Zaphiropoulos (Eds.), *Eating problems. A feminist psychoanalytic treatment model* (pp. 205–226). New York: Basic Books.

Hall, J.R., & McGill, J.C. (1986). Hypnobehavioral treatment of self-destructive behavior: Trichotillomania and bulimia in the same patient. *American Journal of Clinical Hypnosis, 29,* 39–46.

Hall, R.C.W., Tice, L., Beresford, T.P., Wooley, B., & Hall, A.K. (1989). Sexual abuse in patients with anorexia nervosa and bulimia. *Psychosomatics, 30,* 73–79.

Hambidge, D.M. (1988). Incest and anorexia nervosa: What is the link? [Letter to the editor]. *British Journal of Psychiatry, 152,* 145–146.

Hartland, J. (1971). Hypnosis in anorexia nervosa. In J. Hartland, *Medical and dental hypnosis and its clinical application* (pp. 265–268). London: Baillière Tindall.

Hastings, T., & Kern, J.M. (1994). Relationship between bulimia, childhood sexual abuse, and family environment. *International Journal of Eating Disorders, 15,* 103–111.

Herzog, D.B., Stoley, J.E., Carmody, S., Robbins, W.M., & van der Kolk, B.A. (1993). Childhood sexual abuse in anorexia nervosa and bulimia nervosa: A pilot study. *Journal of the American Academy of Child & Adolescent Psychiatry, 32,* 962–966.

Holgate, R. (1984). Hypnosis in the treatment of bulimia nervosa: A case study. *Australian Journal of Clinical and Experimental Hypnosis, 12,* 105–112.

Jackson, C., & Davidson, G. (1986). The anorexic patient as a survivor: The denial of death and death themes in the literature on anorexia nervosa. *International Journal of Eating Disorders, 5,* 821–835.

Kaffman, M. (1981). Monoideism in psychiatry: Theoretical and clinical implications. *American Journal of Psychotherapy, 35,* 235–243.

Kaffman, M. (1991). Monoideistic disorders and the process of suggestion: Anorexia nervosa as a paradigm. In J.F. Schumaker (Ed.), *Human suggestibility. Advances in theory, research, and application* (pp. 289–308). New York: Routledge.

Kaffman, M., & Sadeh, T. (1989). Anorexia nervosa in the kibbutz: Factors influencing the development of a monoideistic fixation. *International Journal of Eating Disorders, 8,* 33–54.

Kaner, A., Bulik, C.M., & Sullivan, P.F. (1993). Abuse in adult relationships of bulimic women. *Journal of Interpersonal Violence, 8,* 52–63.

Katz, B.E. (in press-a). Autohypnosis, hypnotic aneasthesias, hypnoid states, hidden ego states, depersonalization and other dissociative phenomena underlying anorexia nervosa and bulimia nervosa case studies: methods of treatment. *Dissociation.*

Katz, B.E. (in press-b). Dissociative symptoms among patients with eating disorders: Associated feature or artefact of a comorbid dissociative disorder? *Dissociation.*

Kearney-Cooke, A. (1988). Group treatment of sexual abuse among women with eating disorders. *Women and Therapy, 7,* 5–22.

Kearney-Cooke, A., & Striegel-Moore, R.H. (1994). Treatment of childhood sexual abuse in anorexia nervosa and bulimia nervosa: A feminist psychodynamic approach. *International Journal of Eating Disorders, 15,* 305–319.

Kinzl, J.F., Traweger, C., Guenther, V., & Biebl, W. (1994). Family background and sexual abuse associated with eating disorders. *American Journal of Psychiatry, 151,* 1127–1131.

Kranhold, C., Baumann, U., & Fichter, M. (1992). Hypnotizability in bulimic patients and controls: A pilot study. *European Archives of Psychiatry and Clinical Neuroscience, 242,* 72–76.

Lacey, J.H. (1990). Incest, incestuous fantasy & indecency: A clinical catchment area study of normal-weight bulimic women. *British Journal of Psychiatry, 157,* 399–403.

Levin, A.P., & Spauster, E. (1994). Inpatient cognitive-behavioral treatment of eating disorder patients with dissociative disorders. *Dissociation, 7,* 178–184.

Loiselle, R.H. (1993). Sexual abuse and its relationship to eating disorders. In A.J. Giannini & A.E. Slaby (Eds.), *The eating disorders* (pp. 128–132). New York: Springer-Verlag.

Lynn, S.J., Eisen, M.R., Horevitz, R., Araoz, D.L., Zeig, J.K., Garske, J.P., et al. (1991). Perspectives on clinical hypnosis in the treatment of anorexia nervosa. *Contemporary Hypnosis, 8*(2), 63–93.

McCallum, K.F., Lock, J., Kulla, M., Rorty, M., & Wetzel, R.D.(1992). Dissociative symptoms and disorders in patients with eating disorders. *Dissociation, 5,* 227–235.

McCarthy, M.K., Goff, D.C., Baer, L., Cioffi, J., & Herzog, D.B. (1994). Dissociation, childhood trauma, and the response to fluoxetine in bulimic patients. *International Journal of Eating Disorders, 15,* 219–226.

McClelland, L., Mynors-Wallis, L., Fahy, T., & Treasure, J. (1991). Sexual abuse, disordered personality and eating disorders. *British Journal of Psychiatry, 158* (Suppl. 10), 63–68.

McFarlane, A.C., McFarlane, C., & Gilchrist, P.N. (1988).Post-traumatic bulimia and anorexia nervosa. *International Journal of Eating Disorders, 7,* 705–708.

McGillicuddy, P., & Maze, S. (1993). Women embodied and emboldened: Dealing with sexual violence. In C. Brown & K. Jasper (Eds.), *Consum-*

ing passions: Feminist approaches to weight preoccupation and eating disorders (pp. 219–234). Toronto: Second Story Press.

McManus, F. (1995). Dissociation and the severity of bulimic psychopathology among eating-disordered and non-eating-disordered women. *European Eating Disorders Review, 3,* 185–194.

Mehler, P.S., & Weiner, K.L. (1993). Medical presentations of covert sexual abuse in eating disorder patients. *Eating Disorders, 1,* 259–263.

Meignant, P. (1948). Anorexie mentale guérie par narcoanalyse [Anorexia nervosa healed by narcoanalysis]. *Revue Medicale de Nancy, 73,* 180.

Miller, D.A.F., & McCluskey-Fawcett, K. (1993). The relationship between childhood sexual abuse and subsequent onset of bulimia nervosa. *Child Abuse and Neglect, 17,* 305–314.

Miller, K.J. (1993). Prevalence and process of disclosure of childhood sexual abuse among eating-disordered women. *Eating Disorders, 1,* 211–225.

Mizes, J.S., & Fleece, E.L. (1986). On the use of progressive relaxation in the treatment of bulimia: A single subject design study. *International Journal of Eating Disorders, 5,* 169–176.

Oppenheimer, R., Howells, K., Palmer, L., & Chaloner, D. (1985). Adverse sexual experiences in childhood and clinical eating disorders: A preliminary description. *Journal of Psychiatric Research, 19,* 157–161.

Palmer, R. (1995). Sexual abuse and eating disorders. In K.D. Brownell & C.G. Fairburn (Eds.), *Eating disorders and obesity: A comprehensive handbook* (pp. 230–233). New York: Guilford Press.

Palmer, R.L., & Oppenheimer, R. (1992). Childhood sexual experiences with adults: A comparison of women with eating disorders and those with other diagnoses. *International Journal of Eating Disorders, 12,* 359–364.

Palmer, R.L., Oppenheimer, R., Dignon, A., Chaloner, D., & Howells, K. (1990). Childhood sexual experiences with adults reported by women with eating disorders: An extended series. *British Journal of Psychiatry, 156,* 699–703.

Perry, P.J. (1992). Sexual abuse groups. In H. Harper-Giuffre & K.R. MacKenzie (Eds.), *Group psychotherapy for eating disorders* (pp. 217–230). Washington, DC: American Psychiatric Press.

Pettinati, H.M., Horne, R.J., & Staats, J.M. (1982). Hypnotizability of anorexia and bulimia patients [Abstract]. *International Journal of Clinical and Experimental Hypnosis, 30,* 332.

Pettinati, H.M., Horne, R.J., & Staats, J.M. (1985). Hypnotizability in patients with anorexia nervosa and bulimia. *Archives of General Psychiatry, 42,* 1014–1016.

Pettinati, H.M., Kogan, L.G., Margolis, C., Schrier, L., & Wade, I.H. (1989). Hypnosis, hypnotizability and the bulimic patient. In E.K. Baker & L.M Hornyak (Eds.), *Handbook of experiential techniques in the treatment of eating disorders* (pp. 34–59). New York: Guilford Press.

Pettinati, H.M., & Wade, J.H. (1986). Hypnosis in the treatment of anorexic and bulimic patients. *Seminars in Adolescent Medicine, 2,* 75–79.

Pitts, C., & Waller, G. (1993). Self-denigratory beliefs following sexual abuse: Association with the symptomatology of bulimic disorders. *International Journal of Eating Disorders, 13,* 407–410.

Pope, H.G., & Hudson, J.I. (1992). Is childhood sexual abuse a risk factor for bulimia nervosa? *American Journal of Psychiatry, 149,* 455–463.

Pope, H.G., & Hudson, J.I. (1996). "Recovered memory" therapy for eating disorders: Implications of the Ramona verdict. *International Journal of Eating Disorders, 19,* 139–146.

Pope, H.G., Hudson, J.I., & Mialet, J.P. (1985). Bulimia in the late nineteenth century: The observations of Pierre Janet. *Psychological Medicine, 15,* 739–743.

Pope, H.G., Mangweth, B., Brooking Negrão, A., Hudson, J.I., & Athanássios Cordás, T. (1994). Childhood sexual abuse and bulimia nervosa: A comparison of American, Austrian, and Brazilian women. *American Journal of Psychiatry, 151,* 732–737.

Reto, C.S., Dalenberg, C.J., & Coe, M.T. (1993). Dissociation and physical abuse as predictors of bulimic symptomatology and impulse dysregulation. *Eating Disorders, 1,* 226–239.

Rogers, P.J. (1994). Sexual abuse and eating disorders: A possible connection indicated through music therapy? In D. Dokter (Ed.), *Arts therapies and clients with eating disorders* (pp. 262–278). London: Jessica Kingsley Publishers.

Root, M.P. (1991). Persistent, disordered eating as a gender-specific, posttraumatic stress response to sexual assault. *Psychotherapy, 28,* 96–102.

Root, M.P., & Fallon, P. (1988). The incidence of victimization experiences in a bulimic sample. *Journal of Interpersonal Violence, 3,* 161–173.

Root, M.P., & Fallon, P. (1989). Treating the victimized bulimic: The functions of binge-purge behavior. *Journal of Interpersonal Violence, 4,* 90–100.

Rorty, M., & Yager, J. (1993). Speculations on the role of childhood abuse in the development of eating disorders among women. *Eating Disorders, 1,* 199–210.

Rorty, M., Yager, J., & Rossotto, E. (1994a). Childhood sexual, physical, and psychological abuse in bulimia nervosa. *American Journal of Psychiatry, 151,* 1122–1126.

Rorty, M., Yager, J., & Rossotto, E. (1994b). Childhood sexual, physical, and psychological abuse and their relationship to comorbid psychopathology in bulimia nervosa. *International Journal of Eating Disorders, 16,* 317–334.

Rosen, E.F., & Petty, L.C. (1994). Dissociative states and disordered eating. *American Journal of Clinical Hypnosis, 36,* 266–275.

Schaaf, K.K., & McCanne, T.R. (1994). Childhood abuse, body image disturbance, and eating disorders. *Child Abuse & Neglect, 18,* 607–615.

Schechter, I.D., Schwarts, H.P., & Greenfeld, D.G. (1987). Sexual assault and anorexia nervosa. *International Journal of Eating Disorders, 6,* 313–316.

Schmidt, U., Slone, G., Tiller, J., & Treasure, J. (1993). Childhood adversity and adult defense style in eating disorder patients: A controlled study. *British Journal of Medical Psychology, 66,* 353–362.

Schmidt, U., Tiller, J., & Treasure, J. (1993). Setting the scene for eating disorders: Childhood care, classification and course of illness. *Psychological Medicine, 23,* 663–672.

Schumaker, J.F. (1990). Thinness: An unlikely god. In J.F. Schumaker, *Wings of illusion: The origin, nature, and future of paranormal belief* (pp. 111–124). Cambridge: Polity Press.

Schumaker, J.F., & Groth-Marnat, G. (1988). The role of suggestibility in the understanding and treatment of anorexia nervosa. *Corrective and Social Psychiatry, 35,* 24–27.

Schumaker, J.F., Warren, W.G., Schreiber, G.S., & Jackson, C.G. (1994). Dissociation in anorexia nervosa and bulimia nervosa. *Social Behavior and Personality, 22,* 385–392.

Schwartz, M.F., & Gay, P. (1993). Physical and sexual abuse and neglect and eating disorder symptoms. *Eating Disorders, 1,* 265–281.

Scott, D.W. (1987). The involvement of psychosexual factors in the causation of eating disorders: Time for a reappraisal. *International Journal of Eating Disorders, 6,* 199–213.

Scott, R., & Thoner, G. (1986). Ego deficits in anorexia nervosa patients and incest victims: An MMPI comparative analysis. *Psychological Reports, 58,* 829–846.

Scouras, P. (1959). Anorexie mentale d'origine complexuelle: Action combinée de l'electrochoc et de la narco-analyse [Anorexia nervosa of complex origin: Combined action of electroshock and narco-analysis]. *Encéphale, 39,* 545–553.

Sloan, G., & Leichner, P. (1986). Is there a relationship between sexual abuse or incest and eating disorders? *Canadian Journal of Psychiatry, 31,* 656–660.

Smolak, L., Levine, M., & Sullins, E. (1990). Are child sexual experiences related to eating-disordered attitudes and behaviors in a college sample? *International Journal of Eating Disorders, 9*, 167–178.

Solursh, L.P., Bissett, A.D., & Fournier, J.A.A. (1990). Bulimia associated with sexual trauma [Letter to the editor]. *American Journal of Psychiatry, 147*, 373.

Steiger, H., & Zanko, M. (1990). Sexual traumata among eating-disordered, psychiatric and normal female groups. *Journal of Interpersonal Violence, 5*, 74–86.

Stermac, L., Piran, N., & Sheridan, P.M. (1993). Sexual abuse, eating disorders, and prevention: Political and social realities. *Eating Disorders, 1*, 250–258.

Sullivan, P.F., Bulik, C.M., Carter, F.A., & Joyce, P.R. (1995). The significance of a history of childhood sexual abuse in bulimia nervosa. *British Journal of Psychiatry, 167*, 679–682.

Thackwray, D.E., Smith, M.C., & Bodfish, J. (1991). Unsolicited reports of sexual abuse in a comparative study of treatments for bulimia [Letter to the editor]. *American Journal of Psychiatry, 148*, 1754.

Thakur, K. S. (1980). Treatment of anorexia nervosa with hypnotherapy. In H.T. Wain (Ed.), *Clinical hypnosis in medicine* (pp. 147–163). Chicago: Year Book Medical Publishers.

Thakur, K. S. (1984). Hypnotherapy for anorexia nervosa and accompanying somatic disorders. In W.C. Wester & A.H. Smith (Eds.), *Clinical hypnosis: A multidisciplinary approach* (pp. 476–493). Philadelphia: J.P. Lippincott.

Thiessen, T. (1983). Using fairy tales during hypnotherapy in bulimarexia and other psychological problems. *Medical Hypnoanalysis, 4*, 139–144.

Tobin, D.L. (1995). Treatment of early trauma and dissociation in eating disorders of late onset. *European Eating Disorders Review, 3*, 160–173.

Torem, M.S. (1986a). Dissociative states presenting as an eating disorder. *American Journal of Clinical Hypnosis, 29*, 137–142.

Torem, M.S. (1986b). Eating disorders and dissociative states. In F.E.F. Larocca (Ed.), *Eating disorders: Effective care and treatment* (pp. 141–150). Saint Louis, MO: Ishiaky Euro-America.

Torem, M.S. (1986c). Psychodynamic ego-state therapy for eating disorders. *New Directions for Mental Health Services, 31*, 99–107.

Torem, M.S. (1987). Ego-state therapy for eating disorders. *American Journal of Clinical Hypnosis, 30*, 94–103.

Torem, M.S. (1990). Covert multiple personality underlying eating disorders. *American Journal of Psychotherapy, 44*, 357–368.

Torem, M.S. (1991). Eating disorders. In W.C. Wester & D.J. O'Grady (Eds.), *Clinical hypnosis with children* (pp. 230–260). New York: Brunner/Mazel.

Torem, M.S. (1992). The use of hypnosis with eating disorders. *Psychiatric Medicine, 10,* 105–118.

Torem, M.S. (1993). Eating disorders in patients with multiple personality disorder. In R.P. Kluft & C.G. Fine (Eds.), *Clinical perspectives on multiple personality disorder* (pp. 343–353). Washington, DC: American Psychiatric Press.

Tury, F. (1991). *Hypnotizability in bulimics.* Paper presented at the Second Meeting of the European Council on Eating Disorders, Leuven, Belgium.

Tury, F., & Szabo, P. (1990). Hypnotherapy in a special dissociative state: Nocturnal bulimia. A case study. *Hypnos, 13,* 155–161.

Valdiserri, S., & Kihlstrom, J.F. (1995). Abnormal eating and dissociative experiences. *International Journal of Eating Disorders, 17,* 373–380.

Vanderlinden, J. (1993). *Dissociative experiences, trauma and hypnosis: Research findings and clinical applications in eating disorders.* Delft: Eburon.

Vanderlinden, J., Spinhoven, P., Vandereycken, W., & Van Dyck, R. (1995). Dissociative and hypnotic experiences in eating disorders: An exploratory study. *American Journal of Clinical Hypnosis, 38,* 25–36.

Vanderlinden, J., & Vandereycken, W. (1988). The use of hypnotherapy in the treatment of eating disorders. *International Journal of Eating Disorders, 7,* 673–679.

Vanderlinden, J., & Vandereycken, W. (1990). The use of hypnosis in the treatment of bulimia nervosa. *International Journal of Clinical and Experimental Hypnosis, 38,* 101–111.

Vanderlinden, J., & Vandereycken, W. (1993). Is sexual abuse a risk factor for developing an eating disorder? *Eating Disorders, 1,* 282–286.

Vanderlinden, J., & Vandereycken, W. (1995). *Hypnose bei der Behandlung von Anorexie und Bulimie* [Hypnosis in the treatment of anorexia and bulimia]. Munich: Quintessenz.

Vanderlinden, J., Vandereycken, W., & Probst, M. (1995). Dissociative symptoms in eating disorders: A follow-up study. *European Eating Disorders Review, 3,* 174–184.

Vanderlinden, J., Vandereycken, W., & Van Dyck, R. (1995). Trauma en dissociatie bij patiënten met eetstoornissen [Trauma and dissociation in patients with eating disorders]. In O. van der Hart (Ed.), *Trauma, dissociatie en hypnose* (pp. 373–391). Amsterdam: Swets & Zeitlinger.

Vanderlinden, J., Vandereycken, W., Van Dyck, R., & Delacroix, O. (1992). Hypnotizability and dissociation in a group of fifty eating disorder patients: Preliminary findings. In W. Bongartz (Ed.), *Hypnosis: 175 years after Mesmer* (pp. 291–295). Konstanz: Universitäts-Verlag.

Vanderlinden, J., Vandereycken, W., Van Dyck, R., & Vertommen, H. (1993). Dissociative experiences and trauma in eating disorders. *International Journal of Eating Disorders, 13,* 187–194.

Waller, G. (1991). Sexual abuse as a factor in eating disorders. *British Journal of Psychiatry, 159,* 664–671.

Waller, G. (1992a). Sexual abuse and the severity of bulimic symptoms. *British Journal of Psychiatry, 161,* 90–93.

Waller, G. (1992b). Sexual abuse and bulimic symptoms in eating disorders: Do family interaction and self-esteem explain the links? *International Journal of Eating Disorders, 12,* 235–240.

Waller, G. (1993a). Sexual abuse and eating disorders: Borderline personality disorder as a mediating factor? *British Journal of Psychiatry, 162,* 771–775.

Waller, G. (1993b). Sexual abuse as a factor in anorexia nervosa: Evidence from two separate case series. *Journal of Psychosomatic Research, 37,* 1–7.

Waller, G. (1994). Childhood sexual abuse and borderline personality disorder in the eating disorders. *Child Abuse and Neglect, 18,* 97–101.

Waller, G., Everill, J., & Calam, R. (1994). Sexual abuse and the eating disorders. In L.A. Alexander-Mott & D.B. Lumsden (Eds.), *Understanding eating disorders* (pp. 77–97). London: Taylor & Francis.

Waller, G., Halek, C., & Crisp, A.H. (1993). Sexual abuse as a factor in anorexia nervosa: Evidence from two separate case series. *Journal of Psychosomatic Research, 37,* 873–879.

Waller, G., Hamilton, K., Rose, N., Sumra, J., & Baldwin, G. (1993). Sexual abuse and body-image distortion in the eating disorders. *British Journal of Clinical Psychology, 32,* 350–352.

Waller, G., & Ruddock, A. (1993). Experiences of disclosure of childhood sexual abuse and psychopathology. *Child Abuse Review, 2,* 185–195.

Waller, G., Ruddock, A., & Pitts, C. (1993). When is sexual abuse relevant to bulimic disorders? The validity of clinical judgments. *European Eating Disorders Review, 1,* 143–150.

Weene, K.A. (1993). Is childhood sexual abuse a risk factor for bulimia? [Letter to the editor]. *American Journal of Psychiatry, 150,* 357 (reply by H.G. Pope & J.I. Hudson, pp. 357–358).

Weiner, E.J., & Stephens, L. (1993). Sexual barrier weight: A new approach. *Eating Disorders, 1,* 241–249.

Welch, S.L., & Fairburn, C.G. (1994). Sexual abuse and bulimia nervosa: Three integrated case control comparisons. *American Journal of Psychiatry, 151,* 402–407.

Williams, H.J., Wagner, H.L., & Calam, R.M. (1992). Eating attitudes in survivors of unwanted sexual experiences. *British Journal of Clinical Psychology, 31,* 203–206.

Wooley, S.C. (1994). Sexual abuse and eating disorders: The concealed debate. In P. Fallon, M.A. Katzman, & S.C. Wooley (Eds.), *Feminist perspectives on eating disorders* (pp. 171–211). New York: Guilford Press.

Yapko, M.D. (1986). Hypnotic and strategic interventions in the treatment of anorexia nervosa. *American Journal of Clinical Hypnosis, 28,* 224–232.

Zerbe, K.J. (1993a). Selves that starve and suffocate: The continuum of eating disorders and dissociative phenomena. *Bulletin of the Menninger Clinic, 57,* 319–327.

Zerbe, K.J. (1993b). Swallowing anger and despair: The impact of physical and sexual abuse. In K.J. Zerbe, *The body betrayed: Women, eating disorders, and treatment* (pp. 195–222). Washington: American Psychiatric Press.

Additional References and Readings

LIST II

Banyai, F.I., Zseni, A., & Tury, F. (1993). Active-alert hypnosis in psychotherapy. In J.W. Rhue, S.J. Lynn, & J. Kirsch (Eds.), *Handbook of clinical hypnosis.* Washington, DC: American Psychological Association.

Beck, A.T., Ward, C.H., Hendelson, M., Mock, J.E., & Erbaugh, J.K. (1961). An inventory for measuring depression. *Archives of General Psychiatry, 4,* 561–571.

Benjamin, L.R., & Benjamin, R. (1992). An overview of family treatment in dissociative disorders. *Dissociation, 5,* 236–241.

Benjamin, L.R., & Benjamin, R. (1993). Interventions with children in dissociative disorders: A family treatment model. *Dissociation, 6,* 54–65.

Bernstein, E.M., Carlson, L.R., & Putnam, F. (1993). An update on the Dissociative Experiences Scale. *Dissociation, 6,* 16–27.

Bernstein, E.M., & Putnam, F. (1986). Development, reliability and validity of a dissociation scale. *Journal of Nervous and Mental Disease, 174,* 727–735.

Beumont, P.J.V., Kopec-Schrader, E., & Touyz, S.W. (1995). Defining subgroups of dieting disorder patients by means of the Eating Disorders Examination (EDE). *British Journal of Psychiatry, 166,* 472–474.

Boon, S., & Draijer, N. (1993). *Multiple personality disorder in the Netherlands: A study on reliability and validity of the diagnosis.* Amsterdam: Swets & Zeitlinger.

Braun, D.L., Sunday, R., & Halmi, K.A. (1994). Psychiatric comorbidity in patients with eating disorders. *Psychological Medicine, 24,* 859–867.

Briere, J., & Runtz, M. (1988). Symptomatology associated with childhood victimization in a nonclinical adult sample. *Child Abuse and Neglect, 12,* 51–59.

Briere, J., & Zaidi, L.Y. (1989). Sexual abuse histories and sequelae in female psychiatric emergency room patients. *American Journal of Psychiatry, 146,* 1602–1606.

Brown, D.P., & Fromm, E. (1986). *Hypnotherapy and hypnoanalysis.* Hillsdale, NJ: Erlbaum.

Carlin, A., & Ward, N. (1992). Subtypes of psychiatric inpatient women who have been sexually abused. *Journal of Nervous and Mental Disease, 180,* 392–397.

Cerney, M.S. (1995). Treating the "heroic treaters." In C.R. Figley (Ed.), *Compassion fatigue: Coping with secondary traumatic stress disorder in those who treat the traumatized* (pp. 131–149). New York: Brunner/Mazel.

Cheeck, D.D., & Le Cron, L. (1968). *Clinical hypnotherapy.* New York: Grune & Stratton.

Christenson, G.A., Faber, R.J., de Zwaan, M., Raymond, N.C., Specker, S.M., Ekern, M.D., Mackenzie, T.B., Crosby, R. D., Crow, S.J., Eckert, E.D., Mussell, M.P., & Mitchell, J.E. (1994). Compulsive buying: Descriptive characteristics and psychiatric comorbidity. *Journal of Clinical Psychiatry, 55,* 5–11.

Christenson, G.A., & Mitchell, J.E. (1991). Trichotillomania and repetitive behavior in bulimia nervosa. *International Journal of Eating Disorders, 10,* 593–598.

Conte, H., Plutchik, R., Karasu, T., & Jerret, I. (1980). The borderline syndrome index. *Journal of Nervous and Mental Disease, 168,* 428–435.

Cooper, P.J. (1995). Eating disorders and their relationship to mood and anxiety disorders. In K.D. Brownell & C.G. Fairburn (Eds.), *Eating disorders and obesity: A comprehensive handbook* (pp. 159–164). New York: Guilford Press.

Courtois, C. (1988). *Healing the incest wounds; Adult survivors in therapy.* New York: Norton.

Cross, L.W. (1993). Body and self in feminine development: Implications for eating disorders and delicate self-mutilation. *Bulletin of the Menninger Clinic, 57,* 41–68.

Crowe, M.J. (1978). Conjoint marital therapy: A controlled outcome study. *Psychological Medicine, 8,* 623–636.

Dalgard, O.S., Bjork, S., & Tambs, K. (1995). Social support, negative life events, and mental health. *British Journal of Psychiatry, 166,* 29–34.

Derogatis, L.R. (1983). *SCL-90-R administration, scoring and procedures manual II.* Towson, MD: Clinical Psychometric Research.

Derogatis, L.R., Lipman, R.S., Rickels, K., Uhlenhutz, E.H., & Covi, L. (1974). The Hopkins Symptom Check List. *Pharmacopsychotherapy, 17,* 79–110.

De Wachter, D., & Lange, F. (1996). Dissociatieve stoornissen en gezinstherapie [Dissociative disorders and family therapy]. *Tijdschrift voor Psychiatrie, 38,* 150–158.

Dolan, B., Evans, C., & Norton, K. (1993). Disordered eating behavior and attitudes in female and male patients with personality disorders. *Journal of Personality Disorders, 8,* 17–27.

Dutton, M.A., & Rubinstein, F.L. (1995). Working with people with PTSD: Research implications. In C.R. Figley (Ed.), *Compassion fatigue: Coping with secondary traumatic stress disorder in those who treat the traumatized* (pp. 82–98). New York: Brunner/Mazel.

Edelstein, E.L. (1989). *Anorexia nervosa and other dyscontrol syndromes.* Berlin: Springer-Verlag.

Edelstein, M.G. (1982). *Trauma, trance, and transformation.* New York: Brunner/Mazel.

Ensink, B. (1992). *Confusing realities: A study on child sexual abuse and psychiatric symptoms.* Amsterdam: VU University Press.

Everill, J., & Waller, G. (1995). Disclosure of sexual abuse and psychological adjustment in female undergraduates. *Child Abuse and Neglect, 19,* 93–100.

Everson, M.D., Hunter, W.M., Runyon, D.K., Edelsohn, G.A., & Coulter, M.L. (1989). Maternal support following disclosure of incest. *American Journal of Orthopsychiatry, 59,* 197–207.

Fanselow, M.S., & Lester, L.S. (1988). A functional behavioristic approach to aversively motivated behavior: Predatory imminence as a determinant of the topography of defensive behavior. In R.C. Bolles & M.D. Beecher (Eds.), *Evolution and learning* (pp. 185–212). Hillsdale, NJ: Lawrence Erlbaum Associates.

Faust, J., Runyon, M.K., & Kenny, M.C. (1995). Family variables associated with the onset and impact of intrafamilial childhood sexual abuse. *Clinical Psychology Review, 15,* 443–456.

Favazza, A.R., DeRosear, L., & Conterio, K. (1989). Self-mutilation and eating disorders. *Suicide and Life-Threatening Behavior, 19,* 352–361.

Fichter, M.M., Quadflieg, N., & Rief, W. (1994). Course of multi-impulsive bulimia. *Psychological Medicine, 24,* 591–604.

Figley, C.R. (Ed.). (1995). *Compassion fatigue: Coping with secondary traumatic stress disorder in those who treat the traumatized.* New York: Brunner/Mazel.

Finkelhor, D., & Brown, A. (1985). The traumatic impact of child sexual abuse: A conceptualization. *American Journal of Orthopsychiatry, 55,* 530–541.

Finkelhor, D., Hotaling, G., Lewis, I.A., & Smith, C. (1990). Sexual abuse in a national survey of adult men and women: Prevalence, characteristics, and risk factors. *Child Abuse and Neglect, 14,* 19–28.

Forward, S., & Buck, C. (1989). *Toxic parents.* New York: Bantam Books.

Friedrich, W.N. (1990). *Psychotherapy of sexually abused children and their families.* New York: W.W. Norton.

Garfinkel, P.E., & Gallop, R. (1992). Eating disorders and borderline personality disorder. In D. Silver & M. Rosenbluth (Eds.), *Handbook of borderline disorders* (pp. 579–598). Madison, CT: International Universities Press.

Garner, D.M. (1991). *Eating disorder inventory—2: Professional manual.* Odessa, FL: Psychological Assessment Resources.

Garner, D., & Garfinkel, P.E. (1979). The Eating Attitudes Test: An index of the symptoms of anorexia nervosa. *Psychological Medicine, 9,* 273–279.

Garner, D.M., Garner, M.V., & Rosen, L.W. (1993). Anorexia nervosa "restricters" who purge: Implications for subtyping anorexia nervosa. *International Journal of Eating Disorders, 13,* 171-185.

Goldman, M.J. (1991). Kleptomania: Making sense of the nonsensical. *American Journal of Psychiatry, 148,* 986–996.

Hawton, K. (1990). Self-cutting: Can it be prevented? In K. Hawton & P. Cowen (Eds.), *Dilemmas and difficulties in the management of psychiatric patients* (pp. 91–103). Oxford: Oxford University Press.

Herman, J.L. (1992). *Trauma and recovery.* New York: Basic Books.

Herman, J.L., Perry, C.J., & van der Kolk, B. (1989). Childhood trauma in borderline personality disorder. *American Journal of Psychiatry, 146,* 490–495.

Herzog, W., Deter, H.C., & Vandereycken, W. (Eds.) (1992). *The course of eating disorders: Long-term follow-up studies of anorexia and bulimia nervosa.* Berlin/New York: Springer-Verlag.

Hollander, E., & Stein, D. (Eds.). (1995). *Impulsivity and aggression.* Chichester: John Wiley.

Jacobs, W.J., & Nadel, L. (1985). Stress-reduced recovery of fears and phobias. *Psychological Review, 92,* 512–531.

Janet, P. (1901). *The mental state of hystericals.* New York: Putnam.

Janet, P. (1907). *The major symptoms of hysteria.* London & New York: Macmillan.

Janet, P. (1911). *L'Etat mental des hystériques* (2nd ed.). Paris: Félix Alcan.

Jehu, D. (1988). *Beyond sexual abuse: Therapy with women who were childhood victims.* Chichester: John Wiley.

Kog, E., Vertommen, H., & Vandereycken, W. (1987). Minuchin's psychosomatic family model revised. *Family Process, 26,* 235–253.

Kog, E., Vertommen, H., & Vandereycken, W. (1989). Self-report studies of family interaction in eating disorder families compared to normals. In W. Vandereycken, E. Kog, & J. Vanderlinden (Eds.), *The family approach to eating disorders. Assessment and treatment of anorexia nervosa and bulimia* (pp. 107–118). New York-London: PMA Publishing.

Krahn, D.D., Nairn, K., Gosnell, B.A., & Drewnowski, A.(1991). Stealing in eating disordered patients. *Journal of Clinical Psychiatry, 52,* 112–115.

Kroll, J. (1993). *PTSD/borderlines in therapy: Finding the balance.* New York: W.W. Norton.

Lacey, J.H. (1993). Self-damaging and addictive behaviour in bulimia nervosa. *British Journal of Psychiatry, 163,* 190–194.

Lacey, J.H., & Evans, C.D.H. (1986). The impulsivist: A multi-impulsive personality disorder. *British Journal of Addiction, 81,* 641–649.

Lange, A., Kooiman, K., Huberts, L., & van Oostendorp (1995). Childhood unwanted sexual events and degree of psychopathology of psychiatric patients: Research with a new anamnestic questionnaire (the CHUSE). *Acta Psychiatrica Scandinavica, 92,* 441–446.

Lee, S. (1994). The heterogeneity of stealing behaviors in Chinese patients with anorexia nervosa in Hong Kong. *Journal of Nervous and Mental Disease, 182,* 304–307.

Linehan, M.M. (1993). *Cognitive behavioral treatment of borderline personality disorder.* New York: Guilford Press.

Loftus, E.F., & Yapko, M.D. (1995). Psychotherapy and the recovery of repressed memories. In T. Ney (Ed.), *True and false allegations of child sexual abuse* (pp. 176–191). New York: Brunner/Mazel.

Lowe, M.R., & Eldredge, K.L. (1993). The role of impulsiveness in normal and disordered eating. In W.G. McCown, J.L. Johnson, & M.B. Shure (Eds.), *The impulsive client: Theory, research, and treatment* (pp. 185–224). Washington, DC: American Psychological Association.

Manlowe, J.L. (1995). *Faith born of seduction: Sexual trauma, body image, and religion.* New York: New York University Press.

McElroy, S.L., Hudson, J.I., Pope, H.G., & Keck, P.E. (1991). Kleptomania: Clinical characteristics and associated psychopathology. *Psychological Medicine, 21,* 93–108.

McElroy, S.L., Pope, H.G., Hudson, J.I., Keck, P.E., & White, K.L. (1991). Kleptomania: A report of 20 cases. *American Journal of Psychiatry, 148,* 652–657.

Miller, D. (1994). *Women who hurt themselves: A book of hope and understand ing.* New York: Basic Books.

Mitchell, J.E., Fletcher, L., Gibeau, L., Pyle, R.L., & Eckert, E. (1992). Shoplifting in bulimia nervosa. *Comprehensive Psychiatry, 33,* 342–345.

Nash, M.R., Hulsey, T.L., Sexton, M.C., Harralson, T.L., & Lambert, W. (1993). Long-term sequelae of childhood sexual abuse: Perceived family environment, psychopathology, and dissociation. *Journal of Consulting and Clinical Psychology, 61,* 276–283.

Ney, T. (Ed.). (1995). *True and false allegations of child sexual abuse.* New York: Brunner/Mazel.

Nijenhuis, E., van der Hart, O., & Vanderlinden, J. (1995). *Vragenlijst belastende ervaringen* [Traumatic Experiences Questionnaire]. Unpublished report, University of Amsterdam.

Nijenhuis, E.R.S., & Vanderlinden, J. (1995). Dierlijke defensieve reacties als model voor dissociatieve reacties op psychotrauma [Similarities between animal and human defense to trauma]. *Tijdschrift voor Psychiatrie, 38,* 135–149.

Norré, J., & Vandereycken, W. (1991). The limits of outpatient treatment for bulimic disorders. *British Review of Bulimia and Anorexia Nervosa, 5,* 55–63.

Norton, K.R., Crisp, A.H., & Bhat, A.V. (1985). Why do some anorexics steal? Personal, social and illness factors. *Journal of Psychiatric Research, 19,* 385–390.

Oliver, J.E. (1993). Intergenerational transmissions of child abuse rates, research, and clinical implications. *American Journal of Psychiatry, 150,* 1315–1323.

Panos, P.T., Panos, A., & Alfred, G.H. (1990). The need for marriage therapy in the treatment of multiple personality disorder. *Dissociation, 3,* 10–14.

Parker, G. (1983). *Parental overprotection.* New York: Grune & Stratton.

Porter, S., Kelly, K.A., & Grama, C.J. (1993). Family treatment of spouses and children of patients with multiple personality disorder. *Bulletin of the Menninger Clinic, 57,* 371–379.

Probst, M., Vandereycken, W., Van Coppenolle, H., & Vanderlinden, J. (1995). The Body Attitude Test for patients with an eating disorder: Psychometric characteristics of a new questionnaire. *Eating Disorders, 3,* 133–144.

Putnam, F.W. (1989). *Diagnosis and treatment of multiple personality disorder.* New York: Guilford Press.

Resick, P.A., & Snicke, M.K. (1992). Cognitive processing therapy for sexual assault victims. *Journal of Consulting and Clinical Psychology, 60,* 748–756.

Resick, P.A., & Snicke, M.K. (1993). *Cognitive processing therapy for rape victims. A treatment manual.* Newbury Park, CA: Sage Publications.

Roesler, T.A. (1994). Reactions to disclosure of childhood sexual abuse. The effects on adult symptomatology. *Journal of Nervous and Mental Disease, 182,* 618–624.

Ross, C.A. (1989). *Multiple personality disorder: Diagnosis, clinical features, and treatment.* New York: John Wiley.

Ross, C.A., Miller, S.D., Reagor, P., Bjornson, L., Fraser, G.A., & Anderson, G. (1990). Structured interview data on 102 cases of multiple personality disorder from four centers. *American Journal of Psychiatry, 147,* 596–601.

Russell, G.F.M. (1979). Bulimia nervosa: An ominous variant of anorexia nervosa. *Psychological Medicine, 9,* 429–449.

Sachs, R.G., Frischolz, E.J., & Wood, J.I. (1988). Marital and family therapy in the treatment of multiple personality disorder. *Journal of Marital and Family Therapy, 4,* 249–259.

Sainton, K., Ellason, J., Mayran, L., & Ross, C. (1993). Reliability of the new form of the Dissociative Experiences Scale (DES) and the Dissociation Questionnaire (DIS-Q). In B.G. Braun & J. Parks (Eds.), *Dissociative disorders 1993: Proceedings of 10th International Conference on Multiple Personality & Dissociative States* (p. 125). Chicago: Rush.

Sanders, S. (1986). The perceptual alteration scale: A scale measuring dissociation. *American Journal of Clinical Hypnosis, 29,* 95–102.

Schlosser, S., Black, D.W., Repertinger, S., & Freet, D. (1994). Compulsive buying: Demography, phenomenology, and comorbidity in 46 subjects. *General Hospital Psychiatry, 16,* 205–212.

Solin, C.A. (1986). Displacement of affect in families following incest disclosure. *American Journal of Orthopsychiatry, 56,* 570–576.

Steinberg, M., Cichetti, D.V., Buchanan, J., Hall, P., & Rounsaville, B. (1993). Clinical assessment of dissociative symptoms and disorders: The structured clinical interview for DSM-IV dissociative disorders. *Dissociation, 6,* 3–16.

Steinberg, M., Rounsaville, B.J., & Cichetti, D.V. (1990). The structured clinical interview for DSM-III-R dissociative disorders: Preliminary report on a new diagnostic instrument. *American Journal of Psychiatry, 147,* 76–82.

Suyemoto, K.L., & MacDonald, M.L. (1995). Self-cutting in female adolescents. *Psychotherapy, 32,* 162–171.

Terr, L.C. (1991). Childhood traumas: An outline and overview. *American Journal of Psychiatry, 148,* 10–20.

Torem, M.S. (1995). A practical approach in the treatment of self-inflicted violence. *Journal of Holistic Nursing, 13,* 37–53.

Van den Broucke, S., Vandereycken, W., & Norré J. (1997). *Eating disorders and marital relationships.* London/New York: Routledge.

Van den Broucke, S., Vertommen, H., & Vandereycken, W. (1995). Construction and validation of a marital intimacy questionnaire. *Family Relations, 44,* 285–290.

Vandereycken, W. (1992). Validity and reliability of the Anorectic Behavior Observation Scale for parents. *Acta Psychiatrica Scandinavica, 85,* 163–166.

Vandereycken, W. (1993a). The Eating Disorder Evaluation Scale (EDES). *Eating Disorders, 1,* 115–122.

Vandereycken, W. (1993b). Naughty girls and angry doctors: Eating disorder patients and their therapists. *International Review of Psychiatry, 5,* 13–18.

Vandereycken, W. (1994). Parental rearing behaviour and eating disorsers. In C. Perris, W. A. Arrindell, & M. Eisemann (Eds.), *Parenting and psychopathology* (pp. 218–234). Chichester: John Wiley..

Vandereycken, W. (1995). The families of patients with an eating disorder. In K.D. Brownell & C.G. Fairburn (Eds.), *Eating disorders and obesity* (pp. 219–223). New York: Guilford Press.

Vandereycken, W., Kog, E., & Vanderlinden, J. (1989). *The family approach to eating disorders: Assessment and treatment of anorexia nervosa and bulimia.* New York: PMA Publishing.

Vandereycken, W., & Pierloot, R. (1983). The significance of subclassification in anorexia nervosa: A comparative study of clinical features in 141 patients. *Psychological Medicine, 13,* 543–549.

Vandereycken, W., & Vanderlinden, J. (1983). Denial of illness and the use of self-reporting measures in anorexia nervosa patients. *International Journal of Eating Disorders, 2*(4), 101–107.

Vandereycken, W., & Van Vreckem, E. (1992). Siblings of patients with an eating disorder. *International Journal of Eating Disorders, 12,* 273–280.

van der Hart, O. (Ed.). (1991). *Trauma, dissociatie en hypnose* [Trauma, dissociation and hypnosis]. Lisse: Swets & Zeitlinger.

van der Kolk, B.A. (1987). *Psychological trauma.* Washington, DC: American Psychiatric Press.

van der Kolk, B.A., & van der Hart, O. (1989). Pierre Janet and the breakdown of adaptation in psychological trauma. *American Journal of Psychiatry, 146,* 1530–1540.

van der Kolk, V., Greenberg, M., Boyd, H., & Krystal, J. (1985). Inescapable shock, neurotransmitters, and addiction to trauma: Toward a psychobiology of post traumatic stress. *Biological Psychiatry, 20,* 314–325.

Vanderlinden, J., Norré, J., & Vandereycken, W. (1992). *A practical guide to the treatment of bulimia nervosa.* New York: Brunner/Mazel.

Vanderlinden, J., Van Dyck, R., Vandereycken, W., & Vertommen, H. (1993). Dissociation and traumatic experiences in the general population in the Netherlands. *Hospital and Community Psychiatry, 44,* 786–788.

Vanderlinden, J., Van Dyck, R., Vandereycken, W., Vertommen, H., & Verkes, R.J. (1993). The Dissociation Questionnaire: Development and characteristics of a new self-reporting questionnaire. *Clinical Psychology and Psychotherapy, 1,* 21–27.

Vanderlinden, J., Van Dyck, R., Vertommen, H., & Vandereycken, W. (1992). De Dissociation Questionnaire: Ontwikkeling en karakteristieken van een nieuwe vragenlijst [The Dissociation Questionnaire: Development and characteristics of a new questionnaire]. *Nederlands Tijdschrift voor de Psychologie, 47,* 134–147.

Van Moffaert, M. (1990). Self-mutilation: Diagnosis and practical treatment. *International Journal of Psychiatry in Medicine, 20,* 373–382.

Vitousek, K., & Manke, F. (1994). Personality variables and diagnoses in anorexia nervosa and bulimia nervosa. *Journal of Abnormal Psychology, 103,* 137–148.

Waller, G. (1993c). Why do we diagnose different types of eating disorder? Arguments for a change in research and clinical practice. *European Eating Disorders Review, 1,* 74–89.

Waller, G. (1994). Borderline personality disorder and perceived family dysfunction in the eating disorders. *Journal of Nervous and Mental Disease, 182,* 541–546.

Waller, G., Quinton, S., & Watson, D. (1995). Dissociation and the processing of threat-related information. *Dissociation, 8,* 84–90.

Walsh, B.W., & Rosen, P.M. (1988). *Self-mutilation. Theory, research, and treatment.* New York: Guilford Press.

Watkins, J.G. (1971). The affect bridge: A hypno-analytic technique. *International Journal of Clinical and Experimental Hypnosis, 19,* 22–27.

Watkins, J.G., & Watkins, H.H. (1982). Ego state therapy. In L.E. Abt & L.R. Stuart (Eds.), *The newer therapies: A sourcebook* (pp. 136–155). New York: Van Nostrand Reinhold.

Weismann Wind, T., & Silvern, L. (1994). Parenting and family stress as mediators of the long-term effects of child abuse. *Child Abuse and Neglect, 18,* 439–453.

Wellbourne, J. (1988). Do bulimics really steal? *British Review of Bulimia and Anorexia Nervosa, 2,* 71–77.

Williams, M.B. (1991). Clinical work with families of MPD patients: Assessments and issues for practice. *Dissociation, 4,* 92–98.

Wilson, G.T. (1995). Eating disorders and addictive disorders. In K.D. Brownell & C.G. Fairburn (Eds.), *Eating disorders and obesity: A comprehensive handbook* (pp. 165–170). New York: Guilford Press.

Wonderlich, S.A., Swift, W.J., Slotnick, H., & Goodman, S. (1990). DSM-III-R personality disorders in the eating disorder subtypes. *International Journal of Eating Disorders, 9,* 607–616.

Wooley, S. (1993). Recognition of sexual abuse: Progress and backlash. *Eating Disorders, 1,* 298–314.

Wright, M.E., & Wright, B.A. (1987). *Clinical practice of hypnotherapy.* New York: Guilford Press.

Wyatt, G.E., & Newcomb, M. (1990). Internal and external mediators of women's child sexual abuse in adulthood. *Journal of Consulting and Clinical Psychology, 58,* 758–767.

Yaryura-Tobias, J.A., Neziroglu, F.A., & Kaplan, S. (1995). Self-mutilation, anorexia, and dysmenorrhea in obsessive compulsive disorder. *International Journal of Eating Disorders, 17,* 33–38.

Ziolko, H.U. (1988). Bulimia and kleptomania: Psychodynamics of compulsive eating and stealing. In H.J. Schwartz (Ed.), *Bulimia: Psychoanalytic treatment and theory* (pp. 523–534). Madison, CT: International Universities Press.

Zweig-Frank, H., Paris, J., & Guzder, J. (1994). Psychological risk factors for dissociation and self-mutilation in female patients with borderline personality disorder. *Canadian Journal of Psychiatry, 39,* 259–264.

Name Index

Subject Index